The
Puzzle
of
9-11

An Investigation Into
The Events of September 11, 2001
and
Why The Pieces Don't Fit Together.

Eric D. Williams

The Puzzle of 9-11

An Investigation Into
The Events of September 11, 2001
and
Why The Pieces Don't Fit Together.

Eric D. Williams

First published in September 2004
Second revised edition published October 2006
Copyright © 2006 Eric D. Williams and Williamsquire Ltd.

ISBN 1-419-60033-8

Published by
Booksurge Publishing

Front cover artwork inspired and painted by
Eric D. Williams
(whatreallyisthematrix.com)

Back cover artwork inspired and painted by
Cat Stone
(cha0scat.deviantart.com)

Dedication

To the victims of September 11, 2001, and to their families, and friends.
May the truth set you free.

The book was the idea of my friend, Veira, on a cold Slovakian Christmas in 2002. So this book is immensely dedicated to you. Ďakujem, Veira!

To my family for their support. Mom I love you!

To my God Mother, Carol. May the Force Be With You!

To my second family, the Magills whom we all watched the events unfold that day.

To my forever friend Arnold! Hey Buster!

To Agnieszka, Alicia, John, Anthony, Baiba, Bozena, Ewa, Farrell, Jaci, Jarka, Josh and Deanna, Keavy, Kristin Krystoph, Mafe, Marta, Marcela, Michal, Monica, Mary, Nichole, Rick, Vanity, Veikra and Jan, and all my other friends I may have forgotten. Your support for this book is more than appreciated!

Also, to the freedom fighters against tyranny, in the past, the present, and in the future.

Contents

"Beware the leader who bangs the drums of war in order to whip the citizenry into a patriotic fervor, for patriotism is indeed a double-edged sword.
It both emboldens the blood, just as it narrows the mind. And when the drums of war have reached a fever pitch and the blood boils with hate and the mind has closed, the leader will have no need in seizing the rights of the citizenry. Rather, the citizenry, infused with fear and blinded by patriotism, will offer up all of their rights unto the leader and gladly so. How do I know? For this is what I have done. And I am Caesar."

- Julius Caesar

"Let us never tolerate outrageous conspiracy theories concerning the attacks of September 11th - malicious lies that attempt to shift blame away from the terrorists themselves, away from the guilty."

"They shouldn't encourage malicious lies and outrageous conspiracy theories concerning the attacks of September the 11th. No government should promote the propaganda of terrorists."

\- U.S. President George W. Bush,
November 10, 2001

"This country, with its institutions, belongs to the people who inhabit it. Whenever they shall grow weary of the existing government, they can exercise their constitutional right of amending it, or their revolutionary right to dismember it or overthrow it."

- Abraham Lincoln,
16th President of the US First Inaugural Address
- March 4, 1861

Introduction

Where were you when the world stopped turning on that September day?

It was a regular day for me. It was to be a day that would have begun like any other day. Wake up next to my girlfriend. Wait for her to wake up and catch me staring into her face, then off to work. A day like any other day.

But the heavy knocking at the door at 6:20 a.m. that morning (in California) alerted me to the fact that this would not be a day like any other.

"Wake up! Wake up! There has been a terrorist attack in New York. Schools have been canceled across the country," shouted my girlfriend's mom as I tried to comprehend what she had just said.

"Terrorist Attack?"

I don't really recall my first thought, but I believe it was along the lines of a large-scale attack to cancel schools nation wide.

I stretched, as did my girlfriend. She was not a morning person and she struggled to "rise and shine."

But what I imagined, as a terrorist attack was nothing like what I saw when I entered the house of my girlfriend's parents to see the horror unfolding on national television.

I had just walked into footage of the Twin Towers in New York. One was on fire and a large airplane aimed at the second tower slammed into the second catching that tower ablaze also.

Damn!

What I had just seen was a reply of live footage catching the horror that made the whole world stop.

All eyes were on New York City.

It was unbelievable.

It was unreal.

As I blocked everything around me off except for the images on the screen, I remember thinking this was not happening.

It isn't real . . .

A trick . . .

A movie . . .

I remember as the day progressed that I still didn't believe it was real.

I had recently been in New York on a flight from London. I had just taken pictures of the Twin Towers that had crumbled before me on live television.

This had to be a dream.

But it was not a dream.

It was a nightmare.

I am not a professional author. I write for fun here and there. And this is actually my first completed book and my first book that I am publishing.

But when the event happened, I knew something beyond belief was going on. And now, three years later, I still believe that many people of the world are still convinced of the "official" story.

I remember the events as they unfolded that day. I am not a professional psychologist either, but my first hint that something was wrong was as the towers were ablaze, the news anchor began to discuss who could be responsible for this? And only one name was believed to be the mastermind: Osama bin Laden.

Soon after the towers collapsed I remember seeing a video of Osama bin Laden declaring his innocence. But as the week progressed, the suspected mastermind became *THE* mastermind. Without a trial or evidence to support the media's claim, Osama bin Laden was GUILTY. No questions asked.

I don't know who is responsible for the attacks, although I have an idea, but I believe whole heartily that Osama bin Laden is INNOCENT.

I soon returned to Europe later after September 11 and noticed that the news in other countries was very different from the news being reported in America.

I began to start collecting these articles and began a website that revealed my opinion of the true facts of the "terrorist" attacks.

Let me make one clear point: No one person knows all the answers. I don't claim to know them, and I challenge anyone who does. But we do all have parts of the answers. And that is what this book is, a piece in this huge puzzle.

When I was in Central Europe, Slovakia, in the fall of 2002, I was talking with some friends of mine about my website. It was then I discovered that even more people in Central Europe believed as I did.

It wasn't until I was in Poland with two Polish friends and an American that I actually took the idea I was given in Slovakia, and made the conscious thought to actually write the book that you have before you.

My original idea was to copy these articles word for word in the order they were released, and like a puzzle, the reader could put these pieces together on their own.

But as I began to copy these articles, I had a lot, and I mean a lot to say about these articles, so I changed the format to the finished work before you.

But just like a painting I want you to take what you see in this book and step away and make your own mind up.

I have gathered this information with an honest intent, without fear, and with the desire to uncover the ills of the attack that changed the world.

Not every fact is 100% accurate. Nor is every assumption believable. That is what makes us human. To take the facts as we see them and make our own decision.

I come from the direction of no religious, racial, or political reasons. Only to challenge what has been reported to be the "truth." I simply come for you to gather your own conclusions. To think for yourself.

Make your own truth.

I am not asking you to believe everything I say. But to use the given information, mixed with mild British sarcasm, to make a coincidence decision of what "truths" you will accept and which ones you will question.

But if we begin to recognize the negative patterns and lies that we are fed every day, and question them, and remove them . . . Our lives and our world will change. And truth and honesty will replace the fear we live under.

In preparation for this book, I noticed several spellings of the "hijackers," Osama bin Laden, the Taliban, Al Qaeda, etc. So I have adapted one spelling that I have found to be accurate, yet in the articles quoted from a direct source use the spelling for these names used in the source.

I conclude this introduction with a quote that I believe sums up the reasons we are given false "truths." The reason such disasters and catastrophes must occur.

"We seek a free flow of information... a nation that is afraid to let the people judge the truth and falsehood in an open market is a nation afraid of its people."

- John F Kennedy 35th President of the United States of America

The truth.
Let it begin in you!
Eric D. Williams

Chapter 1
The Official Story

American Airlines Flight 11

Crashed: 0848 EDT into north tower of World Trade Center.

The Boeing 767 from Boston to Los Angeles, departed from Boston's Logan airport at 08:02 EDT. It hit the north tower between the 95th and the 103rd floors.

Killed: 92, including nine flight attendants and both pilots, plus many others in the tower.

Hijackers: The men who took over the plane are thought to have been armed with knives. The FBI identified Mohamed Atta, who had a United Arab Emirates passport and underwent flight training with a number of the suspected hijackers, as the group's leader and the pilot of Flight 11. His suitcase, found at Logan Airport, contained a video on flying airliners, a fuel consumption calculator and a copy of the Koran.

Other suspected hijackers have been named as: Waleed M Alshehri, and Wail Alshehri, possibly brothers; Abdulaziz Alomari; and Satam Al Suqami.

The FBI is investigating whether the hijackers could have been using false identification.

On board: When the hijackers took over the aircraft, one of the crew managed to hit a control that allows air traffic controllers to hear the cockpit conversation.

"Don't do anything foolish. You are not going to get hurt. We have more planes. We have other planes," a hijacker was claimed to have said at 0828.

United Airlines Flight 175

Crashed: 0903 EDT in to south tower of the World Trade Center.

The second airliner crashed about 15 minutes after the first. It left Boston's Logan airport at 0758 and was en route to Los Angeles when it was hijacked. It hit the south tower at about the level of the 80th floor.

Killed: 65, including cabin crew and pilots, plus many more in the tower.

Hijackers: It is thought the hijackers were armed with knives. The FBI named the suspects as Marwan Al-Shehhi, Fayez Ahmed, Mohald Alshehri, Hamza Alghamdi and Ahmed Alghamdi.

Marwan Al-Shehhi is reported to be the cousin of Mohammed Atta, one of the suspected terrorists on Flight 11. They both received aviation training in Florida.

Mohald Alshehri is thought to be related to the Alshehri brothers who died on Flight 11. The FBI is investigating the possibility that the hijackers were using stolen identities.

On board: Passenger Peter Hanson called his parents in Easton, Connecticut, a short time before the crash and told them hijackers had taken over the plane and stabbed one of the cabin crew.

An unnamed woman flight attendant called an emergency number from a phone at the back of the aircraft. She said her colleagues had been stabbed.

American Airlines Flight 77

Crashed: 0940 into the Pentagon, the U.S. military headquarters, in Washington, D.C.

This plane, a Boeing 757, took off from Dulles Airport, Washington, at 08:10 and was en route to Los Angeles when it was hijacked.

It was seen approaching Washington from the southwest. Just a few miles outside the city it made a 270-degree turn and lined up on the Pentagon. The impact and resulting fireball caused a five-story section of the building to collapse.

Killed: 64, including four flight attendants and two pilots and 190 in the Pentagon.

Hijackers: Suspected hijackers were named by the FBI as Khalid Almidhar, Majed Moqed, Nawaq Alhamzi, Salem Alhamzi and Hani Hanjour. The FBI suspect it was Hanjour who piloted the jet.

Investigators believe the passengers were herded into the rear of the plane. The jet dropped off radar after the transponder in the cockpit was switched off.

Air force jets were alerted - but they arrived after the plane had crashed.

On board: Among the passengers was TV commentator Barbara Olson, wife of US Solicitor General Theodore Olson. She called her husband twice. She said the hijackers were armed with knives and she asked him, "What should I tell the pilot to do?"

During the second call he told her a plane had crashed into the World Trade Center.

United Airlines Flight 93

Crashed: 1003 EDT 80 miles (128 km) southeast of Pittsburgh.

Flight 93, a Boeing 757, took off from Newark, New Jersey, at 0801 bound for San Francisco. It crashed into the rural Somerset County in Pennsylvania.

Killed: 45, including five cabin crew and two pilots.

Hijackers: It is believed the hijackers were armed with knives and a box they claimed was a bomb. Their intended target was probably Washington, D.C.

The FBI named the suspected hijackers as Ahmed Alhaznawi, Ahmed Alnami, Ziad Jarrahi and Saeed Alghamdi.

On board: At least four passengers made mobile phone calls to relatives and the emergency services.

One of the passengers who made a call was sales manager Jeremy Glick who told his wife that he and some others had taken a secret vote and had decided to tackle the hijackers.

Another passenger, Thomas Burnett told his wife, "I know we're all going to die . . . There's three of us who are going to do something about it."

It is thought these passengers may have averted a more serious attack.

The US Senate is considering posthumously awarding the Congressional Gold Medal, the highest civilian honor in the US, to all those on board.

North Tower crash

American Airlines Flight 11 from Boston crashed into the upper floors of the north tower of the World Trade Center at 0848 Eastern Daylight Time. It hit the building between the 95th and 103rd floors.

Thousands of people were already at their desks in both towers. About 80 chefs, waiters and kitchen porters were also in the 'Windows on the World' restaurant on the 106th floor. Many who worked for

3

firms located in the crash zone were killed instantly.

Those on the floors above were already doomed; their escape routes cut off by fire.

South Tower crash

United Airlines Flight 175 crashed into the south tower 15 minutes later (0903).

The plane caused an explosion on impact and sent a plume of fire out of the opposite side of the building.

Many people in the south tower witnessed the first crash and were already trying to leave the building. Some office workers had been told to remain at their desks, resulting in possibly fatal delays. Some people above the fires chose to jump to their death rather than wait for the flames.

Hundreds of firefighters and police arrived at the scene to help the office workers escape.

Fires rage in the towers

At the heart of the towers were vertical steel and concrete cores, housing lift shafts and stairwells. The towers were built to be tough enough to withstand the impact of a plane. The steel was covered in concrete to guarantee firefighters a minimum period of one or two hours in which they could operate if a fire developed.

But the fires on 11 September were fed by thousands of gallons of jet fuel. The steel cores within the towers heated up to above 800C and the protective concrete cladding on the cores could only keep the heat at bay for a short time. Once the steel frame on one floor had melted, it collapsed, inflicting massive forces on the already-weakened floor below.

0925

The Pentagon and FAA ban all commercial takeoffs nationwide.

0929

Rescue workers and firefighters rushed to the foot of the World Trade Center as the upper floors blazed. On an ordinary day, up to 50,000 people would be working in the Trade Center.

0930

A grim-faced President Bush declared, "We have had a national tragedy. Two airplanes have crashed into the World Trade Center in an apparent terrorist attack on our country. Ladies and gentlemen, this is a difficult moment for America. Two airplanes have crashed into the World Trade Center in an apparent terrorist attack on out country, I am going to conduct a full-scale investigation and hunt down and find those folks who committed this act. Terrorism against our nation will not stand."

0940

American Airlines Flight 77, carrying 64 people from Washington to Los Angeles, crashed into the Pentagon in Washington. The nerve center of the US military burst into flames and a section of the five-sided structure collapsed.

F-16 fighters were still 100 miles away when the plane crashed. President Bush authorized fighters to shoot down any other aircraft that threatened targets in Washington.

0945

The White House and The Capitol were evacuated amid further threats.

1000

Bush places the US military on high alert status.

1003

United Airlines Flight 93 crashed 80 miles (128 km) south east of Pittsburgh. It had been bound for San Francisco from Newark, New Jersey.

South Tower collapses 1005

Once one floor had melted, the collapse became inevitable, as each new falling floor added to the pressure on the floor below. Further down the building, even steel at normal temperatures gave way under the enormous weight - an estimated 100,000 tones.

Just over an hour after the second crash, the south tower, which had been the second tower to be hit, crumbled to the ground. Hundreds of firefighters, police officers and people who were trying to escape the towers were crushed in the collapse.

1012

At the Pentagon, a cross-section of the building collapsed, but only after enough time had elapsed for rescue workers to evacuate all injured employees.

The fire was so hot that firefighters could not approach the impact point itself until approximately 1300.

The collapse and roof fires left the inner courtyard visible from outside through a gaping hole. The area hit by the plane was newly renovated and reinforced. The areas surrounding the impact zone were closed in preparation for renovation, had the plane struck another area, the death toll could have been much higher.

North Tower collapses 1029

Twenty-four minutes later the north tower joined its twin. The floors "pancaked" down and crushed the many people who remained inside.

People on the ground ran for their lives as a cloud of debris hit the streets of lower Manhattan. The dust clouds coated the city.

Rescuers search rubble

After the collapse of the World Trade Center more than 5,000 people were declared missing. Rescuers worked around the clock, carefully searching the ruins in the hope of finding people alive. Five survivors were found in the first 24 hours.

Often people can survive for many days in collapsed buildings, but the weight of the floors and scale of the disaster made this possibility unlikely in New York. Initial hopes that many people would be discovered alive soon began to fade.

A city devastated

After the collapse, police cordoned off the city below 14th street. The place where the twin towers once stood became known as "Ground Zero."

A number of other buildings in the same block were also severely damaged. Engineers on the site said they were concerned that the Trade Center foundations may have been severely weakened by the collapse of the twin towers. If the foundations cave in, it could allow the Hudson River to flood the area.

1239

President Bush made a second statement, in which he vowed to hunt down and punish those responsible.

1320

President Bush left Barksdale Air Force Base in Louisiana and flew to Omutt Air Force Base in Nebraska.

1344

The Pentagon deployed five battleships and two aircraft carriers along the East Coast of the US to provide upgraded air defense for the New York and Washington areas.

1350

Washington, D.C. Mayor Anthony Williams declared a state of emergency in the US federal capital.

1448

New York's mayor Rudy Giuliani said the eventual death toll from the attacks may be, "More than any of us can bear."

1630

President Bush left Omutt Air Force Base aboard Air Force One to return to the White House in Washington.

1720

Number 7, World Trade Center, a 47 story building adjacent to the ruins of the twin towers, collapsed.

2030

President Bush addressed the nation on TV and hinted at a strong U.S. response against the, "terrorists who committed these acts and those who harbor them." He continued, "Today our fellow citizens, our freedom, and our way of life came under attack."

There you have it, the Official Story

Here we have briefly reviewed the 11 September, 2001 tragedy.

We have to now Re-review the original story to find out what happened and how it was that this tragedy not only did happen, but was allowed to happen.

With one of the most, if not *THE* most, advanced technological nations in the world, what went wrong?

The puzzle pieces are out of the box and on the table. Now it is time to evaluate the picture on the box and review the pieces.

One hint of advice for any puzzle is to complete the boarder, and then work in. So, we have the pieces, now we must put together the edges and work our way in.

Let's put this puzzle together, shall we?

Chapter 2
Overview of the Official Story: What Went Wrong?

0759

American Airlines Flight 11 (Boeing 767) takes off from Logan International Airport, Boston heading for Los Angeles with 81 passengers, two pilots, and nine flight attendants.

John Ogonowski (pilot) and Tom McGuinness (co-pilot and former F-14 Navy Tomcat pilot who was described as "big and burly").

0801

United Airlines Flight 93 (Boeing 757) pulls back from gates at Newark, New Jersey but is delayed from take off (for reasons not explained by anyone at United Airlines).

0810

American Airlines Flight 77 (Boeing 757) leaves Washington Dulles International Airport for Los Angeles with 58 passengers, two pilots, and four attendants.

Captain Charles F. "Chic" Burlingame III, 51, and first officer David Charlebois, 39 take off from Washington Dulles. Burlingame was a graduate of the "Top Gun" fighter pilot school and a "perfectionist."

Burlingame had once worked at the Pentagon while Navy Reservist.

Among the passengers: Wilson "Bud" Flagg, a retired Navy Admiral once posted to the Pentagon: and former American Airlines pilot; Brian Jack one of the heads of the fiscal economics in the office of Defense Secretary Donald Rumsfeld at the Pentagon, where he was employed for the last 25 years; three Boeing engineers; and Barbara Olson, wife of Theodore "Ted" Olson, the US Solicitor General, and a contributor to CNN.

The pilots of Flight 11 are instructed by air traffic control to make a 20-degree turn to the right around 14 minutes into the flight.

9

0813

Air Traffic Control attempts contact to take Flight 11 to 35,000 feet, but no response is given.

0814

United Airlines Flight 175 departs also from Boston to Los Angeles carrying 56 passengers, two pilots, and seven flight attendants.

Captain Victor J Saracini, 51, and first officer Michael Horocks, 38 were at controls of Flight 175.

0820

According to FAA, Flight 11's IFF beacon, which allows an aircraft to be more easily tracked on radar, is switched off, over the Hudson River.

0824

Accordingly to recordings released from American Airlines, a voice is heard from Flight 11, "We have some planes. Just stay quiet and you will be OK. We are returning to the airport. Nobody move."

0833

Again from Flight 11, "Nobody move please. We are going back to the airport. Don't try to make any stupid moves," was heard. But even after the first odd voice is heard, it is another 16 minutes before the FAA alerted NORAD that the plane had been hijacked!

0835

"Everything will be OK. If you try to make any moves, you'll endanger yourself and the airplane. Just stay quiet," is heard over the airways from Flight 11.

0837

With Flight 11 now known to be in trouble, Air Traffic Control is said to have asked Flight 175, which ironically also is hijacked SIX minutes later, "Do you have traffic?" (or can you see American Flight 11?)

UAL175 responds, "Affirmative we have him . . . (at) 28,000 (feet)."[1]

We are told there are no other communications between the ground and Flight 175 until 0841, five minutes before American Flight 11 crashed into the WTC.[2]

0840

The Federal Aviation Administration alerted NORAD (North American Aerospace Defense Command: the military organization which monitors the skies over the United States and Canada) that American Airlines Flight 11 had been hijacked.

- Thirty minutes AFTER NO CONTACT WITH PILOT!!!

The four-digit code for hijacking was NEVER sent to Air Traffic Control – According to FBI reports.

According to BBC – Flight attendant Madeline Amy Sweeney made a call to American Airlines Flight Services Manager Michael Woodward at Boston Logan Airport. She reported four hijackers (the FBI claims that here were five). She also stated that they had stabbed two flight attendants and, "A hijacker cut the throat of a business class passenger and he is dead." She also claimed, "The hijackers had just accessed the cockpit." She also gave the hijackers' seat numbers (which were different from the FBI's claims of where the hijackers were sitting).[3]

American Airlines later released an account of a conversation it says took place during the flight between attendant Betty Ong and airline officials which took place 12 minutes after cockpit first failed to respond to ATC. This report states that, "Two attendants were stabbed and one was being given oxygen. And a passenger was cut at the throat and appeared to be dead." Again she also claimed there were four hijackers and NOT five as the FBI claims.[3]

If all this is going on, why was the four digit "hijacker code" not sent to Air Traffic Control?

According to the FBI, the FIVE hijackers were Mohamed Atta, and Egyptian, who they claim was at the controls and the ringleader over all the terrorists, Satam Alsuqami, from United Arab Emirates, and Abdulaziz Alomari, Wail Alshehri, and Waleed M Alshehri all from Saudi Arabia.

Also at the same time, Flight 77 is turned around 180 degrees near the West Virginia and Ohio borders, with its transponder signal turned off, and heads back toward Washington.

11

0841

One of Flight 175 pilots called the controller using code for Boston claiming to have a suspicious transmission, "We heard a suspicious transmission on our departure from B-O-S. Sounds like someone keyed the mike and said, 'Everyone stay in your seats'."

According to United, 90 seconds later Flight 175 veered off course over Northern New Jersey and headed south before turning back toward New York at some 400 miles an hour. 90 seconds between A-OK and the hijacking and being flown off course!!!!

0842

United Airlines Flight 93 leaves Newark for San Francisco with 38 passengers, two pilots, and five attendants.

Captain Jason Dahl, 43, from Littleton, Colorado and first officer Leroy Homer, 36, of Marlton, New Jersey.

FAA told its military colleagues at NORAD at 0916 that Flight 93 might have been hijacked.

The FBI however reports that it was not until 0940 that the transponder signal was lost.

It is believed that the cockpit was hijacked 30 minutes after take off. (0912)

An unnamed government official released the four phrases heard:
- "Get out of here." – from the pilot(s)
- "Bomb on Board."
- "Our demands."
- "Keep Quiet."

ABC News claims to have a tape of the conversations in which a hijacker says, "We'd like you all to remain seated. There is a bomb on board. We are going to turn back to the airport. And they had our demands, so please remain quiet."[4]

Passengers then used their cellular and seat back phones to call loved ones.

0843

FAA notified NORAD that United Airlines Flight 175 from Boston to Los Angeles had also been hijacked. Two F-15 jet fighters took off from Otis Air National Guard Base in Falmouth, Massachusetts.[5]

Once again, the transponder was switched off and there was no highjacking code from the pilots.

A female flight attendant is reported to have called and spoken with a mechanic in San Francisco that takes calls from flight attendants to report of items to be repaired or replaced. We are told the mechanic reported the conversation about 0850 to Rich "Doc" Miles, the manager of United Airlines System Operations Center in Chicago. The attendant told him, "Oh my God. The crew has been killed; a flight attendant has been stabbed. We've been hijacked," and the line went dead.[6]

This meant that the hijackers, stormed the cockpit, killed the pilots, stabbed the attendant, and took control of the plane in 6-7 minutes.

May I bring up that in ten minutes, this aircraft will strike the South Tower of the World Trade Center?

According to a November 11, 2001 broadcast on Radio Free America, Walter Burien said:

> "I Don't Buy It . . . I was one of the first tenants in the World Trade Center back in 1979. Back then, over 20 years ago, it was known to all the tenants that the WTC was a "no fly" zone. If you came within 12 miles of the WTC, flying outside of a pattern where you were supposed to be, you were warned to back off. If you came within five miles, they would threaten to shoot you down. If you came within three miles, they could shoot you down. If I remember correctly, on the roof of tower No. 2 they had surface to air missiles for that purpose, plus also the Spatz helicopters for that purpose. I had a friend who was flying a small plane who got warned away and they almost blew him out of the sky 20 years ago because he was showing somebody a close view of the towers. I can see the first tower getting hit by surprise, but 15 minutes later the second tower also gets hit? I don't buy it."[7]

So ten minutes away from flying directly into a no fly zone, and NORAD scrambles jets FROM MASSACHUSETTS! And why were these alleged surface to air missiles NOT USED?

0846

At the height of New York's morning rush hour American Airlines Flight 11 crashed into the north tower of the World Trade Center, 48 minutes after leaving Boston.

0847

NORAD is, "Informed of the plane striking the World Trade Center."[8]

I thought this was one of the most, if not *THE* most sophisticated military surveillance operation on this planet! According to the NORAD web site;

> "Today the NORAD (North American Aerospace Defense Command) Combat Operations Center has evolved into the Cheyenne Mountain Operations Center which collects data from a worldwide system of satellites, radar, and other sensors and processes that information on sophisticated computer systems to support critical NORAD and U.S. Space Command missions. The Cheyenne Mountain Operations Center provides warning of ballistic missile or air attacks against North America, assists the air sovereignty mission for the United States and Canada, and, if necessary, is the focal point for air defense operations to counter enemy bombers or cruise missiles. In support of the U.S. Space Command mission, the Cheyenne Mountain Operations Center provides a day-to-day picture of precisely what is in space and where it is located. The Cheyenne Mountain Operations Center also supports space operations, providing critical information such as collision avoidance data for space shuttle flights and troubleshooting satellite interference problems. Since the Persian Gulf War, the Cheyenne Mountain Operations Center has continued to play a vital and expanding role in supporting our deployed forces with warning for short-range ballistic missiles such as the Iraqi SCUDs."[9]

So, let me see if I understand this. (If anyone out there could explain this to me, please, see the contact the author info at the end of the book.) NORAD has this massive collection of worldwide surveillance systems, and they had to be "informed" that a plane has crashed into the World Trade Center? Brilliant!

0850

We are told that the cockpit of Flight 77 stopped responding to Air Traffic Control.[10]

0856

Flight 77's transponder was turned off. Still some 40 minutes from impacting with the Pentagon but the air controller is said to have told American Airlines, "We lost control of the guy... We can't get a hold of him."

0858

Jim McDonnell, a representative of American Airlines, is contacted regarding Flight 77.[11]

0900

Flight 175 Passenger Peter Hanson, a software salesman, phoned his parents in Easton, Connecticut using his mobile phone and stated that hijackers with knives had taken over the plane and stabbed a stewardess.[12]

He rang again and told his father the plane was, "Going down," and the line was lost.

Hanson's wife Sue, son Peter and their two-year-old daughter Christine were also on the plane.

Bush and his pet goat story

At Emma E. Booker Elementary School at Sarasota Florida, President Bush entered a classroom of second graders after coming from a private room and being told by his Chief of Staff Andrew Card about Flight 11.

Through "Breaking News" reports, we were made to believe that Flight 11 could have been just a terrible accident. (Yeah right.)

Bush sits down in front of eighteen children. At one point Bush says to them, "Really good readers – whew!"

Bush interrupts the children and says, "This must be Sixth Grade."[13]

He must be at his grade level because this is the President of the United States of America who was just told of a commercial airplane that smashed into one of the tallest buildings in America.

0903

News cameras turned on the burning tower captured the horrifying view of another passenger jet, United Airlines Flight 175, crashing into the south tower of the World Trade Center causing a massive devastating explosion. It had left Boston for Los Angeles carrying 65 passengers and crew. As millions watched around the world, it became clear that the catastrophe was not at all an accident.

0910

In Florida President Bush was reading to children in a classroom when his chief of staff, Andrew Card, whispered news of the second plane crash into his ear.

This goat story must REALLY be at Bush's interest level because two of the tallest buildings in America have both been struck by airliners and thousands of Americans are presumably killed, and the Commander and Chief sits listening to the story about the pet goat for twenty-six minutes. (A total of thirty minutes after the second plane and forty-five after the first strike the World Trade Center.)

0920

The FBI announced that it was investigating reports of planes being hijacked.

0924

The FAA told NORAD that Flight 77 was troubled.

0925

The Pentagon and FAA ban all commercial take offs nationwide.

Barbara Olson, on board Flight 77, phoned her husband, Ted Olson. There are many versions of the conversation, but allegedly, Barbara told her husband the plane had been hijacked using box cutters and knives, and did not mention the nationality or the number of the hijackers. Ted then told his wife about the WTC attacks.

The passengers on Flight 77 are now aware of the two planes that crashed into the World Trade Center. The FAA is aware of the two planes that crashed into the World Trade Center. NORAD, I'm not too sure with all their technology gizmos, but I can assume someone somewhere made them aware of the second plane crashing into the other building of the World Trade Center (as I made the point they were told of the first crash earlier). George W. Bush was told, but we cannot

16

assume he understands that two airplanes have crashed into the World Trade Center. The Pentagon also knows that there were two airplanes that crashed into the World Trade Center. AND there is another airliner, with NO communication between Air Traffic Control and Flight 77, and heading RADICALLY off course, and NO FIGHTERS HAVE BEEN DISPATCHED to intercept it.

Unless everyone who didn't know FAA regulations were at work that day and everyone who did were on vacation on September 11, those people sitting on their leather wrapped swivel armchairs, forgot what EVERYONE sitting in that seat should know:

Section 2. Emergency Assistance [14]

10-2-1. INFORMATION REQUIREMENTS

a. Start assistance as soon as enough information has been obtained upon which to act. Information requirements will vary, depending on the existing situation. Minimum required information for in-flight emergencies is:

NOTE: In the event of an ELT signal see para 10-2-10 Emergency Locator Transmitter (ELT) Signals.

1. Aircraft identification and type.

United Airlines Flight 175 (Boeing 767). CHECK.

2. Nature of the emergency.

Let's see:

- World Trade Center has been attacked with two similar airplanes. CHECK;
  - No contact for thirty-five minutes, CHECK;
  - Unable to locate Flight 77 on radar for ten minutes, CHECK;
  - All takeoffs around the country have been halted, CHECK;
  - Flight 77 has dramatically changed course without approval, CHECK;
  - No contact for thirty-five minutes, CHECK;
  - No contact for thirty-five minutes, CHECK;

3. Pilot's desires.

Let's see. I DON'T KNOW! We haven't had contact for at least thirty-five minutes!!

So, I guess we have no emergency!

b. After initiating action, obtain the following items or any other pertinent information from the pilot or aircraft operator, as necessary:

NOTE: Normally, do not request this information from military fighter-type aircraft that are at low altitudes (i.e. on approach, immediately after departure, on a low-level route, etc.). However, request the position of an aircraft that is not visually sighted or displayed on radar if the location is not given by the pilot.

Well, we have already established that NO emergency situation exists, so . . . The rest of this that I am about to quote DIRECTLY from the FAA web site has no relevance what so ever. Or, at least it made no relevance on September 11, 2001:

10-2-5. EMERGENCY SITUATIONS

Consider that an aircraft emergency exists and inform the RCC or ARTCC and alert the appropriate DF facility when:

NOTE-

1. USAF facilities are only required to notify the ARTCC.
2. The requirement to alert DF facilities may be deleted if radar contact will be maintained throughout the duration of the emergency.
a. An emergency is declared by either:
1. The pilot.
2. Facility personnel.
3. Officials responsible for the operation of the aircraft.
b. There is unexpected loss of radar contact and radio communications with any IFR or VFR aircraft.
c. Reports indicate it has made a forced landing, is about to do so, or its operating efficiency is so impaired that a forced landing will be necessary.
d. Reports indicate the crew has abandoned the aircraft or is about to do so.
e. An emergency radar beacon response is received.

NOTE: EN ROUTE. During Stage A operation, Code 7700 causes EMRG to blink in field E of the data block.

18

f. Intercept or escort aircraft services are required.

g. The need for ground rescue appears likely.

h. An Emergency Locator Transmitter (ELT) signal is heard or reported.

REFERENCE:

FAAO 7110.65, Providing Assistance, Para 10-1-3.
FAAO 7110.65, Emergency Locator Transmitter (ELT) Signals, Para 10-2-10.

10-2-6. HIJACKED AIRCRAFT

When you observe a Mode 3/A Code 7500, an unexplained loss of beacon code, change in direction of flight or altitude, and/or a loss of communications, notify supervisory personnel immediately. As it relates to observing a Code 7500, do the following:

NOTE: Military facilities will notify the appropriate FAA ARTCC, or the host nation agency responsible for en route control, of any indication that an aircraft is being hijacked. They will also provide full cooperation with the civil agencies in the control of such aircraft.

EN ROUTE. During narrowband radar operations, Code 7500 causes HIJK to blink in the data block.

NOTE: Only non discrete Code 7500 will be decoded as the hijack code.

a. Acknowledge and confirm receipt of Code 7500 by asking the pilot to verify it. If the aircraft is not being subjected to unlawful interference, the pilot should respond to the query by broadcasting in the clear that he/she is not being subjected to unlawful interference. If the reply is in the affirmative or if no reply is received, do not question the pilot further but be responsive to the aircraft requests.

PHRASEOLOGY- (Identification) (name of facility) VERIFY SQUAWKING 7500.

NOTE: Code 7500 is only assigned upon notification from the pilot that his/her aircraft is being subjected to unlawful interference.

Therefore, pilots have been requested to refuse the assignment of Code 7500 in any other situation and to inform the controller accordingly.

b. Notify supervisory personnel of the situation.

c. Flight follow aircraft and use normal handoff procedures

without requiring transmissions or responses by aircraft unless communications have been established by the aircraft.

d. If aircraft are dispatched to escort the hijacked aircraft, provide all possible assistance to the escort aircraft to aid in placing them in a position behind the hijacked aircraft.

NOTE: Escort procedures are contained in FAAO 7610.4, Special Military Operations, Chapter 7, Escort of Hijacked Aircraft.

e. To the extent possible, afford the same control service to the aircraft operating VFR observed on the hijack code.

REFERENCE:

FAAO 7110.65, Code Monitor, Para 5-2-13.[14]

0929

Rescue workers and firefighters rushed to the foot of the World Trade Center as the upper floors blazed. On an ordinary day, up to 50,000 people would be working in the Trade Center.

0930

A grim-faced President Bush declared, "We have had a national tragedy. Two airplanes have crashed into the World Trade Center in an apparent terrorist attack on our country."

"Ladies and gentlemen, this is a difficult moment for America. Two airplanes have crashed into the World Trade Center in an apparent terrorist attack on out country, I am going to conduct a full-scale investigation and hunt down and find those folks who committed this act. Terrorism against our nation will not stand."[15]

"These folks" must be from the little children's book about the goat, fresh in his head.

0940

American Airlines Flight 77, carrying 64 people from Washington to Los Angeles, crashed into the Pentagon in Washington. The nerve center of the US military burst into flames. About thirty minutes later, this section of the five-sided structure later collapsed.

F-16 fighters were still 100 miles away when the plane crashed. President Bush authorized fighters to shoot down any other aircraft that threatened targets in Washington.

20

190 people were killed in total at the Pentagon.

The FBI claims five hijackers were on board. This group was allegedly lead by Hani Hanjour, a Saudi who had a commercial pilot license, although according to his flight instructors, was a terrible pilot, even in small planes.

The other hijackers named by the FBI as being on the plane were Majed Moqed, Salem Alhamzi, Khalid Almidhar, and Nawaq Alhamzi, all from Saudi Arabia.

0945

The White House and The Capitol were evacuated amid further threats.

On Flight 93 a 15-minute conversation between Todd Beamer, a 32-year-old employee of Oracle Software, and his air-phone supervisor, Lisa Jefferson, claims that the pilot and co-pilot appeared to be dead and the hijackers were flying the plane.

Beamer is said to have stated that two hijackers were in the cockpit, one was guarding first class, and the fourth was guarding a group of passengers (27 or so) in the back of the plane with what he stated as a bomb around the hijacker's waist.

Yet another report from passenger Lauren Grandcolas, after phoning her husband in San Francisco, claims that, "We have been hijacked. They are being kind. I love you."

Other phone calls from other passengers (Flight attendant Sandy Bradshaw, and Mark Bingham) claim that there were only three hijackers.[16]

0955

Two fighter planes scrambled to intercept Flight 77 arrive to see the Pentagon on fire, which has been burning for fifteen minutes.

0958

An emergency dispatcher in Pennsylvania received a call from a passenger on United Flight 93 who says, "We are being hijacked, we are being hijacked!"[17]

Several passengers continue to call relatives and told them they intended to try to overpower the terrorists.

1000

Bush places the US military on high alert status.

SOME 55 minutes AFTER he is notified of the second plane hitting the tower.

TWENTY minutes AFTER the Pentagon is hit.

What I am thinking now, is I *MUST* GET THAT GOAT BOOK! What a story!!!

1003

United Airlines Flight 93 crashed 80 miles (128 km) south east of Pittsburgh. It had been bound for San Francisco from Newark, New Jersey.

There are at least three different times reported for when United Flight 93 "crashed": 1003, 1010, and 1037.

The hijackers named by the FBI were Saeed Alghamdi, Ahmed Alhaznawi, Ahmed Alnami, and Ziad Jarrahi.

1005

The south tower of the World Trade Center suddenly collapsed sending a massive pall of smoke across Manhattan. Many emergency workers and firefighters were crushed, as all those who could not get out of the tower.

1029

The north tower of the World Trade Center collapsed as well, adding to the devastation and loss of life. The southern part of Manhattan Island was covered in a thick layer of debris and dust.

Among the dead at the World Trade Center were 341 Fire Fighters and other Rescue workers who had rushed into the buildings to help.

1239

President Bush made a second statement, in which he vowed to hunt down and punish those responsible.

1320

President Bush left Barksdale Air Force Base in Louisiana and flew to

Omutt Air Force Base in Nebraska.

1344

The Pentagon deployed five battleships and two aircraft carriers along the east coast of the US to provide upgraded air defense for the New York and Washington areas.

    - I thought lightning didn't strike the same place twice.

1350

Washington, D.C. Mayor Anthony Williams declared a state of emergency in the US federal capital.

1448

New York's mayor Rudy Giuliani said the eventual death toll from the attacks may be, "more than any of us can bear."

1630

President Bush left Offutt Air Force Base aboard Air Force One to return to the White House in Washington.

1720

Number 7, World Trade Center, a 47-story building adjacent to the ruins of the twin towers, collapsed, blamed only on small fires.

2030

President Bush addressed the nation on TV and hinted at a strong U.S. response against the, "Terrorists who committed these acts and those who harbor them."[18]

    "Today our fellow citizens, our freedom, and our way of life came under attack."

So what went wrong?

On September 11, 2001, a tragedy occurred.

    So we have reviewed the original story, and established the boarder of the puzzle.

    We have RE-reviewed the original story, and the puzzle pieces.

So what went wrong? Or, how could everything go so right for the "terrorist?!"

As we continue to take the puzzle pieces and assemble the picture, we will begin to see that nothing went wrong on 11 September for those who want to control every aspect of the world's population.

Now we must look at a few more puzzle pieces a little more closely.

SOURCES

(1) http://www.observer.co.uk/Print/0,3858,4258186,00.html
(2) http://news.bbc.co.uk/1/low/world/americas/1556096.stm
(3) http://www.flightattendants.org/Memorials/AA_FA_Betty_Ong.htm
(4) http://www.boston.com/news/packages/underattack/news/planes
  _reconstruction.htm
(5) http://www.cnn.com/2001/US/09/16/inv.hijack.warning/
(6) http://www.boston.com/news/packages/underattack/news/planes
  _reconstruction.htm
(7) http://www.worldofislam.netfirms.com/terrorism.html
(8) http://www.cnn.com/2001/US/09/16/inv.hijack.warning/
(9) https://www.cheyennemountain.af.mil/today.htm
(10) http://www.usatoday.com/news/sept11/2002-08-12-clearskies_x.htm
(11) http://www.jethros.i12.com/FACT/Sep11/AA77.htm
(12) http://old.smh.com.au/news/0109/14/world/world4.html
(13) http://www.stltoday.com/stltoday/news/special/skyterror.nsf/
  other/8B8F4C8DD63893E186256AC400609220?OpenDocument
(14) http://www.faa.gov/ATpubs/ATC/Chp10/atc1002.html
(15) http://news.bbc.co.uk/hi/english/static/in_depth/americas/2001/
  day_of_terror/timeline/default.stm
(16) http://www.post-gazette.com/headlines/20010916phonecallnat3p3.asp
(17) http://news.bbc.co.uk/hi/english/static/in_depth/americas/2001/
  day_of_terror/timeline/default.stm
(18) http://usembassy.state.gov/islamabad/wwwhbush2.html

Chapter 3
Mommy, Can I be a Terrorist When I Grow Up?

A double check of the pieces

OK, let's consider the following . . . And this much we know . . . On September 11, 2001, four commercial airliners were hijacked.

- Three strike targets.
- One strikes a field in Pennsylvania.

There is an organization to help identify and escort hijacked planes in America and Canada called NORAD (North American Aerospace Defense Command).

> "NORAD is the military organization formed by treaty between the U.S. and Canada to monitor and defend North American skies against enemy aircraft, missiles, and space vehicles. In the US, NORAD has an agreement with the Federal Aviation Administration, to cooperate in emergency civil aviation situations. NORAD helps when aircraft go off course or are hijacked."

> "NORAD uses a network of ground-based radar, sensors and fighter jets to detect, intercept and, if necessary, engage any threats to the continent."[1]

> "In the event of a hijacking, the NMCC will be notified by the most expeditious means by the FAA. The NMCC will, with the exception of immediate responses...forward requests for DOD [Department of Defense] assistance to the Secretary of Defense for approval."[2]

NORAD in action

On October 25, 1999, golfer Payne Stewart's personal plane lost contact with Air Traffic Control minutes after takeoff from Orlando, Florida heading toward Dallas. ATC contacted NORAD and fighter jets were scrambled to check it out. There was an air pressure failure and the pilot and passengers were unconscious. The aircraft was flying on auto-pilot.

CNN reported:

"Pilots on two U.S. Air Force F-16 fighters, sent up by the Oklahoma Air National Guard to track the civilian aircraft as it flew over the Midwest, said the occupants were "non-responsive."

"Officials said the Lear jet took off from Sanford, Florida -- near Orlando at 920 EDT with a flight plan giving its destination as Dallas, Texas.

"Air traffic controllers lost radio contact with the plane about 20 minutes later, as it passed Gainesville, Florida. They said the Lear jet's windows frosted over, an indication that the plane might have lost pressure and that its occupants were already dead."[3]

ABC reported:

"On October 25, 1999, at 0933 air traffic controllers in Florida lost touch with a Lear jet carrying golfer Payne Stewart and several companions after it left Orlando headed for Dallas, Texas.

"Nineteen minutes after Air Traffic Control realized something was wrong, one or more US Air Force fighter jets were already on top of the situation, in the air, close to the Lear jet. Moreover, throughout the course of its flight, Payne Stewart's jet was given escort from National Guard aircraft coordinated across state lines."[4]

Obviously NORAD responded in a timely matter and did there job, escorting the plane until it crashed.

In fact in 2000, NORAD scrambled jets on more than 120 circumstances.

It does not require the approval of the President or other government official. It is a routine response to check what is going on and who is flying the plane. Approval by the President is needed only to "down" the plane.[5]

Let's pretend I am a TERRORIST

Hello boys and girls. I am an (Islamic) Terrorist. And that I am going to organize the largest terrorist plot to terrorize America, just because I hate the American way of life. Never-mind the fact that the American Military will retaliate and kill many thousands of my own countrymen when they bomb my (Islamic) country.

If I was a "highly trained" Arab terrorist from the "brilliantly organized" network (of which we are told was capable of hijacking four commercial aircraft AT THE SAME TIME) of Osama bin Laden, one of my OBVIOUS and FUNDAMENTAL calculations would be the possible reaction time of NORAD once it had known the plane you hijacked had been seized. And looking at the mentioned case above (October 25, 1999 Golfer Payne Stewart), I know that I have about 15 – 20 minutes to proceed with my terrorizing mission.

Flight 11 from Boston lost contact at 8:13am. **32 Minutes Later** Flight 11 strikes the World Trade Center at 8:45!

So why did they choose to hijack the planes that hit the WTC from Boston with the flight time well in excess of NORAD reaction time?

Why also would they fly Flight 77 and 93 toward Mid-America before turning around and going all the way back? Flight 77 had to fly back for 45 minutes from the approximate time of hijacking!!!

Even the smallest glimpse of information on the NORAD website would have alarmed the hijackers that Air Force jets would be scrambled to intercept them, and even possibly shoot them down if they threatened US cities.

This means, that under normal, every-OTHER-day, reaction times (25 October, 1999 for instance) of NORAD, they would have to complete the mission as soon as possible.

BUT, if those who were planning the attacks SOMEHOW knew that NORAD would not be reacting THAT day, these details would no longer be a problem or have to be taken into account when planning the operation.

NORAD Failed to respond to ANY of the four hijackings on September 11, between 8:13 (when communication was lost with Flight 11) and at least 9:38 (when Flight 77, officially reported to have performed a U-turn from its authorized course and fly for 40 minutes before it crashed into the Pentagon).

THAT IS MORE THAN 90 MINUTES!!!

FAA Official Regulations and Procedures Chapter 7 deals with the, "Escort of hijacked aircraft," and says that an FAA, "hijack co-ordinator" on duty at Washington, D.C. will request the military to provide an escort aircraft for a confirmed hijacked plane to:

"Assure positive flight information (or authorized course); report unusual observances; and aid search and rescue in the event of an emergency."[6]

Chapter 7 continues . . .

"The control tower shall coordinate with the designated NORAD military unit advising of the hijack aircraft's location, direction of flight, altitude, type of aircraft and recommend flight plan to intercept the hijack aircraft."[7]

Small private plane ordered to land in vicinity of Bush Ranch
Shortly after 11 September, a small unauthorized private plane flying in the vicinity of President Bush's ranch near Crawford, Texas was ordered by the military to land.

> "The Federal Aviation Administration declared that the plane was unauthorized and ordered its occupants detained," Plemons said.

> "At that point military officials, flying in two jets beside the plane, got on the pilot's radio frequency and ordered the Cessna to land. "The plane landed on a private landing strip near State Highway 6, about eight miles from the Bush ranch near Crawford.

> "In [a second incident, in] Wood County, Sheriff's senior Dispatcher Rodney Mize said a private plane was forced down by two military pilots in A-10 Warthog jets about 11:30 a.m. The jets flew one above and one below until the private plane's pilot landed at Wisener Field near Mineola."[8]

It would seem, that Bush's Ranch is far more important that the Pentagon and the World Trade Center.
    The *Boston Globe* reported that:

> "[Marine Corps Major Mike] Snyder, the NORAD spokesman, said its fighters routinely intercept aircraft.

> "When planes are intercepted, they typically are handled with a graduated response. The approaching fighter may rock its wingtips to attract the pilot's attention, or make a pass in front of the aircraft.

> "Eventually, it can fire tracer rounds in the airplane's path, or, under certain circumstances, down it with a missile."[9]

Mommy, Can I be a Terrorist When I Grow Up?

Obviously, if bin Laden and the Taliban /Al-Qaeda Network were behind the attacks, they had some help from or inside NORAD.

Based on information at the NORAD web sites (www.cheyennemountain.af.mil / http://www.faa.gov/Atpubs/MIL), the technology they have to intercept enemy and hijacked aircraft, left the window open for the world governments to intercept the freedoms and privacy of the World's people.

I don't know about the puzzle you are putting together, but the one in front of me has pieces that are not fitting together very well.

And there are still a lot more pieces to yet examine.

SOURCES

(1) http://www.cheyennemountain.af.mil
http://www.faa.gov/Atpubs/MIL
(2) CJCSI 3610.01A, 1 June 2001
(3) http://www.cnn.com/US/9910/25/wayward.jet.05/
(4) http://abcnews.go.com/sections/us/DailyNews/plane102599.html
(5) http://www.faa.gov/Atpubs/MIL
(6) Ibid
(7) www.faa.go/Atpubs/AIM/Chap5/aim0506.html#5-6-4
(8) AP, 13 September 2001
(9) Boston Globe, 15 September 2001

Chapter 4
The "Hijackers"

Ladies and Gentlemen, I would like us all to review the following pieces of our puzzle:

Aboard American Airlines Flight 11, which crashed into the North Tower of the World Trade Center after taking off from Boston's Logan International Airport en route for Los Angeles:

1. Alshehri, Wail — Passenger No. 1, Seat 2A
2. Alshehri, Waleed — Passenger No. 2, Seat 2B
3. Alomari, Abdulaziz — Passenger No. 14, Seat 8G
4. Al Suqami, Satam — Passenger No. 20, Seat 10B
5. Atta, Mohamed — Seat 8D[1]

Aboard United Airlines Flight 175, which left Boston for Los Angeles but crashed into the South Tower of the Word Trade Center:

1. Alghamdi, Ahmed — Passenger No. 2
2. Alghamdi, Hamza — Passenger No. 3
3. Alshehhi, Marwan — Passenger No. 4
4. Alshehri, Mohald — Passenger No. 5
5. Ahmed, Fayez — Passenger No. 6[2]

Aboard American Airlines Flight 77, which took off from Washington Dulles Airport for Los Angeles and crashed into the Pentagon.

1. Alhamzi, Nawaq — Passenger No. 12
2. Almidhar, Khalid — Passenger No. 20, Seat 12B
3. Alhamzi, Salem — Passenger No. 13, Seat 5F
4. Moqed, Majed — Passenger No. 19, Seat 12A
5. Hanjour, Hani – apparently he wasn't assigned a seat.[3]
- Standing Room Only I suppose.

Aboard United Airlines Flight 93, which departed Newark, NJ, for San Francisco and crashed outside of Shanksville, Pa.:

1. Alghamdi, Saeed — Passenger No. 2 (Nothing like being

first in the queue)

       2. Alhaznawi, Ahmed — Passenger No. 3
       3. Alnami, Ahmed — Passenger No. 4
       4. Jarrahi, Ziad — Passenger No. 26 [4]

The hijackers from the beginning

The accepted truth of September 11, 2001 is that 19 hijackers working for Osama bin Laden hijacked four commercial aircraft, and flew them into the World Trade Center, the Pentagon, and a field in Pennsylvania.

    The hijackers are reported as speaking good English.

    According to the reports, they learned to fly at flight schools based in the US. Mind you, they learned to fly small planes like the Cessna. But as we will soon learn, they failed their test repeatedly, and were not allowed to fly a small Cessna solo. This must be the reason for the group of terrorists on each plane, a team effort I guess.

    But first a sample from the "Official Story":

> "At 9:33 the plane crossed the Capitol Beltway and took aim on its military target. But the jet, flying at more than 400 mph, was too fast and too high when it neared the Pentagon at 9:35. The hijacker-pilots were then forced to execute a difficult high-speed descending turn.

> "Radar shows Flight 77 did a downward spiral, turning almost a complete circle and dropping the last 7,000 feet in two-and-a-half minutes.

> "The steep turn was so smooth, the sources say, it's clear there was no fight for control going on. And the complex maneuver suggests the hijackers had better flying skills than many investigators first believed.

> "The jetliner disappeared from radar at 9:37 and less than a minute later it clipped the tops of street lights and plowed into the Pentagon at 460 mph." [5]

Now, the real story:

> "Once (Khalid al-Mihdhar, who died in the Pentagon attack) had entered the US in January on a Saudi passport, the FBI picked up his trail in San Diego where he took flying lessons at Sorbi's Flying Club in May 2000. Rick Garza, al-Mihdhar and al-Hazami's flight instructor at the school, has said that al-Mihdhar spoke little English but was able say that he wanted

31

to obtain a private pilot licence.

"'They were impatient students, Garza said, saying they wanted to learn to fly jets, specifically Boeings. 'They had zero training before they got here, so I told them they had to learn a lot of other things first,' he told the New York Times. 'It was like Dumb and Dumber. I mean, they were clueless. It was clear to me they weren't going to make it as pilots.'"[6]

And the flight instructors at Freeway Airport in Bowie figured that one of them, Hani Hanjour, was just a bad pilot.

"Hanjour, the suspected pilot on the Dulles flight, went aloft three times in a week in August with flight instructors from Freeway Airport in Bowie. Although he had a pilot's license, Hanjour needed to be certified because he wanted to rent a plane, said Freeway's chief flight instructor, Marcel Bernard.

"But after supervising Hanjour on a series of oblong circles above the airport and Chesapeake Bay, the instructors refused to pass him because his skills were so poor, Bernard said."[7]

It was clear to flight instructors Mr. Garza and Mr. Bernard that they wouldn't make good pilots, as I guess Yoda felt Luke was too impatient to become a Jedi. But students sure fool their teachers, don't they! But surely we could look to the flight data recorders to dig deep into the investigation to determine who really was behind the helm of the doomed planes.

"Both the Flight Data Recorder and the Cockpit Voice Recorder have proven to be valuable tools in the accident investigation process.

"They can provide information that may be difficult to obtain by other means.

"The FDR onboard the aircraft records many different operating conditions of the flight. By regulation, newly manufactured aircraft must monitor at least twenty-eight important parameters such as time, altitude, airspeed, heading, and aircraft attitude. In addition, some FDRs can record the status of more than 300 other in-flight characteristics that can aid in the investigation.

"The items monitored can be anything from flap position to autopilot mode or even smoke alarms.

"The CVR records the flight crew's voices, as well as other

sounds inside the cockpit. The recorder's "cockpit area microphone" is usually located on the overhead instrument panel between the two pilots. Sounds of interest to an investigator could be engine noise, stall warnings, landing gear extension and retraction, and other clicks and pops.

"From these sounds, parameters such as engine rpm, system failures, speed, and the time at which certain events occur can often be determined. Communications with Air Traffic Control, automated radio weather briefings, and conversation between the pilots and ground or cabin crew are also recorded."[8]

Although investigators look for an entire black box, sometimes the only parts of the device that survives are the recorder's crash survivable memory units (CSMU).

THE CSMU IS ALMOST INDESTRUCTIBLE!!

It is housed within a stainless-steel shell that contains titanium or aluminum and a high-temperature insulation of dry silica material.

It is designed to withstand HEAT OF UP TO 2,000 DEGREES FAHRENHEIT FOR ONE HOUR, salt water for at least 30 days, immersion in a variety of liquids such as jet fuel and lubricants, AND AN IMPACT OF 3,400 G's by comparison, astronauts are typically exposed to up to six G's during a shuttle takeoff.[9]

Oh that's right, the indestructible black boxes, built to withstand almost anything, except what happened on 11 September, I guess, did not survive from ANY of the four planes.

Investigators are less confident they will recover the black boxes buried underneath the rubble of the World Trade Center.[10]

Darn. One more missing puzzle piece in our box. I guess the designs that have stood up and survived time and time again, the one found at the bottom of the ocean from Egypt Air Flight 990 and TWA Flight 800 which exploded in the air after takeoff, had a defect that was overlooked. Perhaps it was stamped with the marking "Good for Use any Date EXCEPT September 11, 2001."

The plane hit the ground at 500 mph taking the weight of the plane, its speed of descent, the G's end up much, much lower than 3,400.

Something to think about.

Who knows, anything is possible it appears. And speaking of anything is possible . . .

"Pennsylvania Senators Rick Santorum and Arlen Spector, visiting the site of the crash in Shanksville, Pa., today, said they had examined the transcripts of cell phone calls made from the plane before the crash and concluded that the passengers tried to overcome the hijackers. Santorum and Spector's hunch was that the plane was headed toward Washington, but the passengers' actions diverted its course."[11]

I never knew that from a missing, or destroyed, or partially destroyed, whichever story you want to believe, you could retrieve transcripts from cell phone calls. I didn't even know that all cell phone calls could be, or would be rather, recorded. And is this procedure of recording cellular phone calls common practice, or just when you think you are going to have a heroic end to a hijacking story?

Amazing how you can get word for word conversations between the passengers and loved ones, and yet not send fighter jets to intercept hijacked aircraft.

What a beautiful and wonderful blessing technology is.

Makes me think twice about making a cellular phone call again.

And if they are recording all cellular phone conversations, are land line home telephone conversations being monitored as well? So much for free speech, huh!?

And while we are still in Never Never Land ... where everything that is supposed to happen doesn't, and things that you would never guess imaginable, happen ...

"Each plane has two separate Black Boxes that are designed to be indestructible in the event of a tragedy that makes a total of EIGHT BLACK BOXES. If we are to believe that all the Black Boxes were damaged beyond use, then that is to say EIGHT BLACK BOXES in total were destroyed, while a measly paper passport survived.

"With no hope of recovering indestructible black boxes from the rubble of the World Trade Center, a simple paper passport has survived in a perfect state that has become a "significant piece of evidence?"[12]

One question, where did he get his passport? My U.S. Government-issued passport has been through thirty some countries, countless times, not to mention how many times back into the United States or United Kingdom, and this passport that survived an explosion,

34

and then falling several hundred feet from the air, is in better shape than my passport.

And never mind how the passport was removed from the hijacker's breast pocket or even trousers' pocket. Perhaps it was being used as a bookmark within the Koran. What a wonderful coincidence that would be, huh!?

> "The searchers found several clues, he said, but would not elaborate. Last week, a passport belonging to one of the hijackers was found in the vicinity of Vesey Street, near the World Trade Center. 'It was a significant piece of evidence for us,' Mawn said." [13]

> "In New York, several blocks from the ruins of the World Trade Center, a passport authorities said belonged to one of the hijackers was discovered a few days ago, according to city Police Commissioner Bernard Kerik."[14]

It is well known that paper was displaced all over the streets surrounding the World Trade Center after the plane crash.[15] This was due to the sudden shattering of the windows that would immediately eject all paper (and other) materials out of the building before incineration.

A passport in someone's pocket that is sitting on a plane that explodes will suffer the same fate as the person whose pocket it is in, and the plane they are sitting in: Absolute cremation. The only explanation I can think of is that this passport must have been used as a bookmark in their Koran, and therefore Allah protected the passport and delivered it safely to the ground. Praise Allah!

Aside from the idiocy of any suggestion that a passport could even survive a plane crash that is allegedly so severe it destroys the virtually indestructible Black Box, we are also led to believe that the passport of one hijacker flew away, and down a few blocks from the WTC grounds. Why a few blocks away? Could it be because it was a place out of everyone's sight? Consider once again the mentality of the people involved in this investigation that is not too much of a statement.

Maybe O. J. Simpson should consider a career with the FBI.

> "Investigators, saying it is possible that other personal effects from the hijackers might have been expelled from the crash scene when the planes made impact with the skyscrapers,

have decided to launch an intensive grid search of the area near the World Trade Center disaster zone Sunday, in the hopes of finding other important evidence."[16]

Perhaps they are looking for a shaving kit, or Koran, or even one of them small travelers' kits with the toothbrush that has the toothpaste already on the brush. Who knows!?

Back to reality ... and for the sake of argument lets say that the passport *DID* survive. If the passport did indeed survive then so did the black boxes. If the black box did indeed survive as we have proven beyond a shred of doubt, then why the complete and utter lie that they were damaged beyond use?

What are they hiding?

And the fact that the name of the hijacker, whose passport was found, cannot be released because it could jeopardize the investigation, why release the fact that you have it in the first place?

And what about the Cockpit recording from Flight 93 which excerpts were played ONLY to the relatives of those who died? With all the information I have already presented to you, is it not safe to assume that it may not have been original.

Think of the smoking gun Osama bin Laden "I did it " video.

What was heard on that recording has yet to surface, as the only people who heard it were the relatives, and they were asked not to repeat the information they were given by listening to it because of the "ongoing investigation."

No prior warning

The FBI and CIA claim that there was no prior warning of the disaster that happened on 11 September but within days of the attacks, all 19 hijackers were named and claimed to be in cahoots with Osama bin Laden. Imagine that! This is clearly nonsense.

Why is this nonsense? Seven, maybe even more, of the terrorist named behind the attacks are still alive! Wow, Allah is greater than I thought! You walk on a plane to destroy the sinning enemy, destroy the target, and turn up, alive, thousands of miles away! What a GREAT GOD, (cough) Allah, sorry.

What wonderful investigators we have working for the American people at the FBI and CIA. The reward for this incompetence was an increased budget on behalf of President George W.

Bush.

Saudi Arabian Foreign Minister, Prince Saud Alfaisal, revealed through the Arabic Press and the Arabian Embassy in New York that five Saudi men named by the FBI were not dead.

At least eight of the men whose photographs were released Thursday by the FBI were thought to be Saudi nationals, but officials at the Saudi Arabian embassy in Washington said the photographs do not resemble Saudi citizens with the same name, most of whom are pilots or work in the aviation industry.

Speaking on the condition that he was not named, a Saudi diplomat said his government was doing a "thorough review" of the photos to see if they are of actual Saudi citizens.

Even before the photos were released, the Saudi government had said four men named as dead hijackers, Abdulaziz Alomari, Saeed Alghamdi, Salem Alhamzi and Mohald Alshehri, were alive and were not in the United States at the time of the hijackings.

Alhamzi/Alhazmi told his government he was not on American Flight 77, which crashed into the Pentagon, has never been to the United States, and has been living in fear since his name appeared on the FBI's hijackers list. He said his passport was stolen in the United Arab Emirates, where some of the hijackers allegedly lived.

Alomari was listed as sitting next to Mohamed Atta, whom authorities believe was the ringleader of the suicide hijacking plot on American Flight 11, which was the first to crash into the World Trade Center towers.

But a Saudi government spokesman said Alomari is a Saudi pilot who went to flight school in Florida, as did many of the hijackers, but had moved back to Saudi Arabia before the hijackings.

A Saudi diplomat said the pilot Abdulaziz Alomari is 43, while the photo released by the FBI shows a man who appears to be in his 20s.

Alghamdi, the diplomat said, is a Saudi pilot on loan to Tunisia's national airline. He was in Tunis when the hijackings took place and looks nothing like the photo released by the FBI.

He said the photos showing two brothers, Waleed and Wail Alshehri, are not the pair originally believed to be among the dead hijackers. The Alshehri brothers were initially thought to

37

be the sons of a Saudi diplomat posted in India, but the embassy said the photos are not those of the diplomat's sons.

"Whoever stole these identities knew what they were doing," said an embassy spokesman. "These are very common names in Saudi Arabia."

Two of the hijackers attended the University of Colorado, according to officials there. One was Alomari, the other Ahmed Alghamdi, who was on United Flight 175 out of Boston. Larry Bell, the director of International education at the University of Colorado, told the Globe that the FBI took their records.

Patricia Hagelberg, who rented a room to Alghamdi in Golden, Colo., for about a year, said the FBI had interviewed her. She said she didn't think Alghamdi was one of the hijackers, but the FBI confiscated photographs of him.

"He was quite and he was shy," she said. "He wasn't too friendly."

The Saudi government also confirmed an earlier Globe report that a reputed associate of the hijackers, Amer Kamfar, who is being sought by police in Florida, is a Saudi airlines employee who had moved back to Saudi Arabia a week before the hijackings.[17]

So, who are we to believe? The FBI and CIA who claim to have had no prior warning put names on the "hijackers" while the US Congress sped terrorism legislation (i.e. the Patriot Act, which robs more and more freedoms from the American people) through into law. I wonder if this legislation had been waiting around in the event of a terrorist attack seeing how fast it was written and presented before Congress?

After September 11, The Congress of the United States was able to draft and introduce an "Anti-Terrorism" Bill which was 151 pages long.[18] How could such a huge Bill be formulated in such a short time, covering vast amounts of legal matters? Perhaps, just perhaps, the Bill was drafted long in advance of the attacks, and merely introduced afterwards? Coincidence I'm sure.

Does this not hint at members of Congress themselves having advance knowledge of the attacks?!

This "Anti-Terrorism" Bill has given police sweeping new powers, previously unthinkable in the US, when measured against the Fourth Amendment to the US Constitution, which protects citizens from "unreasonable search and seizure." This Bill, now signed into law, does to the US Constitution, what those airplanes did to the World Trade Center. If you think this an exaggeration, consider the "Homeland Security's" Internal Security Checkpoints in the US where every one of us will have to produce several ID cards proving who we are, in order to travel. People without "proper ID" or those "deemed to be suspicious" will be detained.[19] Any detainee attempting to leave will be shot! It's coming. Consider yourself warned.

Amazing how things all come together in the end, isn't it. And yet the names of the walking dead are still used to identify the dead hijackers.

And if there was no "prior" knowledge of the attacks, why was FEMA (the Federal Emergency Management Agency) stated to be in place and ready to move the day BEFORE the attacks?

During an interview with CBS News anchor Dan Rather, Tom Kennedy, a member of FEMA's "National Urban Search and Rescue Team" let it slip that the Urban Search and Rescue Team was sent to New York City the night before the attacks occurred!

Mr. Kennedy tells Dan Rather:

> "We're currently one of the first teams that was deployed to support the City of New York in this disaster. We arrived on late Monday night and went right into action on Tuesday morning."[20]

They, "Arrived on late Monday night," (10 September) and then, "Went right into action on Tuesday morning," (11 September). What state of "emergency" was New York City in "late Monday night?"

The attacks and collapse of the World Trade center happened on Tuesday, 11 September. Surely it did not take FEMA almost an entire additional week, the following Monday, to send the Urban Search and Rescue Unit to help New York? Well this is something with the name "Federal" at the beginning, so anything is possible.

And Mr. Kennedy says his team was, "One of the first," deployed to assist New York City. Arriving a week after the attacks, points directly to the fact that he surely wasn't talking about the following Monday. Mr. Kennedy certainly couldn't have claimed to have, "been one of the first deployed."

In fact by MONDAY, 17 September, nine teams were working

at Ground Zero. Mr. Kennedy's team was surely not, "One of the first deployed."[21]

Its amazing really, when there was no communication between Air Traffic Control and the hijacked planes, and no black boxes to tell of what really was going on inside the captain's chair that CNN reported that the men who "hijacked " those aircraft "were using phony IDs."[22]

Even Robert Mueller admitted that there is, "No legal proof to prove the identities of the suicidal hijackers,"[23] we are made to believe:

American Airlines Flight 11

Mohamed Atta: the Egyptian by nationality, was the ringleader of the group, and also the pilot who slammed Flight 11 into the WTC.

Mohamed also met with Islamic extremists at the resort of Salou, Spain.[24] Atta arrived to the US with Marwan al-Shehhi (his cousin believed to be on Flight 175) in May 2000.[25] They lived in Florida and were seen five days before 11 September drinking and playing video games.[26]

Abdulaziz Alomari: the Saudi national was a pilot and flight engineer and worked for Saudi Flight Ops, a flight maintenance company at JFK in New York.[27] He lived in Vero Beach, Florida with his wife and four children who told his landlord on 3 September, he was returning to his home in Saudi Arabia.[28] Video surveillance cameras show Alomari and Atta boarding the airport in Portland, Maine on the morning of 11 September.[29] (Picture Section)

Waleed M Alshehri: "possible" Saudi national[30] who lived in the US from 1994 had a Social Security Number,[31] Florida Drivers License,[32] as well as a Commercial Pilot's License.[33] He graduated from Embry- Riddle Aeronautics University in Daytona Beach, Florida.[34] He moved to Virginia, near CIA headquarters and told his landlord he was returning to Saudi Arabia.[35]

Wail Alshehri: a Saudi national is said to have also been a pilot, and may have lived in Florida and Massachusetts.[36]

Satam al-Suqami: from the United Arab Emirates with an address in Boynton Beach, had a Florida Driver's License and a Saudi Arabian License.[37]

For starters, with no evidence, how is it known Mohamed Atta was the pilot?

There is even no evidence to support the meeting in Spain.

Fundamentalist/Extremist Muslims do not drink,[38] mind you, none the less would they be drinking days before a massive holly attack that would require a vast amount of prayer and fasting.[39]

Alomari did in fact return to Saudi Arabia, and walked into the US Consulate in Jedddah to demand why the FBI was reporting him as a dead hijacker.[40]

Another Saudi national, an electrical engineer named Abdulaziz Alomari said he lost his passport while studying in Denver, Colorado. He stated, "I couldn't believe it when the FBI put me on their list. I am alive. I have no idea how to fly a plane. I had nothing to do with this."[41]

Imagine that.

Walled M Alshehri is still alive too. He is a pilot with Saudi Airlines who is taking up further airline training in Morocco.[42]

Oh man. Another one is alive. Wail Alshehri is the name of the son of a Saudi diplomat in Bombay.[43]

As far as Satam al-Suqami being involved, remember that the flight attendants called with the terrorist information claimed there were four hijackers,[44] yet with all the information the FBI has, the FBI claim five.

Brilliant, absolutely brilliant.

United Airlines Flight 175

Marwan al-Shehhi: born in the United Arab Emirates and cousin of Mohamed Atta,[45] was known to hold conversations in Hamburg, Germany (with Atta) with Islamic groups planning attacks on American targets.[46]

Fayez Ahmed: lived in Delray Beach, Florida and has a pilot's license from the Spartan School of Aeronautics, Tulsa, Oklahoma.[47]

Ahmed Alghamdi: lived in Virginia near the CIA in a boarding house sponsored by an Islamic Scholarship. He is also reported to have been living in Delray Beach, Florida.[48]

Hamza Alghamdi: lived in Delray Beach, Florida.[49]

Mohald Alshehri: lived in Delray Beach, Florida.[50]

Marwan al-Shehhi is said to still be alive and living in Morocco.[51]

Mohald Alshehri never boarded the plane, let alone helped hijack it, as according to the Saudi Embassy, he is still alive.[52]

41

American Airlines Flight 77

Hani Hanjour: had a Taif, Saudi Arabia address,[53] and also lived in Phoenix, Arizona where he joined the Sawyer School of Aviation flight simulator club, and also took English lessons at the University of Arizona in 1991.[54] He may have lived in Oakland California in 1996. He is believed to be the pilot who crashed Flight 77 into the Pentagon.[55]

Khalid Almidhar: lived in San Diego, California in 2000[56] and joined Gold's Gym in Maryland[57] weeks before 11 September. He also had two expired visas.[58] The FBI also claims that he was caught on a surveillance videotape in Malaysia showing a meeting with one of the suspects connected with the USS Cole bombing.[59]

This connection therefor links the "terrorists" with Osama bin Laden.

Nawaq Alhamzi: bought a Toyota Corolla with Almidhar[60] (I hope they got the name right on the registration, seeing how nobody knows who Almidhar really is, explain that the loan officer).

Salem Alhamzi: brother of Nawaq[61] and may have lived in Fort Lee and Wayne, New Jersey.[62] He also held a membership at Gold's Gym in Maryland.[63]

Majed Moqed also held a membership at Gold's Gym.[64] An employee claimed that the terrorist paid for the memberships with, "wads of cash" instead of signing a long-term membership plan.[65] Moqed also was caught on a surveillance camera with Hani Hanjour while using an ATM in Laurel, Maryland on 5 September.[66] (Picture Section)

Instructors at Freeway Airport in Bowie, Maryland said that Hani Hanjour was so poor at flying, that he was even refused renting a plane for a solo flight.[67] When he stayed with a family in Miramar, Florida, the family described him as a, "kind and gentle man," who loved children.[68] Just the quality I look for in an Islamic terrorist. Come to mention it, I could use a good baby sitter at the moment.

Khalid Almidhar, as mentioned above by flight instructor Rick Garza, was like, "Dumb and Dumber."[69] It is also reported that he would become so paranoid during lessons that he would pray to Allah for safety.[70]

As for the connection between Almidhar and bin Laden, American investigators, "Are not certain that his name is really Khalid Almidhar."[71]

So, tell me why the FBI claims he was on Flight 77? I didn't quite catch that. And how can you say that this man, who may not even be Almidhar, is the man, or isn't that man, on the video in Malaysia, if they don't know, or is it they do know who he is?

And are you ready for this … Reported in the Arab News, a young Saudi computer programmer named Khalid Almihammadi was confused with Almidhar and had the, "shock of his life" when he saw HIS picture was among the terrorists who had hijacked Flight 77.[72]

I hope you are still sitting down … HIS PICTURE IS STILL BEING USED TO IDENTIFY SOMEONE THE FBI CANNOT CONFIRM THE IDENTITY OF.

Almihammadi had been in the US studying English for nine months in 2000 and returned that same year to Saudi Arabia.[73]

Nawaq Alhamzi was the apparent other half of "Dumb and Dumber." His landlord in San Diego helped him to open an account at the Bank of America[74] and even how to write an advertisement in English for a Mexican wife.[75] (Explain that one to me.) He was described as a model tenant who dropped in often for coffee and cookies.

Flight instructor Rick Garza described Alhamzi as having a, "Great, great personality," and, "Someone you could become attached to quickly."[76] Garza also said that he came back to say goodbye and how nice he was. Garza also said that Alhamzi promised to return once his English improved.[77]

Alhamzi's father released a picture of a different image of what is claimed by the FBI,[78] surprising. There is no word on whether or not he is still alive, but it is a good chance he is, seeing how the man pictured by the FBI is not the man pictured as released by his father.

There is word that Nawaq's brother, Salem Alhamzi, IS in fact alive and works at a petrochemical plant in Yanbou, Saudi Arabia. His father also issued a photograph that bears no resemblance to the hijacker claimed to be Salem by the FBI.[79]

And all of the sudden ATM surveillance photos are readily available to identify a terrorist, just as personal and private cellular conversations are readily available for transcripts. What a wonderful thing technology is. Honey, where are the credit cards and the cell phone?

United Airlines Flight 93

Saeed Alghamdi lived in Delray Beach, Florida with Fayea Ahmed,

Ahmed Alghamdi, Hamza Alghamdi, and Mohald Alshehri.[80]

Ziad Jarrahi "may" have been the pilot.[81]

Ahmed Alnami lived in Delray Beach, Florida.[82]

Ahmed Alhaznawi is said to also have lived in Delray Beach, Florida, with the others mentioned above.[83]

Saeed Alghamdi, still lives in Saudi Arabia and works for Tunis Air.[84] "I was completely shocked. For the past ten months I have been based in Tunis with 22 other pilots learning to fly an Airbus 320. The FBI provided no evidence of my presumed involvement in the attacks," stated Alghamdi.[85] I guess he is training with the other 22 pilots for the NEXT terrorist attack, in which after he hijacks another plane, slams it into another field, or perhaps a building this time, he will miraculous STILL be alive to do it again.

Ziad Jarrahi was engaged to be married to his Turkish girlfriend.[86] He also attended an evangelical Christian school in Lebanon.[87]

Yep, you heard it here first folks, now Osama bin Laden has Christian extremist as well as the Islamic ones. Imagine that.

Ahmed Alnami is still alive,[88] imagine that. And as the others, was shocked to be named as a hijacker.

I sit here writing this chapter almost two years after the attack, and yet the main stream media still refers to the names and photographs supplied by the FBI.

Even on April 19, 2002, Director Robert Mueller admitted in a speech to the Commonwealth Club in San Francisco:

> "In our investigation, we have not uncovered a single piece of paper – either here in the United States or in the treasure trove of information that has turned up in Afghanistan and elsewhere- that mentioned any suspect of the September 11 plot."[89]

Yet Attorney General John Ashcroft described the, "Most massive and intensive investigation ever conducted in America," which consisted of 4000 special agents, and 3000 support workers that were assigned to the case of determining the names of the hijackers.[90]

The first list of these, well, I guess we can't really call them the hijackers, because we really don't know who hijacked the planes. But anyway, the FBI released the first list on 14 September and the second "updated" list was the 27th of September. This update listed added slightly different spelling and additional names and aliases. Yet, seven, at least seven of the "known" hijackers are still alive!

And after all these people, who probably worked overtime, and maybe even received a raise thanks to Little Boy Bush, at the tax payers expense, claim that what I mentioned above about the hijackers is truth. I think I am going to throw up. Or apply at the FBI. Maybe both.

One disappearing act deserves another

Another odd shaped puzzle piece is that fact that on the "partial" passenger lists released by American and United Airlines, the terrorists' names do not appear. Although quoted three days after the attack, ABC News released their names and the seats they were sitting in. (I used this information to open the chapter.)

So where did their names go all of the sudden?

As I write this chapter in February 2003, I can still only find a partial list, and not one includes ANY name of the "terrorists."

In this partial list I found floating around on various Internet news sites, I found discrepancies between them. This is what I found:

American Airlines Flight 11 has variations of missing between five and eight passengers from the list.

American Airlines Flight 77 has between eight and ten missing names.

United Airlines Flight 175 also had between eight and ten names missing from their list.

United Airlines Flight 93 however, no matter which news web site you looked at came up with twelve missing passenger names.

Going with the lowest number of missing names on the list, the five unaccounted names on Flight 11 confirm that there might have been five hijackers, but the names of the people mentioned in the introduction to this chapter are not named.

Flight 77 with a minimum of eight names, gives at least three more helpers on board. And Flight 175 respectfully.

Even Flight 93 had either eight more heroes, or eight more terrorists.

Interesting.

I placed a phone call to the United Airlines Reservations and asked for information regarding the names of the passengers on Flights 175 and 93. I was referred to Jenna Ludgate, which wasn't a toll free number, nor who was an easy person to get to take my calls.

45

I asked Jenna about the missing names on the flight lists as well as there being more names missing than were hijackers being reported by the FBI. She responded very coldly, "United Airlines has not released a complete passenger list, pending notification of the victims' families."[91]

Ahhh, that explains it. Almost two years after the attacks, everyone in the world knows of the horrible attacks on that day. But yet at least fourteen families of the missing names have not been contacted yet? And if you go with the highest number of missing names eighteen families are either taking it too hard or have yet to wonder why Cousin Ralph and Auntie Edna have not shown up for Christmas dinner the last two years without any calls or cards!!

But yet ABC reported the seat numbers of the "terrorists" just three days after the attacks?!

And now, almost two years later, they are not on any passenger list, as well as a few more names of people whose families have yet to be notified.

And if you take off the number of LIVING terrorists, the number of unnamed passengers grows to AT LEAST TWENTY-ONE! But yet the FBI has it all figured out? Right! Sure they do.

When I tried to find the same answers with American Airlines I was told there was no number I could call. But they did refer me to their web site for related information and to better help address my questions, I should phone the FBI directly.

Sure, I'm sure I will have only more unanswered questions then, not the answers to my simple questions if I phoned the FBI.

According to Stanley Hilton, a California-based lawyer who has filed a $7 billion lawsuit against the United States government for prior knowledge of the attacks, his "Clients have been placed under very tough gag orders." His clients include the families of the pilots, and flight attendants of American Airlines.[92]

It is also alleged that if anyone involved with either American or United Airlines who speaks of their knowledge publicly are subject to IMMEDIATE TERMINATION.[93]

What are they hiding? Really? What is it that is so important that cannot be said publicly?

It's all in the numbers

One other interesting puzzle piece is the number of people on the flights

46

"hijacked."

I don't know how many flights I have been on from Seattle to New York, Washington, D.C. to San Francisco, New York to San Francisco, Chicago to Seattle to New York, Cleveland to Toronto, Detroit to Minneapolis, etc. on various days of the week, with flights nearly full to capacity, if not completely full. Yet these flights were not even half of the capacity.

Flight 11 had 81 passengers on a plane built for 158.[94]

Flight 175 had only 56 passengers with a capacity of 168.[95]

Flight 77 carried 56 passengers also on a plane with 176 total seats available.[96]

Flight 93 had just 38 aboard a plane that could cram in 182.[97]

Combined, the average passenger capacity was at 34%. Damn, why can't I fly when there are so few passengers? Not only would I avoid useless small talk, I would be able to relax and even stretch my legs or even lie down in the center seats.

Had the flights even been filled to 75% or even 50%, the casualties would be even higher than they already are, with more families in turmoil, and possibly even more unnamed passengers.

OK, all jokes aside, the fact is, these planes were not nearly as full as they could have been. Is that a clue?

No wonder these flights were so easy to be hijacked. There wasn't anyone to fight the hijackers, whoever they were. And surprisingly the flight with the least amount of passengers was the flight that was "supposedly" brought down by the passengers.

While on the phone with Jenna Ludgate, I asked if she could reveal if certain seats were blocked from purchase, or if she could release to me the average passenger totals on all the other United Airline Flights 175 and 93?

"This information is not made public, and is proprietary."[98]

Well perhaps I could phone the FBI!

I did contact the FBI on February 26, 2003 and was asked to "Type up my questions and fax them to Rex Tomb." I submitted my fax on March 3, 2003. I am sure the answers to my questions will be answered promptly and be included in this book.

YEAH RIGHT!

The "Ringleader"

As revealed above, the alleged hijackers were, well those still alive are normal people with normal lives. It is amazing how such normal people could have carried out such abnormal and furious attacks on the American people.

Friendly neighbors, serious students and model dads. The men suspected of hijacking the jets that carried out history's deadliest terror strikes looked a lot more like the guy next door than the incarnation of the devil.

The most disturbing common element that has emerged from the FBI investigation into the 19 men who are now believed to have cold-bloodedly rained destruction on the U.S. political and economic capitals is how ordinary their behavior was.

They were aged between 21 and 40. They were of Arab extraction. Many had lived for years in the United States without raising suspicion.

One of the suspects, Mohamed Atta, considered by FBI chief Robert Mueller as one of the main leader in the devastation, was typical of what investigators have found.[99]

Known as a polite student to acquaintances who got to know him over the past few years, Atta, aged around 33, had taken the care to shave his beard and put away his long kaftan, changing his appearance from when he previously lived in Hamburg, Germany.[100]

It seems he first came to the United States in 1989. He stayed several times in Florida, notably in a charming small pink house close to Daytona Beach, where he sometimes received neighbours or Elaine Brinkley, the real estate agent looking after the property.

"How can you suspect someone like that of being a terrorist?" Brinkley asked, recalling how he offered her biscuits or coffee. "They are not like you see in the movies."

Still, this polite tenant and attentive host was aboard the doomed American Airlines Boeing 767 that slammed into the first tower of the World Trade Center on Tuesday.[101]

And speaking of Mohamed Atta the, "Polite tenant and attentive host,"[102] and the alleged ringleader of the terrorist. Lets look a little into his life.

Egyptian man denies son's involvement in hijackings, calls

48

accusations 'nonsense'

CAIRO — Sometimes shouting, sometimes crying, sometimes shaking his head, Mohamed al-Amir Atta said Tuesday that his son and namesake was a shy man who could not possibly have sent a hijacked jet slicing through the first World Trade Center tower.

"Mohamed. Oh God! He is so decent, so shy and tender," said the father, a 65-year-old retired lawyer. "He was so gentle. I used to tell him, 'Toughen up, boy!'"

Atta stood on the barren concrete doorstep of his 11th-floor Cairo apartment on Tuesday in a cream leisure suit, alternating between rage at the picture being painted of his son as one of the attack's ringleaders and pride that his boy had done well abroad after graduating with average marks in architecture from Cairo University's Faculty of Engineering.

The FBI has identified the 33-year-old son of Atta as one of the hijackers. He has been traced to at least two flying schools in Florida in the 14 months before last week's attack.

The elder Atta laced his conversation with fierce attacks against the United States, a "tyrant nation" that he blasted repeatedly for supporting Israel and for moral contagions like adultery and same-sex marriage.

Some of his son's university friends in Germany have described Mohamed Atta as a sharply intelligent, strict, serious man who seemed to retreat socially, seeking solace from religion.

The elder Atta said he never encouraged his children to be social, even avoiding the incessant contact between relatives so common in Egypt. Neighbors in their slightly tattered, middle class neighborhood in Giza, just off the road to the Pyramids, confirmed that family members rarely said more than hello.

"We keep our doors closed, and that is why my two daughters and my son are academically and morally excellent," Atta said.

He was outraged at reports that his son was seen drinking in a Florida bar on the eve of the attacks.

"My son is a hijacker and drinks vodka!" yelled Atta, his face reddening to the roots of his short white hair and his hands waving in the air. "It is like accusing a decent, veiled religious girl of smuggling prostitutes into Egypt. It is nonsense, imagination!"

Indeed, two German students who spent the months of August

49

to October 1995 in Cairo with Atta while completing an urban renewal field study said they did not drink alcohol around him because it made him uncomfortable.

The elder Atta said that while his son was also religious, that fervor did not extend to politics.

He had refused, his father said, to take part in a neighborhood basketball league when he found out it was organized by the Muslim Brotherhood, Egypt's most established religious political organization.

"He was a donkey when it came to politics," his father said. "I advised him, like my father advised me, that politics equals hypocrisy." [103]

Hijacking suspect's father says son `hates bin Laden,' isn't terrorist

CAIRO - Mohamed Al-Amir, the father of a hijacking suspect in the Sept. 11 attack on the World Trade Center, said Monday that his son hated Osama bin Laden and would never commit terrorism.

The FBI has called Al-Amir's son, Mohamed Atta, 33, the "axis" of a terrorist network that carried out the bloodiest attack on U.S. soil.

"I challenge any person who has any proof that one member of this family belongs to any political party," said Al-Amir, shaking a forefinger as his face reddened. "My son hates bin Laden - and this is the only political opinion he had in his life."

Al-Amir's crowded afternoon news conference dissolved into a shouting match with reporters. He said Atta hated bin Laden because the accused mastermind of the recent terrorist strike in New York also attacked the Egyptian embassy in Pakistan in the mid-1990s.

In a quivering voice that rose to a shout, he blamed Israel's intelligence service, Mossad, for the attacks: "America knows that it was the Mossad who did this operation!" He accused Mossad or another intelligence agency of kidnaping his son.

Al-Amir, a middle-class lawyer in Cairo, described his son as a quiet, happy child who grew into a hard-working, religious man "like all the people in our family . . . He only had one hobby; that was playing chess with me."

Atta graduated from Cairo University with a degree in

architecture in 1990. He studied English at American University in Cairo and wrote and spoke English perfectly, according to his father.

He studied German before studying urban planning at a technical university in Hamburg, Germany.

Al-Amir admitted he did not know much about his son's life in Germany. But he insisted that Atta visited only Turkey, Syria and Saudi Arabia, not the United States.

His son phoned home 12 to 36 hours after the Sept. 11 attacks, he said, in what was "a normal phone conversation."

Pressed to explain where the call came from, Al-Amir said he did not know, screaming back: "Is it written on the telephone where he is?"

Airport security videotapes of his son on the morning of the terrorist attacks were "falsified," he declared.

"That is not my son," he shouted, pointing to a security-camera photo published in an Arabic newspaper. "This person has more muscle than my son. He has a big nose, and he apparently is wearing a mask. This is not my son!"

Other individuals initially identified as hijackers, he said, were found to be living in Saudi Arabia.

Al-Amir also warned that U.S. retaliation against Afghanistan will not stop terrorism. "There will be different generations of Americans who will suffer," he shouted. "For God's sake, don't fight terrorism with terrorism. America has to think in a wise way and understand why this enemy became an enemy."[104]

Could it be that the identity of Mohamed Atta was also stolen or used? Who could identify his own son better than his own father who stated, "That is not my son," looking at the surveillance video of Atta "boarding" the plane?

Someone claimed for being in bed with bin Laden sure fooled his father into believing he hated him. I do not believe bin Laden did anything in the 11 September attacks. Bin Laden is a terrorist. I do not dispute this. But surely evidence is stronger to support the fact that Mohamed Atta was not the ringleader of the terrorist, let alone the pilot who slammed Flight 11 into the World Trade Center.

Yet the FBI, yes those guys again, believes that Atta first arrived in the United States sometime in 2000.[105] (I love their precise estimations, don't you!) In November and December of 2000 he purchased flight deck videos for various airplanes at Sporty's Pilot Shop in Ohio. [106]

Nawaq Alhamzi, the supposed pilot of Flight 77, and Zacharias Moussaoui, the "20th hijacker" (more on him in a second), are believed to have bought similar videos at this same pilot's store.[107] Perhaps they should have come in together and received the special group terrorist discount, or something.

And here is where our puzzle continues to get even more odd. It is believed that Atta was originally given his visa to America on May 18, 2000 from the US Consulate in Berlin, Germany.[108] He overstayed his visa more than 30 days.[109] But when he returned from Europe without a visa, he was permitted to pass through customs, and therefor into the streets of America. And then, as the FBI claims, into the pilot seat of Flight 11. Amazing!

Atta is also claimed: to have been seen in Norfolk, Virginia surveying the US naval base as a possible target;[110] to have been surveying Boston Logan Airport;[111] to be a member of Egyptian Jihad with ties to Osama bin Laden;[112] to have flown from Miami, Florida to Madrid, Spain;[113] to have rented a car ordered over the internet[114] (this is a crime, I suppose); to have spent at least one night at the Montsant Hotel in the resort town of Salou, Spain;[115] to have met an Al-Qaeda operative named Ramzi bin Shibh in Salou;[116] to have shared an apartment with Shibh in Germany;[117] and plotted the attacks.[118] Man this guy gets around more than my ex-wife does!

And this is all reported with only "sources" to support the fire burning crueler and crueler terrorist in America.

One-source claims that on August 28, 2001, Atta purchased two one-way tickets on the internet for Flight 11 with a visa card and a frequent flier membership number issued only three months before the departure.[119] Can I ask a question here? Why would one need to rack up frequent flier miles for a free trip, if you knew you were going to be dead in less than three months? Maybe the miles rollover in Heaven. Who knows. One thing is for certain, frequent flier and supermarket membership cards were created with the intention of monitoring and tracking its owner. Would a terrorist be so stupid to leave a trail that could be easily tracked back to him?

Another source claims that Atta racked up more than 3000 miles on rental cars between 6 August and 9 September.[121]

So? I have driven between California and Montana more than

four times in the period of less than six weeks. I also put more than 100,000 miles on a car in one year's time. Am I a terrorist? Let me check in the mirror. Be right back. Nope. Not that I can tell.

Warrick Rent-A-Car in Pompano Beach, Florida owner, Brad Warrick, said Atta, "Carried a briefcase, was polite, and looked like a professional businessman."[122] (I wonder if the Enterprise Rent-A-Car in Fortuna, California will state to the reporters, after I perform my "terrorist " act, whatever that may be, that I wore jeans and T-shirts and rode a 18-speed bicycle to pick up my rental cars?) Warrick continued:

> "He didn't spend money like there was an unlimited source. He squabbled a little bit over mileage."[123]

Although others claimed Atta had unlimited funds from bin Laden and wads of cash in his pocket, Warrick also noted that he switched to a Ford Escort because it was $10 less than the Chevy Corsica.[124] Now we have a conservative Islamic extreme terrorist. And I am sure it is all in the act. You know the one, to draw attention to themselves. Yeah, that one.

Brad Warrick continued:

> "He appeared to me to be just a very conscientious, nice businessman," Warrick said. "I'm really just a little small, hole-in the-wall rental office . . . We're an inconspicuous place to go."
> [125]

> "They were just great customers," said Brad Warrick, the Pompano Beach businessman who rented cars to Atta and Al-Shehhi. For years, Warrick has conducted a quick "gut check" of everyone who walks through his door, declining to rent to those who give him a bad feeling. "Didn't have it with these guys,"[126]

If can be said that Atta cared deeply about people. It is not just that he cared about the Muslim poor. He even cared about the next American to rent his rental car. Brad Warrick continued by saying that Atta had called him to say the car's oil light was on. When he returned it on 9 September, Atta reminded him about the light. This unconsciously echos the many Germans who experienced Atta's consideration, Warrick continued, "The only thing out of the ordinary was that he was nice enough to let me know that the car needed an oil change."[127]

When Brad Warrick saw Atta's picture on television, he

instantly recognized him as the polite, well-spoken man to whom he had rented a car three times in the last six weeks. Warrick, said Atta first came into his office on 6 August and appeared to be someone who had lived in the country for years and "Seemed pretty friendly."[128]

So who really was Mohamed Atta? We don't really know.

We don't really know who any of them really were. But we do know who they were supposed to be. Or, what we are meant to believe they were.

Islamic Fundamentalist in Strip Clubs

Mohamed Atta is said to have been at Shuckums Oyster Pub and Seafood Grill in Hollywood, Florida along with Marwa al-Shehhi and another unidentified man. The manager claims they stayed from around 4:30pm until around 7pm. Their waitress, Patricia Idrissi told the press that the unidentified individual went off to play a video game while Atta and Al-Shehhi sat drinking rum and coke and Stolichnaya Vodkas with O.J. and argued a bit. Even their bill of $48 was argued with the manager.[129]

Atta is said to have yelled "You think I can't pay my bill? I am a pilot for American Airlines. I can pay my fucking bill."[130]

OK, I have been a manager of a restaurant. Three actually, and I don't recall everyone in the restaurant and at what time they arrived and what time they left. I have also have had to serve regular guests, frequent regulars mind you, and I couldn't remember what each of them drank for the life of me. (But I know that many servers do remember frequent customers.) I do not even remember all the arguments over bills I have had to settle. But apparently someone who is a first time customer at this restaurant, someone who is about to die in a few days flashing "wads of cash" is arguing over $48. Why?

The manager claimed he did settle to pay the $48 and paid using a "thick wad of 50s and 100s."[131]

I thought you can't take it with you? And the "fact" that he mentioned American Airlines? Anyway, we are fed this garbage as fact.

For one, Islamic law, let alone fundamental Islamic law, strictly forbids drinking alcohol.

Atta's father mentioned he was, "Very shy, very polite, and would never swear."[132]

Azzan Ali, a friend of Atta from the Florida flying school said, "They were very religious."[133]

On 13 September, the *USA Today* ran a story that on the night before 11 September, the "fundamentalists" were drinking in a strip bar in Daytona Beach, Florida.

> MIAMI (AP) — The night before terrorists struck New York and Washington, three men spewed anti-American sentiments in a bar and talked of impending bloodshed, according to a strip club manager interviewed by the FBI. John Kap, manager of the Pink Pony and Red Eyed Jack's Sports Bar in Daytona Beach, said the men made the claims to a bartender and a patron. "They were talking about what a bad place America is. They said 'Wait 'til tomorrow. America is going to see bloodshed,'" Kap said.
>
> He said he told FBI investigators the men in his bar spent $200 to $300 apiece on lap dances and drinks, paying with credit cards.
>
> Kap said he gave the FBI credit card receipts and a business card left by one man and a copy of the Quran that was left at the bar.[134]

There you have it... "real" (and drunk) Extreme Islamic Fundamentalist. Would an Islamic Extremist for one, take a copy of the Koran into a strip club, and then leave his sacred text to be found by an infidel? Perhaps he wanted to do some witnessing or converting.

But that's not all. It was reported that these extremist hijackers left copies of the Koran EVERYWHERE. What a great detective movie script. Coming Soon to a Movie Cinema near you: ISLAMIC GIDEONS.

As American demands for a violent act of revenge grow louder, the Western media have still not addressed many questions and contradictions. They remain buried under the tons of Western newsprint propagating the kind of hatred and desperation that presumably motivated those who committed the acts of terror themselves. How could Osama Bin Laden have organized such an attack from a cave in the middle of a country that has neither electricity nor modern telecommunications? How could the hijackers themselves have been "Islamists" if they frequented bars, drank in some cases, beer and wine, and one even attended an evangelical Christian school and stated that he would not have minded marrying a non-Muslim?

How can we have faith in the investigations when almost half of the original list of hijackers have turned out to be alive and well in other parts of the world? Could all of this really be only a battle between "good" and "evil?"[135]

Is this a coincidence that we are seeing staged events designed to build a story to back up the FBI's "official"one?

The mainstream media only reports what they are given. They never question it. And therefore the mass population of America believes what the media tells them. A never-ending chain that must be broken!

One story that the media has not reported is on Atta's miraculous journey. One day before he returned his rental car to Daytona Beach on 9 September, Atta was seen walking into the control tower at Boston Logan Airport. The rental car didn't have any extra mileage. There is no account of another rental car other than the one in Boston rented on 10 September. So he must have flown to Boston, then had flown back to Florida to return the car, then flew back to Boston to rent the car to then go to Portland on 10 September.

The media has released the surveillance video of Atta and Alomari boarding the plane in Portland, Maine (picture section). So why are we not shown video clips of the flights between Florida and Boston, and back to Florida, then from Florida back to Boston? Where are the tickets to get there? Which library computer did Atta use to purchase them on, and did he use his frequent flier membership? Where again is the check in staff testimony, "Oh yes, sure I remember him boarding the plane in Florida to Boston ... the Islamic Extremist, right?"

Well this footage is not available, yet the footage of Atta and Alomari is? Um, well, no, that isn't right. Alomari is still alive, and according to Atta's father, he was too, at least he was on 12 September.

But never-mind that, we have to stick to the "official" lie of bullshit. And in this line of shit, we are made to believe that the people responsible for pulling off the largest hijacking in history would risk being on a delayed or late plane arriving into Boston to catch the predetermined flights to their destiny. I mean come on, how many transfer flights have you been on that were late, or were very close together?

I am remembered of a connecting flight from London to Berlin, and then Berlin to New York. I had four hours between the scheduled landing in Berlin and the departure for New York. But when I arrived three hours and 25 minutes late from London, I had already missed the final boarding call and just as I was exiting the plane from London, my flight destined for New York had left the airport heading for the runway, and for New York, without me.

It's a good thing I didn't plan to hijack that plane to crash it into Berlin's Financial District. But never the less we are made to believe that these two individuals left from Portland to catch a connecting flight from Boston.

The FBI claims that Atta left, and checked out of his hotel at 5:33am, with 27 minutes to spare before take off to Boston.[136]

The image that records "Atta" and "Alomari" boarding the flight in Portland was at 05:53:41. Only six minutes till take off. At least they had six minutes to catch their first flight.

Why was he running late? Cold feet?

Not only did the ringleader of the biggest hijacking in history take the chance of missing his connecting flight, he also took the chance of missing his flight to getting to Boston.

When I fly, I always plan for the worst. These guys can plan and prepare the largest hijacking, yet run late, risking the chance of messing everything up? Well there is always the next flight, right?

But it gets even more complex.

Take a look at the image from the Security camera. (Picture Section) There are two times. 05:53:41 and 05:45:13.

No wonder planes never leave airports on time. They are going by two different times! All our questions about airline travel have been answered!

But this question still remains. If Atta and Alomari did check out at 5:33, they made it to the airport, returned the car, checked in and went through screening in 12 minutes! And they still have 15 minutes to spare. How?

Man these guys are good!

And let me ask this. What other images have you seen in the media that show Atta, or any of the other hijackers boarding the plane or even in the lounge at Boston Logan International Airport?

That's right. None. Nil. Zero. Zilch.

Isn't it ironic, or just a matter of connivance that there are no security camera images available from Boston Logan of any of the identified hijackers?

Would you believe me if I told you that up until the time of the attacks, Boston International Airport did not have security cameras installed in the waiting lounge? I didn't think you would so let me give you an article from the *Boston Globe*:

Logan lacks video cameras
by Doug Hanchett and Robin Washington
Saturday, September 29, 2001

In perhaps the most stunning example of Massport's lax security safeguards, Logan International Airport is missing a basic tool found not only in virtually every other airport, but in most 7-Elevens. Surveillance cameras.[137]

So now we don't even know if the "hijackers" even boarded the plane. Would explain why they are not named on any of the passengers' list, wouldn't it?!

The luggage of the hijackers

It would appear that the gods above would like to help in the investigation, by surprisingly delaying the luggage of many of the hijackers onto their flights. So that explains all the times that I have lost luggage, or had to wait days for it to turn up. Divine intervention. They say god works in mysterious ways. Um, sure.

Anyway, the FBI "investigators" have seized articles belonging to the "hijackers" that surprisingly never made it on their flights.[138]

One of the most surprising items that did not make it on any of the doomed airliners was Mohamed Atta's luggage. We are told, although his name does not appear on any passenger list, that he brought two suitcases with him. I would assume to not arise suspicion, but I know many people who fly first class that check nothing in and carry only a carry-on. But Mr. Atta apparently had two suitcases. I guess in the event that the attack didn't go as planned he would need some things to get on after he arrived in Los Angeles.

But what were in his suitcases?

Although it was a little too convenient for the FBI that these two suitcases that did not make it from his connecting flight onto his suicidal flight, the articles also conveniently included: a copy of the Koran; a handheld flight computer; flight simulator manuals; two videotapes about Boeing aircraft; a slide rule flight calculator; numerous documents including a letter of recommendation and education related documents; a Saudi passport; his will; and lots of socks and underpants.[139]

If he was really committing an act of suicidal Jihad would he not have brought his Koran on board? And surely the handheld flight computer, and slide rule flight calculator do a lot of help in flying a plane when they are in your checked luggage! Yet, they didn't even make it onto the plane. And it looks to me like he had items that would be handy for a job interview, not a suicide attack. This isn't a McDonald's interview he would have attended, where they hire anyone off the street, hence the reason I don't eat fast food, let alone many restaurants. But sense most of this book is based on "speculation" lets speculate that he was not on a mission of a suicide attack, and a job interview. Would it not make sense to have tapes to view to refresh knowledge learned in school prior to an interview? Makes sense to me. The more you know, the less a company has to train you, and the greater chance the employee is to stay with the company.

Why an Egyptian national has a Saudi passport is beyond me. Must be an Islamic Extremist thing. And correct me if I'm wrong, but don't you need photo identification, i.e. a passport, to check in at an airport? How did he get on the plane without identification?

Among other documents that were found in his suitcase was a five-page letter handwritten to his fellow hijackers. The FBI claimed to be the same handwritten letter found in the wreckage of Flight 93 in Pennsylvania.[140] Everything is blown to bits or incinerated, and yet one five-page letter escapes the flames of the wreckage to be that which is similar, if not identical to the note that didn't make it onto a doomed flight? What are these letters written on? Obviously the same thing one of the hijacker's passports, like what was "found"blocks from the World Trade Center, was printed on. Amazing, isn't it!

Also found in his suitcase was his will. In a document dated April 11, 1996, he gave instructions that he be buried next to good Muslims, that his body pointed east toward Mecca, that strict Muslim traditions are followed for his burial, and that no women be allowed at his funeral.[141] The FBI claims that Atta must have been planing suicide attacks sense 1996. Yeah like my last will and testament is for the suicide bombing I'm planning, and have been planning sense I had it written in July 2001. Oh that's right, I am a Caucasian, so they would never assume that about me. They are racially profiling again.

But again, why is a man about to plow an airliner into the World Trade Center check baggage anyway?

The "20th hijacker"

Zacharias Moussaoui was arrested on 16 August, 2001, and in custody on September 11, 2001 for immigration offences, and had he not been arrested, would have been the fifth hijacker on Flight 93, according to the FBI.[142] Or would that make Moussaoui the third hijacker sense two named "hijackers" are still alive and well? Who knows?

Moussaoui, 33, entered the United States last February and immediately began trying to learn to fly. He washed out of flight school in Norman, Okla., and moved onto the Pan Am International Flying Academy in Eagan, Minn., where he paid $8,000 to use flight simulators designed to train commercial pilots. His instructors became suspicious, and the school called the FBI, which detained Moussaoui on Aug. 17 on immigration charges. Held as a material witness after Sept. 11, he has been in jail ever since.

At the time of his arrest FBI agents found flight manuals for the Boeing 747-400, a flight-simulator computer program, binoculars, two knives, fighting shields and a laptop computer. They later learned that French intelligence officials suspected Moussaoui of involvement with Islamic extremists. The FBI team applied to Washington for a special warrant to go into Moussaoui's computer but were turned down: as it turned out, a disc contained information about spraying pesticide from a plane.

"All I can tell you is that the agents on the scene attempted to follow up aggressively," FBI director Robert Mueller said this week. "The attorneys back at the FBI determined that there was insufficient probable cause for a [warrant], which appears to be an accurate decision. And September 11 happened." [143]

It is alleged that in the aftermath of the investigations, more bits of "evidence" turned up. Including Moussaoui carrying the phone number assigned to Ramzi bin Alshibh.

Alshibh is allegedly a member of the Hamburg, Germany Al-Qaeda cell that also included Mohammed Atta. Alshibh served as a financial coordinator for the conspiracy, said the FBI, so we know how reliable this information is. Also in early August, Alshibh sent $14,000 in two wire transfers to Moussaoui therefore using some of the cash to enroll at Pan Am.[144] Perhaps when he gets out of prison, he will be a good pilot then.

The FBI also claims there are the disturbing similarities

between Moussaoui and Mohamed Atta:

1) Atta visited the same flight school in Norman, Oklahoma, that Moussaoui attended.

Although Atta attended a flight training in Florida, it is not claimed that Moussaoui and Atta visited each other. They could have, perhaps, even had a beer at the local pub.[145]

2) Atta and Moussaoui both researched using crop dusters for what might have been a biochemical attack, according to the FBI.[146]

3) Atta and Moussaoui both bought "Flight Deck" instructional videos for the Boeing 747 from the same retailer, Sporty's Pilot Shop in Batavia, Ohio.

Newsweek reported in mid-October that Moussaoui ordered videos on the 747-200 and 747-400 - a finding now included in the indictment.[147]

It is also alleged that inmates in jail with Moussaoui said he cheered at the news of the attacks. And interestingly enough, in a letter written to his mother he wrote:

> "As far as the American story is concerned, don't worry, I didn't do anything, and I'll prove it when the time comes. They are going to try to fabricate proofs and witnesses, but I have proofs and witnesses, and Allah will make their plot ridiculous.
>
> "Do not think I am unhappy or that I am desperate. I am fine."
> [148]

Aicha Moussaoui his mother said, in an interview with *Newsweek*, she knew nothing about her son's alleged involvement with Al-Qaeda and had not seen him since 1997. She also said she is "devastated" by his indictment. "I don't trust American justice," she said. "They find somebody and then they charge him with anything. It is just like he wrote in his letter—they make up proofs."[149]

Well, imagine that. That is what 90% of this book is all about.

Moussaoui's lawyer, Donald D. DuBoulay, a court-appointed attorney, was defiant. "We are conceding nothing," he told reporters. He said Moussaoui intended to plead not guilty. "The charges are not true. He maintains his innocence."[150]

When I watch the morning news shows, they almost blast this man as if he has been tried and convicted. There once was a time where someone was innocent until proven guilty.

Sadly—four of the six charges against him carries the death penalty. French officials are ready to oppose the imposition of the death penalty if Moussaoui is convicted.[151]

In Paris, Isabelle Coutant-Peyre, a lawyer who represents Moussaoui's family, asked French Prime Minister Lionel Jospin to intervene in the case and to work to get Moussaoui repatriated to France to stand trial saying Moussaoui could not receive a fair trial in the United States.[152] Imagine that ... could not receive a fair trial.

Moussaoui, while before the judge in a federal courtroom in Alexandria, Virginia, declared that he is a member of Al-Qaeda and wants to plead guilty to his alleged role in the 11 September attacks.

But U.S. District Judge Leonie M. Brinkema declined to accept his request and said she would give him another week to decide whether he still wanted to plead guilty.

"Bet on me," Moussaoui shot back. "I will."[153]

I wish I had a judge who gave me a week to think about my pleading guilty. What right does a judge have to not accept a plea? When the judge decided punishment. Had he pleaded not guilty, would he been locked away never to be heard from again?

Shortly after that warning, Moussaoui did what all lawyers advise their clients not to do: Admitted a role in the crimes. In addition to declaring his allegiance to Osama bin Laden and saying he was a member of the Al-Qaeda terrorist network, Moussaoui said:

"I will be able to prove I have certain knowledge about September 11, and I know exactly who done it. I know which group, who participated, when it was decided. I have many information."

Moussaoui, 34, a French citizen, said he was pleading guilty to the six charges against him in order to move on to the penalty phase and try to save his life. Four of the counts carry the death penalty.

"For the guilt phase, I'm guilty," he told the judge. "But for the death penalty, we will see."

Brinkema told him that if he truly wanted to plead guilty, he should consider negotiating a plea bargain, which could result in the government's dropping its death penalty demand. "I'll give you at least a week to think about that," the judge said.

"I don't need it," Moussaoui replied. "I've been thinking for months."

If Moussaoui is prepared to tell all, it is unclear whether he will discuss his purported role in the attacks or whether he will want to expound on his theory that the U.S. government was complicit in the hijackings -- something he has asserted repeatedly in more than 70 handwritten motions.

Moussaoui has filed dozens of motions seeking evidence to support his contention that he and the 19 hijackers were being watched by the FBI before Sept. 11. He had contended that he was not part of the hijacking group even though he said he is loyal to bin Laden. [154]

I also would like to see this evidence. As I have already presented that at least seven are still alive. And from an attack nobody seen coming, and four flight lists without a single name of the named hijackers on it, what evidence does the FBI have that Moussaoui had any involvement?

Mark Hulkower, a former federal prosecutor, agreed. "The notion that they're going to cut a deal for cooperation with somebody who was planning on piloting a plane into the World Trade Center is inconceivable," he said.

Holder said Moussaoui's self-representation has allowed the proceedings to reach this critical stage. "We're in the nightmare that in some ways was predictable once he made the motion to represent himself," he said.

Initially, Moussaoui said he had consulted Black's Law Dictionary and wanted to plead "an affirmative plea, a pure plea." He explained that this plea would require him to "make a specific statement regarding my involvement, my participation in a known terrorist group since 1995."

Brinkema said she thought Moussaoui was confused. He assured her he was not. The affirmative plead would "reflect the reality of what I did, why I came to the United States . . . especially because the conspiracy that I was involved, it's an ongoing conspiracy who have started since around 1995 and it continues on to this day." [155]

What conspiracy could he be speaking of? And I may be going of the deep end here, but in this fairy tale anything is possible. But many people, more qualified than I, have suggested mind control within several stages of previous U.S. Government programs. Could it not also be safe to assume that some sort of mind game was being played here also? It really isn't far out there if you think about it. Could Moussaoui been involved in such a program, and somehow been de-programmed to be able to come forth with this information? I believe we will never know.

> Moussaoui, a French citizen of Moroccan descent, told the judge, "I want to enter a plea today of guilty, because this will ensure to save my life." He said that he had "certain knowledge about September 11." He also said, "I know exactly who done it, I know which group, who participated, and I know when it was decided."

> He added, "I am a member of al Qaeda. I pledge bayat to Osama bin Laden." Bayat is the loyalty oath taken by members of al Qaeda. He told the judge, "I have many, many information to give to the America[n] people about an existing conspiracy."

> But Brinkema would not allow him to continue. "This is not the forum to do that," she said. She suggested it might be in his best interest to enter into plea bargain negotiations with the government.[156]

Would someone with such a strong tie to fundamental Islam, be willing to die, gloriously before Allah in a terrorist attack against America the "Great Satan" yet admit that he knew "exactly who " was responsible for the attacks, and reveal everything about the, "existing conspiracy" in hopes he could wither away in prison an old man? Some religious extremist!

Also keep in mind that this "mad-mad" with his bizarre and contradictory behavior is claimed by the FBI as being involved to be one of the highly skilled or highly professional individuals behind the brilliant planning of the hijacking.

I would have to disagree. With this kind of sporadic behavior, I would think he was someone behind Air Traffic Control who did not contact NORAD instead of someone who helped mastermind the hijackings.

Moussaoui's trial was set for September 2002. Let me make aware to those who are not up to date yet. September 2002 has come and gone. And yet Moussaoui is still awaiting his day in court to reveal the, "Important part of the conspiracy."

Someone who has nothing to do with 11 September, will be tried with evidence that is fabricated, convicted, given the death sentence, and will be locked away because of his "mental state" so he cannot talk to anyone. He will either then, be mobbed and killed in prison, or executed on public television for the world to take revenge on the "terrorist" attacks while the one who knows the truth is, sadly, then dead. Then there are the others who know the truth who are not dead. Those are the people running the highest offices of the United States of America.

More bizarre puzzle pieces. Here we have the picture of 19 "hijackers" and yet we are in the electronic and digital age. There are no surveillance camera snapshots. Their names do not appear on any of the passenger list. And at least seven are still alive and many of those seven are employed as pilots in which they received their training for in the flight schools we hear so much about in the main stream media.

Piece by piece another image entirely begins to form. Let's continue.

SOURCES

(1) http://abclocal.go.com/kgo/news/091401_nw_terrorist_attack_hijack_
    suspects.html
    http://abcnews.go.com/sections/us/DailyNews/WTC_MAIN010914.html
(2) Ibid
(3) Ibid
(4) Ibid
(5) http://www.cbsnews.com/stories/2001/09/11/national/main310721.shtml
(CBS News 9-26-01)
(6) http://www.observer.co.uk/Print/0,3858,4272043,00.html
(Observer 10-7-01)
(7) http://www.washingtonpost.com/ac2/wp-dyn/A52712-2001Sep18?
    language=printer, September 19, 2001
(8) http://www.ntsb.gov/aviation/CVR_FDR.htm
(9) http://abcnews.go.com/sections/scitech/TechTV/techtv_blackboxes0109
    17.html ABC News
(10) http://abcnews.go.com/sections/us/DailyNews/WTC_MAIN010914.html
(11) Ibid
(12) http://www.cnn.com/2001/US/09/17/inv.investigation.terrorism/
(13) http://asia.cnn.com/2001/US/09/17/inv.investigation.terrorism/index.html
(14) http://asia.cnn.com/2001/US/09/16/gen.america.under.attack/index.html
(15) http://pubs.usgs.gov/of/2001/ofr-01-0429/

(16) http://www1.chinadaily.com.cn/highlights/doc/2001-09-16/33549.html
(17) http://www.nctimes.com/news/2001/20010929/73128.html
(18) http://www.tamil.net/list/2001-10/msg00704.html
(19) Ibid
(20) CBS News deleated from their website, can be found at:
      http://www.newswatchmagazine.org/apr02/
(21) http://www.fema.gov/emanagers//nat091701.htm
(22) http://www.cnn.com/2001/US/09/21/inv.id.theft/
(23) http://www.observer.co.uk/libertywatch/story/0,1373,560613,00.html
(24) http://www.cnn.com/2002/WORLD/europe/01/19/inv.spanish.arrests/
      &e=747
      http://www.cnn.com/2003/US/03/05/wtc.tape/&e=747
(25) http://www.cia.gov/cia/public_affairs/speeches/archives/2002/dci_testi
      mony_06182002/DCI_18_June_testimony_new.pdf&e=747
(26) http://www.freerepublic.com/focus/news/683026/posts&e=747
(27) http://www.cbsnews.com/htdocs/america_under_attack/
terror/team1_right.html
(28) http://www.cbsnews.com/stories/2001/09/14/archive/main311329.shtml
(29) http://www.courttv.com/assault_on_america/1004_hijackers_ap.html
      &e=747
(30) http://www.sun-sentinel.com/news/local/southflorida/sfl-worldtradesus
      pectprofiles.story&e=747
(31) http://hrsbstaff.ednet.ns.ca/waymac/Sociology/A%20Term%201/5.%20
      Research%20Methods/world_trade_centre_assignment.htm
(32) http://www.orlandosentinel.com/news/nationworld/orlasecterrorists15091
      501sep15,0,391120.story
(33) http://www.sun-sentinel.com/news/local/southflorida/sfl-worldtradesus
      pectprofiles.story
(34) http://news.bbc.co.uk/hi/english/world/americas/
      newsid_1567000/1567815.stm
(35) Ibid
(36) http://www.cbsnews.com/stories/2001/09/ 14/archive/main311329.shtml
(37) Ibid
(38) http://www.reeusda.gov/f4hn/fdrm/Muslims-fact%20sheet-2.pdf
(39) Ibid
(40) http://www.corpust.com/CorpusTArchiveFBI70f19Alive.cfm
(41) UK Telegraph September 23, 2001
(42) http://www.ncmonline.com/content/ncm/2001/oct/1005identities.html
(43) http://www.bartcop.com/1106atta.htm
(44) http://news.bbc.co.uk/1/hi/world/americas/1556096.stm
(45) http://www.cbsnews.com/stories/2002/06/05/national/printable511204.
      shtml
(46) http://www.pbs.org/wgbh/pages/frontline/shows/network/personal/
      whowere.html
(47) http://www.telegraph.co.uk/news/main.jhtml?xml=/news/2001/09/20/
      wterr120.xml
(48) http://www.fairus.org/html/04178101.htm
(49) http://www.effroyable-imposture.net/docs/IMG/pdf/doc-1078.pdf

The "Hijackers"

(50) http://www.telegraph.co.uk/news/main.jhtml?xml=/news/2001/09/20/wterr120.xml
(51) http://news.bbc.co.uk/1/hi/world/middle_east/1559151.stm
(52) http://www.washtimes.com/national/20020910-159437.htm
(53) http://www.cbsnews.com/htdocs/america_under_attack/terror/team3_right.html
(54) Ibid
(55) http://www.911-strike.com/remote_skills.htm
(56) http://www.cbsnews.com/htdocs/america_under_attack/terror/team3_right.html
(57) http://www.autentico.org/oa09551.html
(58) http://www.bakudapa.com/america-underattack/Hijackers/team3_files/team3_files/team3_right.htm
(59) http://www.msnbc.com/news/629406.asp
(60) http://www.cbsnews.com/htdocs/america_under_attack/terror/team3_right.html
(61) http://www.arabview.com/article.asp?artID=98
(62) http://www.dallasnews.com/specialreports/2001/attack/hijackphoto.html
(63) http://www.cbsnews.com/stories/2001/09/14/archive/printable311329.shtml
(64) http://www.makethemaccountable.com/articles/Feds_Evidence_suggests_hijackers_support_in_U_S_.htm
(65) http://www.cbsnews.com/htdocs/america_under_attack/terror/team3_right.html
(66) Ibid
(67) http://www.washingtonpost.com/ac2/wp-dyn/A52712-2001Sep18?language=printer
(68) http://www.cbsnews.com/stories/2001/09/14/archive/main311329.shtml
(69) http://www.observer.co.uk/Print/0,3858,4272043,00.html
(70) http://hrsbstaff.ednet.ns.ca/waymac/Sociology/A%20Term%201/5.%20Research%20Methods/world_trade_centre_assignment.htm
(71) http://www.observer.co.uk/Print/0,3858,4272043,00.html
(72) http://www.serendipity.li/wot/adam.htm
(73) Ibid
(74) http://www.wsws.org/articles/2002/sep2002/sept-s12.shtml
(75) http://www.usefulwork.com/shark/deadlymistakes.html
(76) http://www.nctimes.net/news/2001/20010918/62911.html
(77) Ibid
(78) http://www.newsmedianews.com/wtc.htm
(79) http://newsandviews5.tripod.com/news/031502p2.html
(80) http://www.sptimes.com/News/091501/Worldandnation/14_hijackers_spent_ti.shtml
(81) http://news.bbc.co.uk/hi/english/world/americas/newsid_1567000/1567815.stm
(82) http://www.sptimes.com/News/091501/Worldandnation/Names_of_hijackers.shtml
(83) Ibid
(84) http://chicagotribune.com/news/nationworld/chi-0109190363sep19.story

?coll=chinews-hed

(85) http://www.telegraph.co.uk/news/main.jhtml?xml=/news/2001/09/23/widen23.xml

(86) http://www.thisdayonline.com/archive/2001/09/27/20010927lif01.html

(87) http://www.cbc.ca/fifth/featurestories/jarrah_101001/timeline.html

(88) http://www.americanfreepress.net/10_12_01/STILL_ALIVE__FBI_Mixed_Up_on_T/still_alive__fbi_mixed_up_on_t.html

(89) http://news.theolympian.com/specialsections/TerrorinAmerica/20020430/15779.shtml

(90) http://www.usdoj.gov/ag/speeches/2001/0912pressconference.htm

(91) Personal phone call placed January 24, 2003

(92) Another personal phone call placed January 24, 2003

(93) http://www.truthout.org/docs_02/06.21A.pitt.watchtower.htm

(94) http://www.boeing.com/commercial/767family/

(95) Ibid

(96) http://www.boeing.com/commercial/757family/

(97) Ibid

(98) Personal Phone Call placed January 18, 2003

(99) http://www.mugu.com/pipermail/upstream-list/2001-September/003270.html

(100) http://denunge.dk/article/articleview/387/1/14/

(101) http://asia.dailynews.yahoo.com/headlines/world/afp/article.html?s=asia/headlines/010916/world/afp/The_hijack_suspects__ordinary_neighbours_--_and_terrorist__moles__.html

(102) http://www.papillonsartpalace.com/hijack.htm

(103) http://www.maebrussell.com/Articles%20and%20Notes/Eqyptian%20man%20denies%20son's%20involvement%20in%20hijackings.html
San Jose Mercury News - Sept. 19, 2001, pg. 6A
The New York Times - Sept. 19, 2001, pg. B4

(104) http://www.pittsburghlive.com/x/tribune-review/columnists/hiel/s_3023.html

(105) http://www.cia.gov/cia/public_affairs/speeches/archives/2002/dci_testimony_06182002/DCI_18_June_testimony_new.pdf

(106) http://www.timesonline.co.uk/article/0,,2523-305811,00.html

(107) http://www.msnbc.com/news/673068.asp

(108) http://www.cooperativeresearch.org/completetimeline/2001/berlinerzeitung092401.html

(109) http://www.webcom.com/hrin/magazine/la-atta.html

(110) http://bulletin.ninemsn.com.au/bulletin/eddesk.nsf/6df5c28ed2c6c605ca256a1500059f03/408C5CE916694857CA256ACB001D955B?OpenDocument

(111) http://www.cooperativeresearch.org/completetimeline/2001/bostonglobe091401.html

(112) http://news.bbc.co.uk/hi/english/world/americas/newsid_1581000/1581063.stm

(113) http://www.lvrj.com/lvrj_home/2001/Sep-20-Thu-2001/news/17037273.html

(114) http://www.redwhiteandblue.org/news/bnws/PGP2.HTM

The "Hijackers"

(115) http://www.foxnews.com/story/0,2933,60089,00.html
(116) http://www.inptvnews.com/stories.asp?StoryId=86
(117) Ibid
(118) http://www.cbsnews.com/stories/2002/06/06/attack/main511244.shtml
(119) http://ctstudies.com/Document/Indictment_Zacarias_Moussaoui.htm
(120) http://www.spychips.com or http:www.norfid.com
(121) http://www.abc.net.au/4corners/atta/maps/timeline.htm
(122) http://newsandviews8.tripod.com/news/091301tv17.html
      http://www.observer.co.uk/international/story/0,6903,552749,00.html
(123) http://www.observer.co.uk/2001review/story/0,1590,624103,00.html
(124) http://www.ctnow.com/news/nationworld/hc-attacka1-hijackers
      -0914.story
(125) http://cjonline.com/stories/091301/ter_florida.shtml
(126) http://www.sptimes.com/2002/09/01/911/Florida__terror_s_lau.shtml
(127) http://www.observer.co.uk/waronterrorism/story/0,1373,556630,00.html
(128) http://www.thisdayonline.com/archive/2001/09/16/20010916cov05.html
(129) http://www.observer.co.uk/Print/0,3858,4258186,00.html
(130) Ibid
(131) Ibid
(132) http://www.pbs.org/wgbh/pages/frontline/shows/network/etc/script.html
(133) http://www.sptimes.com/News/091401/State/A_trail_of_
      contradict.shtml
(134) http://www.usatoday.com/news/nation/2001/09/14/miami-club.htm
(135) http://www.westerndefense.org/articles/SaudiArabia/october01.htm
(136) http://www.abc.net.au/4corners/atta/maps/usa/default.htm
(137) http://www.bostonherald.com/attack/investigation/aussecu
      09292001.htm
(138) http://www.observer.co.uk/international/story/0,6903,552789,00.html
(139) http://www.the-movement.com/Top_10s/evidence.htm
(140) http://www.usdoj.gov/ag/agcrisisremarks9_28.htm
(141) http://abcnews.go.com/sections/us/DailyNews/WTC_atta_will.html
(142) http://www.cnn.com/2001/US/11/15/inv.ramzi.manhunt/
(143) http://www.msnbc.com/news/673068.asp
(144) http://www.msnbc.com/news/673068.asp
(145) http://multimedia.belointeractive.com/attack/investigation/1211
      investigate.html
(146) http://www.dailyillini.com/apr02/apr25/opinions/stories/opinions_
      column02.shtml
(147) http://www.msnbc.com/news/673068.asp
(148) http://www.dailyillini.com/apr02/apr25/opinions/stories/opinions_
      column02.shtml
(149) Ibid
(150) http://www.msnbc.com/news/673068.asp
(151) Ibid
(152) http://www.foxnews.com/story/0,2933,40985,00.html
(153) http://www.washingtonpost.com/ac2/wp-dyn/A25456-2002Jul18?
      language=printer
(154) http://newsandviews3.tripod.com/news/072002.html

(155) http://www.washingtonpost.com/ac2/wp-dyn/A25456-2002Jul18?
     language=printer
(156) http://www.cnn.com/2002/LAW/07/18/moussaoui.hearing/

"Detailed" Passenger list can be found at:
http://www.msnbc.com/modules/wtc/victims/default.asp?0cb=-81a101489&0
cb=-g1k105604klklk

Chapter 5
George W. Bush
President of the United States of America

Here we have one of the oddest looking puzzle pieces in the box.

Before any other information about "little boy" Bush can be presented, I must bring up the issue of the accountability to the words of the highest position in the United States. As proved in the Clinton Presidency, Presidents lie. This is a given. All humans lie. It is something in the brain. But as another thing in the brain, when we are lied to, credibility in that person becomes questionable. So, although this is out of sequence with the events that I will present regarding President George W. Bush, I have to bring up the lie he has told about the September 11 events.

"I saw an airplane hit the tower"

In a Town Hall Meeting in Orlando Florida with President W. Bush on December 4, 2001, Bush was asked how he felt about when he heard about the attack:

> QUESTION: One thing, Mr. President, is that you have no idea how much you've done for this country, and another thing is that how did you feel when you heard about the terrorist attack?
>
> BUSH: Well . . . (APPLAUSE) Thank you, Jordan (ph). Well, Jordan (ph), you're not going to believe what state I was in when I heard about the terrorist attack. I was in Florida. And my chief of staff, Andy Card -- actually I was in a classroom talking about a reading program that works. And I was sitting outside the classroom waiting to go in, and I saw an airplane hit the tower -- the TV was obviously on, and I use to fly myself, and I said, "There's one terrible pilot." And I said, "It must have been a horrible accident.
>
> "But I was whisked off there -- I didn't have much time to think about it, and I was sitting in the classroom, and Andy Card, my chief who was sitting over here walked in and said, "A second plane has hit the tower. America's under attack."[1]

One small problem Mr. President, there was no live footage of the first plane "hitting the tower."

And people who did happen to be at the "right" place at the right time continued to film the incident. Many of these people were not mass media cameramen, and did not have live feeds to media centers. I do also believe that the video footage of the first plane striking the North Tower of the World Trade Center was not shown on television until 11pm that evening. (Please note, that I was watching footage as much as anyone that day, but I may be wrong about when footage of the first hit did originally air, but I do know that no cameras were live on the World Trade Center.)

And another thing to question, as a former school attendee, and maybe it's just because I wasn't the President of anything then, but there were no televisions OUTSIDE of the classroom (i.e., in the hall) to watch.

And why was the President watching television before he entered the classroom anyway? Shouldn't he have been reviewing note cards, or responses to possible questions that may be asked by reporters following the presentation of the children?

Excuse me, but could Mr. President be lying. He is not under oath, but ask Mr. Clinton, that doesn't even matter for a President, but none the less, why lie about something so obvious.

He also states he used to fly himself, but he was not a good pilot either. He was taken off of flight status for a failure to take a medical exam, which included a drug test.[2] If in fact he did observe the first plane hitting the tower, would not the President of the United States of America would assume that a commercial airplane hitting the World Trade Center (which was a no fly zone) in clear weather was NOT a pilot's error?

The only other known impact between an airplane and a New York Skyscraper was when a military B-25 airplane, in heavy fog mind you, crashed into the Empire States Building July 28, 1945. This accident claimed the life of twelve people and injured many dozen more.[3]

And please remember that even after news of the second impact was told to him, by his own admission, he knew the United States was being attacked, he continued to read to the classroom full of children.

He must have been really concerned about the children and their impressionable young minds in the event that Bush had to leave

72

to do his job to protect his people. No, that couldn't be what he was thinking, too involved for a man of his intelligence. Maybe he was too intrigued in the story line about the goat, something more along his level.

While millions of people around the world stopped doing what they were doing when our lives were interrupted that horrible morning, the President of America continued with his story break.

Just think about that for a while. It's ok, mark your spot and put the book down, and think about what the President of the Free World did when he understood his nation was, "Under attack."

Ok, now that I have you back now, it is unfair to put words and thoughts into the mouth of the President, or at least unfair unless you are the Presidents Press Secretary. The comment to the question continues:

"And Jordan (ph), I wasn't sure what to think at first. You know, I grew up in a period of time where the idea of America being under attack never entered my mind -- just like your daddy and mother's mind probably. And I started thinking hard in that very brief period of time about what it meant to be under attack. I knew that when I got all the facts that we were under attack, there would be hell to pay for attacking America. (APPLAUSE)

"I tried to get as many facts as I could, Jordan (ph), to make sure I knew, as I was making decisions, that I knew exactly what I was basing my decisions on. I've got a fabulous team. A president can't possibly be president without a good team. It starts with having a great wife, by the way. (APPLAUSE)

"And so I got on the phone from Air Force One asking to find out the facts. You've got to understand, Jordan (ph), that during this period of time, there were all kinds of rumors floating around. Some of them were erroneous. For example, there's a news report saying that the State Department had been attacked. I needed to know what the facts were.

"But I knew I needed to ask. I knew that if the nation's under attack, the role of the commander in chief is to respond forcefully to prevent other attacks from happening.

"And so I talked to the secretary of defense. One of the first acts I did was to put our military on alert.

"An interesting thing happened shortly thereafter. Condoleezza Rice who was not with me, but was with the vice president, because they were in the White House compound, called me

73

on the Air Force One after that, and said she'd gotten a call from Russia, from Vladimir Putin, who understood why we were putting our troops on alert, and therefore wasn't going to respond. That was an important phone call, because when I was coming up, and a lot of other older-looking people coming up with me, that would have never have happened in the past. An alert by the United States would have caused Russia to go on an alert, which would've created a complicated situation. But that wasn't the case.

"By the way we're heading into a new era. One of the positive things that come out of evil was a reassessing relationships, in order to make the world more peaceful. I believe it's important for us to have positive relations with our former enemy and to rethink the defenses of the United States of America. (APPLAUSE)

"At any rate, I knew I had a job to do. And I was quoted in the press the other day as saying I haven't regretted one thing I've decided. And that's the truth. Every decision I've made I stand by, and I'm proud of the decisions I've made. (APPLAUSE)[4]

Now we know the "Official" reaction to the attacks. Let us now observe what happened beginning on that day.

0900 Sarasota Florida

On the morning of September 11, 2001, President George W. Bush arrived at Booker Elementary School, Sarasota, Florida for plans to watch a classroom full of children and a new teaching program that helps children learn to read. Then a speech about school programs and government funding, no doubt, was scheduled to have followed afterwards at 9:30am.[5]

Apparently in the hallway he views the first plane striking the World Trade Center, or White House Chief of Staff Andrew Card told him, it is really unclear, and assumes it is just an accident. Bush speaks to National Security Advisor Condoleezza Rice on the phone and she suggests the matter, "Could be just a terrible accident."[6] That must have been reassuring because he proceeded to enter the second-grade classroom.

While Bush is listening to the children read, Andrew Card approaches him and whispers into his hear that a second plane has struck the South Tower.[7]

74

According to the press release page on the White House's official web site, the President delayed plans to address the tragedy, to gather more information first.[8] And I assume the second grade children reading the story about a goat will supply all the information he needs.

Bush's appearance did seam to grow dim, but one odd thing to mention is how Andrew Card reacted to Bush's reaction.

Of course Bush is the President of the United States of America and his job is to make decisions. Andrew Card is the White House Chief of Staff and his job is to make sure that the President's decisions are carried out. But by observing the videotape of when Card whispers into Bush's ear, Bush does not decide to do anything but sit there, for twenty minutes. Card who is supposed to wait for the decision that Bush doesn't make, steps back, without waiting for a reply. Card disappears, and Bush continued to listen to the children and began to smile again. He then joked as they read so well, they are, "Really good readers! Whoo."[9]

Did Bush anticipate the attacks, and did Card know that Bush would not make a decision at that moment?

This video should show that the man elected to the office of the President (oh, wait I'm sorry, this video doesn't show Al Gore) and him going off to the protection of the American people. But it doesn't. It shows a President who is informed of a "surprise" attack, and not being surprised at all. And it also shows that Chief of Staff does not act like a position delivering an unexpected piece of news but instead is merely delivering a progress report to which he already knows Bush will not have an immediate response. Unlike someone waiting for Fed Ex to appear with the prized item they won on eBay.

So let's reexamine this piece carefully before we continue with our puzzle.

Bush knew about the first crash BEFORE entering Booker School

Associated Press reporter Sonya Ross was one of the journalists covering Bush's trip to Florida on the morning of 9-11.

Ms. Ross was at the Booker School already when she learned of the first WTC crash:

> "My cell phone rang as President Bush's motorcade coursed toward Emma E. Booker Elementary School in Sarasota, Fla. A colleague reported that a plane had crashed into the World Trade Center in New York. No further information.

"I called the AP desk in Washington, seeking details. Same scant information. But I knew it had to be grim. I searched for a White House official to question, but none was on hand until 9:05 a.m."[10]

Ms. Ross searched for a White House official' because she knew Bush's people would be better informed than the Associated Press. And who wouldn't look for an official from the White House. The people that the President travels with are paid to know everything, or paid to deny everything, take your pick.

The staff the President travels with is responsible for receiving, filtering and conveying administrative and military information. Chief of Staff Andrew Card organizes and coordinates these staff members and communicates with the President. In addition, Bush has the Secret Service, which is responsible for his safety.

The members of this support team have the best communications equipment in the world. They maintain contact with, or can easily reach, Bush's cabinet, the National Military Command Center (NMCC) in the Pentagon, the Federal Aviation Administration (FAA), and Secret Service agents who are at the White House, etc.

Since this walking information system is far more extensive and sophisticated than what is available to a reporter, it seems more than plausible that by the time Ms. Ross heard about the first WTC crash - that is, as the Bush motorcade was speeding to Booker Elementary School - the President already knew about this tragic event.

Public sources confirm this. But yet we are made to believe that Bush was instructed in the hall outside the second grade classroom. Apparently, Bush also travels in his limo alone, without someone, like Card, to inform him of the information this team receives. Now that is an informed man!

But on that morning, ABC Journalist John Cochran was traveling with the President. When the normal Good Morning America program was interrupted with the incoming news of the first plane crash, Cochran was immediately a chosen candidate for ABC News to get a first hand response from the President. He reported on Tuesday, 11 September, 2001:

"Peter, as you know, the president's down in Florida talking about education. He got out of his hotel suite this morning, was about to leave, reporters saw the White House chief of staff, Andy Card, whisper into his ear. The reporter said to the president, 'Do you know what's going on in New York?' He said he did, and he said he will have something about it later. His first event is about half an hour at an elementary school in Sarasota, Florida."[11]

So, Bush knew about the first WTC incident before leaving his hotel!? What else did Bush know? Perhaps that the attack was going to happen? Why not!?

Upon leaving the classroom, Bush was asked by a shouting reporter, "What should be done?" Bush replied that he would make a statement later. Bush would not have said that without discussing the situation with the Chief of Staff, as well as others. Because obviously the information he was hoping for, was in a story being read to him by second graders, had left him down.

After meeting with Bush's staff and advisers, he entered the media center, which had been prepped for the education speech. He reached the podium composed and sober. At 0930 he delivered the chilling news of "an apparent terrorist attack on our country."[12]

So, it can be said that before President Bush left his hotel, the Secret Service knew a hijacked plane had ploughed into the World Trade Center, a building that symbolized US power. Also, knowing that the President is the most obvious individual target for a terrorist attack, the Secret Service did not prevent him from his publicly known plans. The President was scheduled to visit the Booker School that morning. The visit was of no importance - that is, he could easily cancel it. His schedule was publicly known, down to the minute he would give a televised talk on education at 9:30 that morning. Why was he not whisked away secretly into hiding to avoid being a target? Perhaps that is what he was doing in Florida.

Again, it has been suggested that flight 93 was possibly heading to strike the White House. But why would this plane be going to possibly kill the President when the terrorist would have known his whereabouts?

Now, assuming the official story is entirely true, there was every reason to believe that a terrorist had flown a plane into the World Trade Center. Therefore a terrorist might fly a plane into the Booker School to kill Bush - arguably a bigger victory than destroying the Twin Towers. This danger was increased by the proximity of Sarasota-Bradenton International Airport.

Moreover, the attacks might have signaled the start of a broader terrorist attack. In that case it was certainly possible that heavily armed terrorists would attack the Booker School on the ground.

Given that the Secret Services job and obligation to protect the President, and given the Secret Service's open line to the FAA 14 and therefore its knowledge that a plane had been hijacked and subsequently ploughed into the World Trade Center, the potentially deadly threat to President Bush if he proceeded to a public place, on schedule, as announced the day before and known to everyone in the region, was significantly high.

There is only one explanation for the Secret Service allowing President Bush to take the deadly risk of going to the Booker School on the morning of 11 September; George Walker Bush knew the plans for 9-11.

And because he knew those plans, he knew that nobody was going to attack him, or the Booker School.

President George W. Bush, listening to the children and the story of the goat, was safe from terrorist attacks, and he knew it.

While almost 3,000 people lost their lives. What a guy!

Puzzled? I am!

Here we are given basically two different accounts of what happened that day. The ABC Reporter stated Bush knew of the terrorist attacks while leaving his hotel room. But then later at the Town Hall Meeting, he says he watched the first plane strike the tower at the Booker School before entering the second grade class room.

So which was it? Surely, it couldn't have been both.

And the fact remains: Bush was an easy target that morning.

Why has no one brought this up in the media? Because the media are trained to report on the official story and not to ask questions about what they are presented with, because it is the "Official" story.

And there used to be a thing called Freedom of the Press.

SOURCES

(1) http://www.cnn.com/TRANSCRIPTS/0112/04/se.04.html
(2) http://www.babelmagazine.com/issue74/bushlie.html
(3) http://www.teamtwintowers.org/history.html
(4) http://www.cnn.com/TRANSCRIPTS/0112/04/se.04.html
(5) http://www.miami.com/mld/miamiherald/news/local/4054881.htm
(6) http://www.september11news.com/PresidentBush.htm
(7) http://radified.com/911/
(8) http://www.whitehouse.gov/news/releases/2001/09/20010
    911.html
(9) http://www.stltoday.com/stltoday/news/special/skyterror.nsf/other/
    8B8F4C8DD63893E186256AC400609220?OpenDocument
(10) http://www.christopherlydon.org/viewtopic.php?topic=993&
    forum=4
    The Associated Press - Wednesday 12 September 2001 "Flying
    with President Bush on a day terrorists hit hard" by Sonya Ross.
(11) http://www.visiontv.ca/Archive/Archive5.html
    ABC News Special Report 'Planes crash into World Trade Center'
    (8:53 AM ET) Tuesday 11 September 2001.
(12) http://gov.state.nv.us/pr/2001/09-11TERROR.htm

Chapter 6
Dick Cheney
Vice President of the United States of America

On Sunday, 16 September, 2001, Vice President Cheney met with Tim Russert on NBC's *Meet the Press* talk show.[1] It is from this interview that most of this chapter will be devoted too, and being only five days from the attacks, is very important to the information that was released then, compared to what they are saying now.

> **TIM RUSSERT:** Where were you when you first learned a plane had struck the World Trade Center?
>
> **VICE PRES. CHENEY:** Well, I was in my office Tuesday morning. Monday, I had been in Kentucky, and the president had been in the White House. Tuesday, our roles were sort of reversed. He was in Florida, and I was in the White House Tuesday morning. And a little before 9, my speech writer came in. We were going to go over some speeches coming up. And my secretary called in just as we were starting to meet just before 9:00 and said an airplane had hit the World Trade Center, and that was the first one that went in. So we turned on the television and watched for a few minutes, and then actually saw the second plane hit the World Trade Center. And the — as soon as that second plane showed up, that's what triggered the thought: terrorism, that this was an attack . . .
>
> **RUSSERT:** You sensed it immediately, "This is deliberate?"
>
> **CHENEY:** Yeah. Then I convened in my office. Condi Rice came down. Her office is right near mine there in the West Wing.
>
> **RUSSERT:** The national security adviser.
>
> **CHENEY:** National security adviser, my chief of staff, Scooter Libby, Mary Matalin, who works for me, convened in my office, and we started talking about getting the Counter terrorism Task Force up and operating. I talked with the president. I'd given word to Andy Card's staff, who is right next door, to get hold of Andy and/or the president and that I wanted to talk to him as soon as they could hook it up. This call came in, and the

80

president knew at this point about that.

We discussed a statement that he might make, and the first statement he made describing this as an act of apparent terrorism flowed out of those conversations. While I was there, over the next several minutes, watching developments on the television and as we started to get organized to figure out what to do, my Secret Service agents came in and, under these circumstances, they just move. They don't say "sir" or ask politely. They came in and said, "Sir, we have to leave immediately," and grabbed me and . . .

RUSSERT: Literally grabbed you and moved you?

CHENEY: Yeah. And, you know, your feet touch the floor periodically. But they're bigger than I am, and they hoisted me up and moved me very rapidly down the hallway, down some stairs, through some doors and down some more stairs into an underground facility under the White House, and, as a matter of fact, it's a corridor, locked at both ends, and they did that because they had received a report that an airplane was headed for the White House.[2]

As I noted in the chapter five, the Secret Service is to protect the President and the Vice President from attack. And obviously they felt that the fully publicized whereabouts of the President that day were no need to move him from harms way. But yet the unpublicized whereabout of the Vice President causes for him to be "grabbed" and pulled out of harms way.

But that still raises the question: Did Bush know the accidental plane crash at the World Trade Center was really an accident, or a "terrorist attack?"

Vice President Richard Cheney revealed, probably unwittingly, on *Meet the Press*, Sunday, 16 September, 2001 that Bush did know the World Trade Center "accident" was a Terrorist Attack.

Cheney's comments constitute evidence that before President Bush went to the Booker School he knew a plane had been hijacked and then crashed into the WTC.

Cheney later discussed with *Meet the Press* journalist Tim Russert about the flight path of American Flight 77, which struck the Pentagon:

CHENEY: ...As best we can tell, they [American Flight 77] came initially at the White House and . . .

RUSSERT: The plane actually circled the White House?

CHENEY: Didn't circle it, but was headed on a track into it. The Secret Service has an arrangement with the FAA. They had open lines after the World Trade Center was . . . "

RUSSERT: Tracking it by radar.

CHENEY: And when it entered the danger zone and looked like it was headed for the White House was when they grabbed me and evacuated me to the basement . . . [3]

Cheney stopped before completing his sentence. But it is obvious that the sentence should have ended with the word 'hit' or something similar. Thus:

> "The Secret Service has an arrangement with the FAA. They had open lines after the World Trade Center was hit."

According to this interview, from the time of the first strike on the World Trade Center, the Secret Service (who, mind you, didn't see any reason to protect the President in Florida) had open communication with the FAA.

As mentioned in previous chapters, NORAD was not informed about flight 77, which was known to be in trouble by the FAA, but we are told to believe that there was an open line of communication between the FAA and the Secret Service.

Yeah, right. So let me get this straight, and help me out if you can here too: Flight 11 has struck the World Trade Center, Flight 77's transponder was deactivated and in the jet itself in trouble, the FAA and Secret Service have "open lines" of communication, and the Pentagon and NORAD did not have open lines with the FAA.

OK, I think I know what is going on here. If we are to take Mr. Cheney's comments at face value, these lines of communication surely were opened up at least from the moment of the first strike on the World Trade Center. So, why the delay in contacting NORAD and the deployment of any fighter jets?

Cheney made the claim that the military needed authorization from President George W. Bush before scrambling fighter jets to intercept American Airlines Flight 77.

Meet the Press continued:

RUSSERT: What's the most important decision you think he made during the course of the day?

CHENEY: Well, the — I suppose the toughest decision was this question of whether or not we would intercept incoming commercial aircraft.

RUSSERT: And you decided?

CHENEY: We decided to do it. We'd, in effect, put a flying combat air patrol up over the city; F-16s with an AWACS, which is an airborne radar system, and tanker support so they could stay up a long time. It doesn't do any good to put up a combat air patrol if you don't give them instructions to act, if, in fact, they feel it's appropriate.

RUSSERT: So if the United States government became aware that a hijacked commercial airline was destined for the White House or the Capitol, we would take the plane down?

CHENEY: Yes. The president made the decision, on my recommendation as well, wholeheartedly concurred in the decision he made, that if the plane would not divert, if they wouldn't pay any attention to instructions to move away from the city, as a last resort, our pilots were authorized to take them out.

Now, people say, you know, that's a horrendous decision to make. Well, it is. You've got an airplane full of American citizens, civilians, captured by hostages, captured by terrorists, headed and are you going to, in fact, shoot it down, obviously, and kill all those Americans on board? And you have to ask yourself, "If we had had combat air patrol up over New York and we'd had the opportunity to take out the two aircraft that hit the World Trade Center, would we have been justified in doing that?" I think absolutely we would have. Now, it turned out we did not have to execute on that authorization. But there were some — a few moments when we thought we might, when planes were incoming and we didn't know whether or not they were a problem aircraft until they'd diverted and gone elsewhere and been able to resolve it. It's a presidential-level decision.[4]

"Now, it turned out we did not have to execute on that authorization." Why the hell did you not, "Execute on that authorization, "Mr. Vice President? Thousands of Americans, as well many other nationalities, were killed! Had you executed your "authorization" you would have saved at least 2700 lives! But for some odd reason, Mr. Cheney, you worried about your own self, and in the midst of your selfishness, created this outright straightforward lie to protect your actions.

I already covered this in a previous chapter, but just in case I did not make myself clear what the proper actions are involving hijacked airliners:

10-2-6. HIJACKED AIRCRAFT

When you observe a Mode 3/A Code 7500, an unexplained loss of beacon code, change in direction of flight or altitude, and/or a loss of communications, notify supervisory personnel immediately. As it relates to observing a Code 7500, do the following:

NOTE: Military facilities will notify the appropriate FAA ARTCC, or the host nation agency responsible for en route control, of any indication that an aircraft is being hijacked. They will also provide full cooperation with the civil agencies in the control of such aircraft.

EN ROUTE. During narrowband radar operations, Code 7500 causes HIJK to blink in the data block.

NOTE: Only non-discrete Code 7500 will be decoded as the hijack code.

a. Acknowledge and confirm receipt of Code 7500 by asking the pilot to verify it. If the aircraft is not being subjected to unlawful interference, the pilot should respond to the query by broadcasting in the clear that he/she is not being subjected to unlawful interference. If the reply is in the affirmative or if no reply is received, do not question the pilot further but be responsive to the aircraft requests.

PHRASEOLOGY-

(Identification) (name of facility) VERIFY SQUAWKING 7500.

NOTE: Code 7500 is only assigned upon notification from the pilot that his/her aircraft is being subjected to unlawful interference.

Therefore, pilots have been requested to refuse the assignment of Code 7500 in any other situation and to inform the controller accordingly.

b. Notify supervisory personnel of the situation.

c. Flight follow aircraft and use normal handoff procedures without requiring transmissions or responses by aircraft unless communications have been established by the aircraft.

d. If aircraft are dispatched to escort the hijacked aircraft, provide all possible assistance to the escort aircraft to aid in placing them in a position behind the hijacked aircraft.

NOTE: Escort procedures are contained in FAAO 7610.4, Special Military Operations, Chapter 7, Escort of Hijacked Aircraft.

e. To the extent possible, afford the same control service to the aircraft operating VFR observed on the hijack code.

REFERENCE: FAAO 7110.65, Code Monitor, Para 5-2-13.[5]

The official authorization was not enforced, or followed! And nowhere does it state that, "It's a presidential-level decision," in order to scramble fighter jets!

Dick Cheney spoke that the need for presidential authorization was a commonly accepted fact. Then, based on this fantasy foundation, he emitted a fog of an emotional misinformation to confuse the millions of Americans who had asked themselves: "Why didn't jet fighters intercept any of the airliners before striking its target?" and, "Doesn't the U.S. have radar and an Air Force anymore?"

At around 0927, thirty-four minutes AFTER losing contact, NORAD claims it ordered jets scrambled from Langley Air Force Base, Virginia to intercept Flight 77.[6] The main question, one that still remains unanswered to this day is; Why were three F-16 Fighting Falcons were deployed from Langley Air Force Base, which is 130 miles away from Washington when Andrews Air Force Base is located a little over ten miles from the capital? In fact Andrews is designated to defend Washington,[7] yet the three fighter jets scrambled to intercept Flight 77 departed not 10 miles away, but 130 miles away!

Why? Because 9-11 was allowed to happen.

Langley reported that at 0935, the three fighter jets were in the air.[8] Eight minutes later!

The Air Force boasts that it can scramble a fighter jet to 29,000 feet in two and a half minutes.[9]

TWO AND A HALF MINUTES!

The pilots must have stopped for breakfast before attempting to intercept the plane that struck the Pentagon, a no-fly zone by the way, at 0937.

What good is a No-Fly Zone, if there are no squadrons on standby to defend it? Not to even mention that Andrews is the proud home of the 121st Fighter Quadroon of the 113th Fighter Wing, the

321st Marine Fighter Attack Squadron of the 49th Marine Air Group, AND the same F-16 Fighting Falcons that were deployed from Langley.[10]

The NORAD/Langley jets arrived at 0949. So, I guess back to IHOP and gain the CNN news coverage.

Perhaps CNN would like to do a story on why Andrews Air Force Base's web site "crashed" around 12 September and stayed down for another two months. And when it was resurrected, all links to the mission statement and capabilities of the 113th Fighter Wing Squadron had disappeared.

BUT, the official web site for the District of Colombia National Guard, headquartered at Andrews AFB, states:

> "Throughout its existence, the men and women of the DC Air National Guard have been and will continue to be a vital part of the community and the total force. They stand ready to respond to the needs of the District of Columbia- and the nation- should the need arise."[11]

Except on 11 September. *Meet the Press* continued:

RUSSERT: Were you surprised by the precision and sophistication of the operation?

CHENEY: Well, certainly, we were surprised in the sense that, you know, there had been information coming in that a big operation was planned, but that's sort of a trend that you see all the time in these kinds of reports. But we didn't . . .

RUSSERT: No specific threat?

CHENEY: No specific threat involving really a domestic operation or involving what happened, obviously, the cities, airliner and so forth. We did go on alert with our overseas forces a number of times during the course of the summer when we thought the threat level had risen significantly. So clearly, we were surprised by what happened here. On the other hand, in terms of the sophistication of it, it's interesting to look at, because clearly what happened is you got some people committed to die in the course of the operation, you got them visas, you got them entered into the United States. They came here. Some of them enrolled in our commercial aviation schools and learned to fly, courtesy of our own capabilities here in the United States. Then what they needed in order to execute was some degree of coordination, obviously, in terms of timing. But they knives, cardboard cutters, razor blades, whatever it was, and an airline ticket. And that's it. They then were able to take over the aircraft and use our own, you know, heavily loaded with fuel large aircraft to take over and use it. [12]

So, I assume that the maneuvers performed by these terrorist pilots, who 1) failed numerous flight exams, and 2) were not permitted to fly the simplest of aircraft ALONE, are even more surprising and astonishing. So surprising in fact that no one has yet to bring it up.

Why doesn't the Bush Administration want a real investigation of 9-11? The House and Senate, whose intelligence committees are now meeting in private, are considering bills that would set up limited, closed-door independent investigative panels, but Bush has stymied even those watered-down efforts at openness, arguing they, "Would cause a further diversion of essential personnel from their duties fighting the war."[13] What is he hiding? Americans pay Bush's salary, and Americans deserve to know what he's doing.

> **RUSSERT:** What's the most important decision you think the (President Bush) made during the course of the day?

Finishing the end of the goat story no doubt.

SOURCES

(1) http://emperors-clothes.com/9-11backups/nbcmp.htm#openlines
(2) Ibid
(3) Ibid
(4) Ibid
(5) http://www.faa.gov/ATpubs/ATC/Chp10/atc1002.html
(6) http://billstclair.com/911timeline/2001/cnn091701.html
(7) http://www.defendamerica.mil/profiles/nov2002/pr110402a.html
(8) http://www.flight93crash.com/flight93_timeline.html
(9) http://www.mtmi.vu.lt/wtc/questions/05where_fighters_was.htm
(10) http://www.defendamerica.mil/profiles/nov2002/pr110402a.html
(11) http://www.dcandr.ang.af.mil/aboutDCANG.htm
(12) http://emperors-clothes.com/9-11backups/nbcmp.htm#openlines91
(13) http://www.foxnews.com/story/0,2933,58731,00.html

Chapter 7
The Taliban
The Creation and Rise of the Taliban

In October 29, 1994, a convoy of 30 military trucks driven by ex-army drivers, supervised by a senior ISI official and guarded by Taliban fighters, set off across the long mountainous rugged terrain of Afghanistan.[1] Few anticipated at the time, what was set in motion was a chain of events that would not only give birth to a new regime in the region, but also unleash a new wave of misery and destruction on the impoverished country itself.

Former Premier Benazir Bhutto's Interior Minister, Naseerullah Babar, conceived this idea. The idea was to use the Taliban, who were then, mere armed zealots, for productive purposes. As the convoy proceeded, throughout the country, the Taliban cleared the route by fighting off the regional warlords' fighters who asked for cash payoffs to allow the convoy to continue.[2]

By 5 November, the Taliban had not only cleared the road, but had, with minimal fighting, taken control of Kandahar. In the next three months, the Taliban overtook, without much effort, 12 of Afghanistan's 31 provinces.[3]

Later in October 1995, one year after the original convoy began its trek, UNOCAL, the American oil giant, signed an oil pipeline deal with Turkmenistan.[4]
In September of 1996, the Taliban entered Herat. This effectively cleared a road from Pakistan to Central Asia.[5]

This whole exercise, which also gave birth to the Taliban regime, was originally designed to convince Unocal to go ahead with the pipeline project by guaranteeing safety of the route for laying of the 1,000-mile line which Pakistan was also to greatly benefit from.

It was reported Pakistan was to earn eight billion dollars in transit fees, and get its oil at half price.[6] Later, American policy-makers saw in the Taliban an instrument for furthering US aims in the Caspian and Persian Gulf regions, and placed increased pressure on China and Russia.

With the government of Afghanistan uneasy, and within three years, the communistic regime has been overthrown two times. This presented Unocal with the threat of lawlessness and chaotic, stressful conditions, which endangered the operation through this country. What Unocal needed was a single administration in place before it put millions of dollars into the project.

Enter the rise of the Taliban

Taliban Take Kabul

On September 27, 1996, CNN reported that the Taliban militia seized control of Kabul, Afghanistan, and hanged the former President Najibullah and his brother, former security chief Shahpur Ahmedzi in one of the presidential palace's towers.[7]

A leader in this militia, Mullah Mohammad Rabbani, said Najibullah "deserved his fate."[8]

At a news conference in the presidential palace, Rabbani stated, "He killed so many Islamic people and was against Islam and his crimes were so obvious that it had to happen. He was a communist."[9]

Najibullah's execution closed the chapter that began with the 1979 Soviet invasion of Afghanistan. Najibullah was a former security chief who came to power in 1986, replacing the Soviet installed Babrak Karmal, whose regime sparked an Islamic resistance movement, obviously including the Taliban.[10]

During Najibullah's six-year dictatorship, hundreds, maybe thousands of Afghans were arrested, tortured and killed. With the withdrawal of Soviet forces in 1989, Najibullah was left on his own to defend the capital and eastern Afghanistan from Muslim rebels. He was forced to resign in 1992 and lived since then in a U.N. compound. On 26 September, 1996, the Taliban abducted him from his home within the U.N. compound. He was then beaten, tortured, castrated, dragged behind a truck, shot and hanged.[11]

The Taliban quickly took over all key government installations.

Some reports claim within hours. Among these places to now be controlled by the Taliban, included the presidential palace and the ministries of defense, security and foreign affairs. No government forces, including police, were visible on the city's streets. This action prompted two days of fighting on the capital's eastern side, leaving hundreds dead.

This was the third time in a four-year period of a faction takeover of Afghanistan since Najibullah's communist regime was overthrown in 1992.

Either during this fighting, or perhaps after, it is not stated, massive crowds of Afghan people queued up and cheered at the sight of Najibullah's bloated and heavily beaten body.[12]

Many of Afghanistan's citizens welcomed the Taliban and hoped it would end factional fighting.[13]

"We killed him because he was the murderer of our people," said Noor Hakmal, one of the Taliban's commanders.[14]

Just hours after the takeover, Taliban announced that an interim six-man ruling council would run the country and declared Afghanistan a, "Completely Islamic state," where a, "Complete Islamic system will be enforced."[15]

The Taliban fought to oust the regime of President Burhanuddin Rabbani, apparently no relation to Mullah Mohammad Rabbani.

Diplomats loyal to the Rabbani Government mounted a counteroffensive to recapture the city. It failed.[16]

The Taliban, imposing its strict Islamic rule, then controlled over two-thirds of the country until U.S. Military attacks in October 2001. This version of Islamic rule was believed to include keeping women mostly in home or indoors, and imposing horrible criminal punishments for teaching girls in school, and the teaching Christianity or Judaism, as well as any thing else they seamed fit to punish people for.[17]

US State Department's reaction: "Nothing Objectionable"

When the Taliban had taken over Kabul in late September 1996, the U.S. State Department held a (media public relations) conference. In this conference Glyn Davies (U.S. State Department spokesperson) said:

> **Davies:** Kabul has fallen to the Taliban. Kabul appears to be relatively calm. Taliban leaders have announced that Afghans can return to Kabul without fear and that Afghanistan is the common home of all Afghans. We take this as an indication that the Taliban intends to respect the rights of all Afghans.
>
> **Question:** There are reports the Taliban is imposing strict Islamic law, ordering women to go into purdah. Is that consistent with the government you describe as apparently willing to respect the rights of its citizens?
>
> **Davies:** We've seen some reports that they've moved to

impose Islamic law, but at this stage we're not reading anything into that. There's nothing objectionable at this stage.

Question: Is this a good thing? Will it bring stability to Afghanistan?

Davies: We hope very much and expect the Taliban will respect the rights of all Afghans, and that the new authorities will move quickly to restore order and security, and form a representative interim government on the way to national reconciliation.

Question: Do you have any response to the demise of former president Najibullah?

Davies: We regret the deaths of President Najibullah and his associates.

Question: How can you do anything but condemn it? Regret is different from condemnation.

Davies: It appears as if that was a regrettable development.

Question: Let me get this straight. This Islamic fundamentalist group has taken Afghanistan by force, summarily executed the president and the U.S. is holding out the possibility of relations?

Davies: I'm not going to prejudge where we're going with Afghanistan. Since they appear to hold the majority of the cards, our call on them is to use their new position of authority to establish democratic institutions and move towards national reconciliation.[18]

I wonder how many people around the world would call the abduction, beating, torturing, castration, and shooting and public execution of one of today's political leaders, "Nothing objectionable?"

UNOCAL expressed grand support for the Taliban takeover. Of course it would make the pipeline project easier to complete. But according to their website (after 9-11), the claimed they were "misquoted."[19] SURE!

At the beginning of 1997, the US still had no objection to the Taliban's governing procedures, their lifestyle, and religious perceptions.

A U.S. diplomat told Ahmed Rashid:

"The Taliban will probably develop like the Saudis did. There will be Aramco (meaning a consortium of oil companies as in Saudi Arabia), pipelines, an Emir, no parliament and lots of

Shariat laws. We can live with that."[20]

It seems the Americans, behind Unocal's lead, were ready to go to any extent to promote business interests in Afghanistan.

Senator Hank Brown (R-Colorado), a supporter of the UNOCAL project, said:

"The good part of what has happened is that one of the factions at least seems capable of developing a government in Kabul."[21]

As for the UNOCAL, its Vice –President Miller called the Taliban's success a, "Positive development."[22]

The US-Taliban Coalition begins

The Bush administration is today demolishing the very force the Clinton administration had courted for years on behalf of the US oil barons, one of which is President Bush himself.

The Clinton administration was clearly sympathetic to the Taliban because it served its anti-Iran policy.[23] The US Congress had authorized a covert $20 million budget for the CIA to destabilize Iran, but some of these funds, Iran says, went to the Taliban.[24] In fact, the period from 1994 to 1997 saw a flurry of US diplomatic activity to secure support for the UNOCAL pipeline.[25]

In March 1996, prominent US Senator Hank Brown, a vocal supporter of the Unocal project, visited Kabul and met Taliban leaders.[26]

In the same month, the US government put pressure on the Pakistan government to back the American Company and distance away from the Argentinean rival.[27] The next month, US Assistant Secretary of State for South Asia, Robin Raphel, visited Pakistan, Afghanistan and Central Asia for the same purpose.[28]

That is funny, I don't recall the Senator from Colorado or Mr. US Assistant Secretary of State for South Asia (whew... long name) being interviewed with Larry King or Bill O'Reily after the September 11 attacks. What a better way to understand the heads of these "terrorists" than to talk to people who met and spent time with them. Right?

But then that may bring up suspicion that the US Government would have had some involvement with the "enemy." That's right, forgive my ignorance.

The primary factor in determining the twists and turns in

Washington's policy towards Afghanistan has not been the threat of Islamic extremism (in fact Afghanistan was not even listed on the countries know to harbor terrorists - I will reveal this in the review of 2000, a few paragraphs ahead), but how best to exploit the new opened opportunities of the Soviet Union's collapse in the region.

The key to huge profits lay in transporting oil from this landlocked region to the world markets. The US would surely not favor any pipeline through Iran. The only best route is through Afghanistan and Pakistan and then to the entire South Asia. That is why Islamabad and Washington had backed the Taliban when the latter swept into power in 1996, bringing, some sort of a degree of stability that foreign investors needed to go ahead with any deal.

Are these people's hands itching or are they just really money hungry?

Taliban leaders, in an effort to obtain the most lucrative deal, like they were the greedy ones, were in the meantime playing the US firm off against the Argentinean Oil Company, Birdas. Unocal, with the support of Washington, provided nearly one million dollars to set up a Center for Afghanistan (who funded the terrorist? Please remind me) Studies at the University of Omaha.[29] The money was actually used to set up a school near Kandahar to train the pipe fitters, electricians and carpenters needed to construct the pipeline.[30]

This reminds me of an anti-drug campaign that ran almost immediately after the 11 September attacks. It basically alleges that if you buy illegal drugs, your money goes to support terrorists. So, you pay $25 for a little marijuana, or $100 for a little crack cocaine, some of that money goes to the terrorist. How much of this one million dollars used to train these future constructors of the pipeline, spent this money IN Afghanistan and therefor supported the local economy, which in turn, funded the alleged terrorist of the attacks? I would guarantee more than that from the drug sales in the United States.

1997: A busy year and the Taliban IN America

In January 1997, Turkmenistan signed an exploration agreement with Mobil and Monument Oil.[31] The U.N., under Secretary General Akashi, criticized oil companies and warlords for pipeline projects.[32] Hmmmm, imagine that.

I don't know if you recall any media asking the question, again and again, how these "terrorists" entered the United States. I can tell

93

you. The Oil Companies flew them here.

I will repeat. THE OIL COMPANIES FLEW THEM HERE.

(Perhaps the anti-drug commercials should be replaced with, "If you buy petroleum you support terrorism.")

In February 1998, members of the Taliban flew to Washington to seek recognition. They were also escorted to Sugarland, Texas, the headquarters of UNOCAL to meet everyone within the corporation.[33] They were even flown to Argentina as guests of Bridas.[34] Upon return, Taliban meets with Saudi Intelligence chief, Prince Turki Alfaysal, in Jeddah.[35] These guys really got around, all off the profits the oil companies maid off your Cadillac and SUV sitting in your heated garage.

In March, UNOCAL set up offices in Kandahar (the power seat of the Taliban, mind you); Bridas followed suit in Kabul.[36]

The Taliban, in April, announced criteria for the awarding contract: The company that starts work first, wins. UNOCAL President John Imle was "baffled" by the statement.[37] I can just see millions of dollars dropping out of his wallet as this statement is recited.

UNOCAL struck back in June saying peace is necessary for the construction of the pipeline, otherwise the project could take years.[38]

I'm sorry, I thought that was the reason you sponsored the Taliban, for regional control of Afghanistan.

Bridas officials met the Taliban, stepping up the heat, and said that they were "interested in beginning work in any kind of security situation."[39] Brave people right here, let me tell you. Then when July rolled around, guess what? Pakistan, Turkmenistan, and UNOCAL signed a new contract extending UNOCAL's deadline by one year to start the project by December 1998.[40] In a policy shift, the United States says it will not object to a Turkmenistan-Turkey pipeline through Iran.[41] Sure, if Clinton's support of the Taliban pays off, Iran is no longer a threat. Why not?

Shell's Alan Parsley meet Niyazov and promised to help on the Turkmenistan-Turkey pipeline in August.[42] The Taliban said the Bridas offered better terms and expected to enter into agreement with them.

It's all about resources. It's all about money!

It never has been about terrorism, war, or peace.

It never will be.

While in September, Turkmenistan opened tenders for oil

94

companies to take up new concessions along the Caspian Sea. Niyazov, 57, had a heart operation in Munich, concern grew about his health, and who would replace him, should he die.[43]

Bridas sold 60 percent of the company's stakes in Latin America to Amoco. The two agreed to form a new company to run operations jointly.

Then the Taliban returned for delegation in Argentina to discuss the pipeline deal with Bridas.[44]

So, I guess it was all a bluff, because in October, the Taliban delegation visited Ashkhabad and agreed to set up tripartite commission with Pakistan and Turkmenistan to explore the UNOCAL pipeline project. From this meeting, Centgas Pipeline Ltd. was formed in Ashkhabad.[45]

Before this meeting the shares looked like this:

UNOCAL held a 70 per cent stake.

Saudi oil company Delta-Nimir 15 per cent.

Russia's state-owned gas company Gazporm 10 per cent.

Turkmen state-owned company Turk-menrosgaz 5 per cent.[46]

After the formation of Ashkhabad: in October 1997, after Gazporm left the Cent-Gas, the consortium was expanded:

UNOCAL's share reduced to 54.11 per cent.

Delta still held 15 per cent.

Turk-menrosgaz 7 per cent.

Indonesia Petroleum (Japan) 7.22 per cent.

CIECO Trans-Asia Gas Ltd. (Japan) 7.22 per cent.

Crescent Group (Pakistan) 3.89 per cent.

Hyundai Ltd. (South Korea) 5.56 per cent.[47]

Taliban undecided which consortium to join

Again in November 1997, the Taliban flew back to the United States to visit UNOCAL and U.S. State Department officials. While in December, Turkmenistan and Iran, inaugurated a 120-mile-long gas pipeline between the two countries.[48]

The Taliban again are flown back to Texas. Reuters reported this visit on December 13, 1997, and also in the Sunday Telegraph with a story by Caroline Lees titled "Oil Barons Court Taliban in Texas."[49]

Most of these reports can be summed up by saying that in the second week of December 1997, a Taliban delegation led by Mullah Muhammad Ghaus arrived at a five-star hotel in Houston, Texas. Their itinerary for the next few days included shopping at the city's best supermarkets, for which they did not show any particular interest, except that Mullah Ghaus bought a comb. However, the Taliban delegates were quite excited after visiting the Houston Zoo and the NASA Space Center. They also had dinner with Marty Miller, vice-president of the US Oil Company UNOCAL. The Taliban were quoted as, "admiring his swimming pool," and Mr. Miller's "comfortable house."[50]

The Taliban's sojourn to Texas as VIP guests was part of a series of attempts on the part of UNOCAL to woo the Taliban towards its own pipeline project and forbid them from cutting a pipeline deal with Birdas. The same month, when the Taliban delegation visited Houston, another Taliban delegation was being hosted similarly by Birdas chiefs in Buenos Aires.[51]

As for the US Government, it wanted UNOCAL to build the oil and gas pipelines from the Central Asian states to Pakistan through Afghanistan so that the vast untapped reserves in the Central Asian and Caspian regions could be transported. Marketing these products to markets in South Asia, South-East Asia, the Far East and the Pacific.

No surprise then that the very people who are being accused today by the United States as harboring Osama bin Laden and his Al-Qaeda terrorist networks were courted by Washington for years in order to secure a commercial interest-the UNOCAL pipeline deal.[52]

The US Policy towards Afghanistan continues to improve (sort of)

The Clinton administration ignored the rise of the Taliban from October 1994 onwards, with the active backing of its allies Pakistan and Saudi Arabia. For political reasons as well, Washington did not object to the emergence of an inherently anti-Iran Sunni force in Afghanistan, which secured its first major victory against the then Afghan government of Burhanuddin Rabbani in September 1995, when the Herat province bordering Iran and Turkmenistan fell.

For the next three years, between 1995 and 1998, especially after the fall of Kabul in September 1996, the Clinton administration officials openly lobbied for the UNOCAL before Taliban authorities.

That the American Government ignored the rise of the Taliban and courted them on behalf of the US oil concerns led to a widespread perception in the regional media, also expressed officially by the anti-American Iranian regime, that the CIA was behind the Taliban.[53]

Secretary of State Madeleine Albright visits Pakistan while top US officials continued to pay regular visits to Kabul.[54] They included former US Assistant Secretary of State for South Asia Robin Raphel, her successor Karl Inderfurth, Deputy Secretary for Political Affairs Thomas Pickering, and the US ambassador to the UN Bill Richardson.[55]

Albright was the first U.S. diplomat who came out categorically against the "despicable" attitude of Taliban on women rights. Otherwise, all top U.S. leaders visiting the region, particularly Kabul, since it came under Taliban's occupation, had spoken altogether different words about Taliban.

Inderfurth, who succeeded Raphel in July 1997, was quoted by the *Washington Post* on 12 January, 1998, even after Madeleine's remarks about Taliban, as saying, "We do believe they (Taliban) can modify their behavior and take into account certain international standards with respect to women's rights to education and employment."[56]

The 1,300km/800m pipeline will carry gas across Afghanistan's harsh terrain

The following article ran on the BBC website. I reprint the entire article to show the enthusiasm for this pipeline:

> A senior delegation from the Taliban movement in Afghanistan is in the United States for talks with an international energy company that wants to construct a gas pipeline from Turkmenistan across Afghanistan to Pakistan.
>
> A spokesman for the company, Unocal, said the Taliban were expected to spend several days at the company's headquarters in Sugarland, Texas.
>
> Unocal says it has agreements both with Turkmenistan to sell its gas and with Pakistan to buy it.
> But, despite the civil war in Afghanistan, Unocal has been in competition with an Argentinean firm, Bridas, to actually construct the pipeline.
>
> Last month, the Argentinean firm, Bridas, announced that it was close to signing a two-billion dollar deal to build the pipeline,

which would carry gas 1,300 kilometers from Turkmenistan to Pakistan, across Afghanistan.

Last month the Taleban Minister of Information and Culture, Amir Khan Muttaqi, said the Taleban had held talks with both American and Argentine-led consortia over transit rights but that no final agreement had yet been reached. He said an official team from Afghanistan, Pakistan and Turkmenistan should meet to ensure each country benefited from any deal.

However, Unocal clearly believes it is still in with a chance - to the extent that it has already begun training potential staff.

It has commissioned the University of Nebraska to teach Afghan men the technical skills needed for pipeline construction. Nearly 140 people were enrolled last month in Kandahar and Unocal also plans to hold training courses for women in administrative skills.

Although the Taliban authorities only allow women to work in the health sector, organisers of the training say they haven't so far raised any objections.

The BBC regional correspondent says the Afghan economy has been devastated by 20 years of civil war. A deal to go ahead with the pipeline project could give it a desperately-needed boost.

But peace must be established first -- and that for the moment still seems a distant prospect.[57]

U.S. gives silent backing the Taliban rise to power

Is it not ironic that Washington was courting the very force it is up against today for years in a bid to advance the commercial interests of US oil barons?

I know what you are thinking: This is simply coincidence. Perhaps you can refer the friendship of the Americans with Iraq to fight Iran in the 1980's. But what if it isn't. What if the attack upon the United States on 11 September, 2001 was an event simply to oust the Taliban government?

On 12 February, 1998, Unocal went before the Sub-committee on Asia and the Pacific of the Committee on International Relations at the House of Representatives to bring up the natural resources in the Caspian Sea region and the need to create the pipeline mentioned above.[58] Unocal also stresses about the need for governing stability in this region. I will cover this event in the next chapter. I am briefly mentioning it here, to be concurrent with the time line of who the Taliban are.

I'm sorry, Taliban, who?

In August 1998 the bombing of the two U.S. embassies in East Africa occurred.[59] Then the consequent cruise missile attack on the alleged terrorist camps in Afghanistan of the Al-Qaeda, the organization headed by Osama bin Laden, who allegedly masterminded the bombing of the embassies. U.S. official contact with the Taliban was then restricted.[60]

Yet, according to official U.S. claims, the provision of millions of dollars in humanitarian assistance and the visit of a number of U.S. officials to Kabul until only a couple of months before the 11 September strikes.[61]

As for UNOCAL, it took three months after the August 1998 terrorist act and U.S. military response that is December 1998, to withdraw from the Cent-Gas consortium the US oil company itself had organized to build a gas pipeline from Turkmenistan's old Daulatabad gas field to Pakistan through Afghanistan.[62]

Bill Richardson was the highest-ranking U.S. diplomat to visit Afghanistan since Henry Kissinger.[63] During his visit in April 1998, six months before the U.S. embassies were attacked, and two months after Al-Qaeda issued a declaration of jihad to, "kill the Americans and their allies, civilian and military, "the U.S. Ambassador to the U.N. was reported to have offered U.S. recognition of the Taliban regime in Afghanistan in exchange for the handing over of Osama to the United States. Since then, even after the US embassies bombing in August 1998, the Taliban maintained their official contacts with the State Department through their representatives based in Washington, D.C., urging the U.S. and Bill Clinton's Administration that it should recognize their government since they were now in control of more than 90 percent of Afghanistan, meaning they were in a position to provide safe and secure environment to the American oil concerns.

UNOCAL invited some of the leaders of the Taliban to Houston. This has been documented.[64] Today, if you visit UNOCAL's web site, they claim to be, "misquoted" about their dealings with the Taliban.[65]

So, the lodging of the Taliban in a five-star hotel, visiting the zoo, supermarkets and the NASA space center, was just a nice

American company giving some tours to tourist they just happened to run into in the streets. I'm sure that I am "misquoting" them now too.

Again please remember the printed article in two newspapers of the dinner the Taliban ate at the home of Marty Miller, a senior company executive, where they admired his swimming pool and the large, "comfortable house,"[66] is probably misquoted as well. I'm sure. I would then assume the reporters mixed up the notes about the neighbour's house, not Mr. Miller's. That's it, but I'm sure just a misplacement of notes.

The US dealings with the Taliban, from their emergence in October 1994 to the August 1998 bombing of U.S. Embassies, leave little doubt as to why such speculations should not arise in response to renewed U.S. contacts with the radical Islamic militia. Even if the official U.S. explanations about such contacts are that they are guided by nothing but humanitarian concerns in Afghanistan.

In 1998, the Taliban chose to protect Osama bin Laden,[67] who had taken refuge in Afghanistan after having launched Jihad against the United States and was wanted by Washington, rather than protect the pipeline and get 15 cents per 1,000 cubic feet from Unocal for the service.

So, the pipeline dream went sour and the Taliban became a pariah regime.

OH, you mean *THE* Taliban

The United States, between May and July 2001, donated 3,500 tons of wheat for Afghan "refugees" living in miserable conditions in northern Pakistan. The wheat arrived in the southern port city of Karachi, and was said would, "Help feed at least 65,000 Afghans in refugee camps near the northern border city of Peshawar," according to the World Food Program in a statement.[68]

Then on May 19, 2001, the United States announced a $43 million program of emergency assistance for Afghanistan! $43 million for emergency assistance for Afghanistan! Four months BEFORE the terrorist attacks, therefor five months before the War on Afghanistan. Oops! I'm sorry the war on "terrorism." Then in July 2001, Washington promised another $2.3 million to help Afghan refugees in Pakistan. More than 200,000 refugees have arrived from Afghanistan since September 2000. The new refugees were in addition to the more than two million Afghans who fled to Pakistan since 1989.[69]

So let me see if I understand this: 3,500 tons of wheat and $2.3 million went to Pakistan to feed 65,000 of the 2.2 million refugees. BUT, $43 million went to Afghanistan, NOT Pakistan mind you, AFGHANISTAN. More than likely, in the case of a government so corrupt as the Taliban, the money would go to the Taliban and not the charity intended, correct? Correct!

This figure does not include the year to date assistance given to Afghanistan. Are you ready for this? $124 million.

$124 million!!!

So who is one of the nations "harboring and funding terrorism," President Bush?

> The aid is given through the United Nations and non-governmental organizations because the United States has no official relationship with Afghanistan's ruling Taliban Islamic militia, which Washington accuses of sponsoring terrorism.[70]

So, this report is suggesting that the US aid isn't ACTUALLY from the U.S. It is from the U.N.[71] So, is it then the U.N. who funds and harbors terrorism, is it Mr. President?

Afghanistan: Unlisted as Terrorist Sponsor

The following information has been gathered from the *Washington Post*:

> Monday, November 5, 2001,
>
> By Mary Pat Flaherty, David B. Ottaway and James V.Grimaldi Washington Post Staff Writers
>
> Each year, the U.S. State Department formally rebukes and imposes penalties on governments that protect and promote terrorists. But since 1996, when the Taliban seized power in Afghanistan, the nation harboring Osama bin Laden has never made the department's list of terrorist-sponsoring countries.
>
> The omission reflects more than a decade of vexing relations between the United States and Afghanistan, a period that found the State Department more focused on U.S. oil interests and women's rights than on the growing terrorist threat, according to experts and current and former officials.
>
> Even as its cables and reports showed growing anxiety, the department vacillated between engaging and isolating the Taliban. It was not until 1998, when two U.S. embassy bombings were linked to bin Laden, that officials knew they

must directly address Afghanistan's protection of the terrorist's organization.

U.S. diplomats held out hope that the threat of adding Afghanistan to the terrorism list was "one card we had to play" in pressing the Taliban to turn over bin Laden, according to a former Clinton administration adviser.

The lack of a coherent policy toward Afghanistan was part of a broader miscalculation by the U.S. Government, experts now realize.

By allowing terrorism fueled by anti-American rage to take root in Afghanistan, officials underestimated the potential for danger.

"This is hard to say and I haven't found a way to say it that doesn't sound crass," said former secretary of state Madeleine K. Albright.

"But it is the truth that those [attacks before Sept. 11] were happening overseas and while there were Americans who died, there were not thousands and it did not happen on U.S. soil."

Taliban Not 'Objectionable'

The day after the Taliban seized Kabul in September 1996, State Department spokesman Glyn Davies encountered tough questions from U.S. reporters. Victorious in a brutal fight against rival factions, the Taliban claimed power after castrating and killing former president Najibullah and hanging the corpses of him and his brother from a post at the entrance to the Presidential Palace.

Davies reported the events matter-of-factly and told reporters the United States saw "nothing objectionable" about the Taliban imposing its strict interpretation of Islamic law.

"So let me get this straight," a reporter asked. "This group, this Islamic fundamentalist group that has taken Afghanistan by force and summarily executed the former president, the United States is holding out possibility of relations?"

"I'm not going to prejudge where we're going to go with Afghanistan," Davies said.

For seven years, the State Department had loosely monitored Afghanistan's civil warfare after defeated Soviet troops pulled out of the country in 1989. Prolonged fighting had left Afghanistan devastated, with tides of refugees, a largely illiterate population and a ravaged agricultural economy based heavily on opium production.

Promising to restore law and order, the Taliban said that refugees could return "without fear." The United States hoped the regime would restore stability.

Davies' comments reflected years of U.S. support for Afghan rebels during the war with the Soviets. The U.S. government had covertly supplied aid to religious fighters known as mujaheddin who wanted to restore an Islamic state.

In those ranks was bin Laden, a scion of a wealthy Saudi Arabian family. Bin Laden had arrived in Afghanistan in 1982 to fight the Soviets, and stayed through 1990, forming alliances with fundamentalist leaders, including Mohammad Omar, the Taliban supreme commander.

None of this seemed particularly threatening to most of the diplomatic corps at the State Department, which was consumed with events in Iran and Iraq and the brewing nuclear arms race between Pakistan and India.

In fact, when the Clinton administration took over in 1993, Warren Christopher mentioned bringing peace to Afghanistan in his confirmation hearings for secretary of state, then never made a significant speech about the country again. Christopher declined requests for an interview.

But there were warnings. Peter Tomsen, a longtime State Department official who was a special envoy to Afghanistan, and a few others insisted that the United States should help rebuild the country to protect it from extremists. By disengaging, the United States risked "throwing away the assets we have built up in Afghanistan over the last 10 years, at great expense," he argued in a confidential 1993 memo to top State Department officials.

"The U.S. mistake was to ignore Afghanistan," Tomsen says today.

"We walked away."

After the Cold War, the United States was "weary of Afghanistan," said Robin L. Raphel, the assistant secretary for South Asian affairs at the State Department from 1993 to 1997. "It was really a struggle to get attention and resources."

Yet to a large extent, the United States deferred to Pakistan, its ally against the Soviet Union, as Afghanistan's turbulence dragged on, according to other former officials.

"The U.S. had what I call a derivative policy toward Afghanistan," said Elie D. Krakowski, a former special assistant to the secretary of defense, who has written extensively on Afghanistan. "That is, it had no policy on Afghanistan on its own, and whatever Pakistan said, we bought."

The United States was reluctant to criticize Pakistan as it further aligned itself with the Taliban after Kabul's fall.

With U.S. officials paying more attention to Afghanistan's neighbors, bin Laden returned to the country. The United States had pressed Sudan to evict him for suspected terrorist activities but did not sustain the pressure when Omar welcomed him in as a guest.

Activities at bin Laden's training camps increased. A State Department report in August 1996 labeled him one of the "most significant sponsors of terrorism today."

The Pipeline Connection

Throughout the mid-1990s, a U.S. oil company was tracking the outcome of the Afghan conflict. Unocal, a California-based energy giant, was seeking rights to build a massive pipeline system across Afghanistan, connecting the vast oil and natural gas reserves of Turkmenistan to a plant and ports in Pakistan.

State Department officials promoted Unocal's pipeline project in their role of helping U.S. companies find investments in the region, Raphel said.

Raphel, who shuttled to Kandahar to meet with Taliban leaders and met at other points with different groups, said the agency also thought the project might help rally them around a common goal. "We worked hard to make all the Afghan factions understand the potential, because the Unocal pipeline offered development opportunities that no aid program nor any Afghan government could," she said.

But Unocal faced fierce competition. Because it was unclear which of Afghanistan's factions would ultimately take control, international oil companies jockeyed to build alliances.

Unocal appealed to the Taliban and received assurances that it would support a $4.5 billion project rivaling the Trans-Alaska pipeline.

The deal promised to be a boon for the Taliban, which could realize $100 million a year in transit fees.

But Unocal also needed U.S. backing. To secure critical

financing from agencies such as the World Bank, it needed the State Department to formally recognize the Taliban as Afghanistan's government.

Unocal hired former State Department insiders: former secretary of state Henry A. Kissinger, former special U.S. ambassador John J. Maresca and Robert Oakley, a former U.S. ambassador to Pakistan.

Zalmay Khalilzad, an Afghan-born former Reagan State Department adviser on Afghanistan, entered the picture as a consultant for a Boston group hired by Unocal. Khalilzad and Oakley had dual roles during this period because the State Department also sought their advice. Khalilzad is now one of President Bush's top advisers on Afghanistan.

Officially, Unocal refused to take sides in the Afghan conflict. But its favors to the Taliban sent a clear signal to rivals. Unocal gave the Taliban a fax machine to speed its communications and funded a job training program affiliated with the University of Nebraska that was set up in Kandahar, the Taliban stronghold in southeast Afghanistan.

Before Unocal, the Taliban "were just a bunch of wild jihadists running around. They came out of nowhere," said Richard Dekmejian, a University of Southern California terrorism specialist, using the Islamic term for holy warriors.

In a late 1997 public relations move, Unocal flew Taliban officials to tour the company's U.S. offices. They took a side trip to the beach, then flew to Washington for meetings in the Capitol and at the State Department to press their case for U.S. recognition.

But the visit only fueled the outrage of women's rights groups who were incensed by Unocal's coziness with the regime.

The State Department's human rights division had been chronicling the Taliban's increasingly repressive treatment of women. Women were barred from schools and jobs and required to wear head-to-toe shrouds known as burqas. Secluded inside homes with darkened windows, they could be seen in public only in the company of male relatives.

But reports of these and other human rights violations -- including stonings, amputations and executions -- had little effect until Secretary of State Albright took over in Clinton's second term. She elevated the Afghanistan focus, naming her close colleague Karl F. "Rick" Inderfurth to head the South Asia

Bureau. She also planned a November 1997 trip to meet with Afghan women huddled in refugee camps.

Albright's trip was a sign that the Taliban treatment of women, more than any other issue, "finally sparked their interest on the seventh floor," the State Department's executive suite, said Lee O. Coldren, who directed the little-noticed office on Afghanistan from 1994 to 1997.

Crucial Albright Visit "Despicable."

Albright emerged from a mud-brick camp in Nasir Bagh sheltering 80,000 Afghans, and with that single word, she ratcheted up the U.S. rhetoric.

She had listened as women and girls described deplorable treatment, including a 13-year-old who told of watching her older sister jump to her death out a window rather than live under the regime.

The visit "was one of those watershed events for me," Albright said recently.

Women's groups had been agitating at the State Department since the Taliban's 1996 takeover but believed they were not taken seriously. In meetings, Afghan American women described life before the Taliban, when well-educated, professional women moved freely in some Afghan cities.

But among the State Department's old hands, "there was a lot of putting down, like these women didn't know what they were talking about," said Eleanor Smeal, president of the Feminist Majority Foundation.

The women's effort had an important ally at the White House, first lady Hillary Rodham Clinton. And at the United Nations, the two women who headed the food and children's care programs linked their Afghanistan aid to improved treatment of women.

The issue of international terrorism had no such constituency. A bin Laden fatwa in early 1998 urged followers to target the United States and its citizens, but the notice was largely ignored by U.S. groups and businesses concentrating on Afghanistan.

That July, U.S. women's groups organized protests of Unocal's plans to go ahead with its project despite what Smeal called the Taliban's "horrific gender apartheid."

The pressure from women's groups began to have an impact domestically. It became increasingly clear that U.S. recognition of the Taliban - the seal of approval needed so desperately by Unocal - would be politically implausible.

Why Not on List?

Shortly after Inderfurth took over the State Department office dealing with Afghanistan and Pakistan in 1997, he posed a question: Why isn't Afghanistan on the list of terrorist-sponsoring nations?

Inclusion would have meant a ban on arms sales, constraints on business and a cutoff of economic aid. The same seven countries had been on the list since 1993 -- Cuba, Iran, Iraq, Libya, North Korea, Sudan and Syria.

With Afghanistan, there was a catch. If the Taliban was branded a "state sponsor" of terrorism, that meant the United States would inadvertently be acknowledging the Taliban as the official government. And the State Department had resisted doing so.

Instead, the United States was using other methods to press its case. It leaned on Pakistan to persuade the Taliban to stop harboring bin Laden. Pakistan had developed a close relationship with the Taliban, supplying arms and using camps in Taliban-controlled territory to train its own guerrillas.

Consequently, if Afghanistan made the list, the procedure for designating terrorist sponsors would have argued for also sanctioning Pakistan. "We weren't prepared to totally isolate Pakistan," an official said.

"The whole approach was so absurd," said Phil Smith, a spokesman for Afghanistan's Northern Alliance faction, a Taliban rival. "It ignored the reality that it was the Pakistani military that had helped to create and maintain the Taliban regime."

The 1998 bombings of U.S. embassies in Kenya and Tanzania, which killed 224 people, including 12 Americans, altered the landscape. The attacks were quickly linked to bin Laden, and President Bill Clinton froze bin Laden's assets and prohibited U.S. firms from doing business with him.

Thirteen days after the attacks, the United States directed missile strikes on terrorist camps in Afghanistan and Sudan. Doing more, Albright said, would have been a challenge "since we did not have the kind of support we have now for our actions on terrorism. Back then, we were being criticized both for doing too much and for not doing enough."

The bombings abruptly ended Unocal's hopes of a pipeline project.

The company backed out on Dec. 4, 1998, citing business reasons.

News reports at the time speculated that Unocal feared it could face sanctions for doing business with the Taliban. At the White House, debate resurfaced about adding Afghanistan to the terrorist list.

Officials reasoned that they could use the threat of listing to bargain with the Taliban, according to one former adviser.

By 1999, the United Nations imposed the first of two sets of sanctions that cut off Taliban funds and arms. In that same year, the State Department formally named bin Laden's al Qaeda group as a "foreign terrorist organization," which froze its U.S. assets, barred visas for its members and made it a crime to support the group. Still it did not formally single out Afghanistan or the Taliban as terrorist sponsors.

Inderfurth and others believed that step was unnecessary because Clinton's order and the United Nations sanctions were the "functional equivalent" of declaring the Taliban as a state sponsor. To some analysts, the actions were too little, too late.

"Right up until the embassy bombings, we were willing to believe their assurances," said Julie Sirrs, a former analyst on Iran for the Defense Intelligence Agency who also monitored the Taliban.

"We were not serious about this whole thing, not only this administration, but the previous one," and that holds true until the Sept. 11 attacks, said Middle East specialist Dekmejian.

Albright disagrees. She said terrorism "was not a back burner issue at all. We kept pushing it and pushing intelligence agencies -- the FBI, CIA -- to work on it."

The State Department, she said, "consumed all the intelligence. . . . Given the intelligence we had, we followed through as best we could.

"So the question comes up of how do you fight terrorism," Albright said. "The tragedy of this, and it's horrible, is that it took this kind of event to generate the support we need to do more."[72]

108

Taliban: Come 11 September, 2001

President Bush declared an indefinite and global war on terrorism as America's answer to the 'unthinkable' attacks on New York and Washington, with his top priority being to get a hold of Osama, "dead or alive," and the dismantling of the Taliban regime.

But many analysts insist there is much more to it than meets the eye. The whole world cannot be threatened by the US to rally behind it merely to launch a hunt for one man and re-destroy an already destroyed country.

Since the October 7 invasion of Afghanistan, three distinct features mark Washington's strategy:

First, the endless denomination of Osama bin Laden by the media in all possible forms (to keep public attention away from real war aims).

Second, the perpetuation of a climate of fear in the United States by: Slashing civil liberties, by making laws harsher; Incidences of hate crimes; Forecasts of more terrorist attacks; And the anthrax scare (to demoralize and silence dissidents and critics of all shades).

Third, most of the statements by the president and the key functionaries continue to remind the allies and rival powers that this time the American presence in Afghanistan will be indefinitely long, to rebuild the country and to ensure stability and peace (a warning to Russia not to raise its stakes in the region).

Now that the Taliban regime stands dismantled, and our puzzle pieces are not starting to fit together like the image on the box, what can be the next move of the U.S. in Afghanistan after a new, favorable government is installed in Kabul?

Finding Osama, of course, remains a major objective, or does it?

We have yet to examine his puzzle pieces. But relax, we will.

In September, a few days before the attacks on New York, the US Energy Information Administration had reported:

Afghanistan remains a potential transit route for oil and natural gas exports from Central Asia to the Arabian sea.

This potential includes the possible construction of pipelines through Afghanistan.[73]

The Guardian said:

109

Given that the Bush administration is dominated by former oil industry executives (Cheney was head of the world's biggest oil service company, Haliburton; Condaleeza Rice has been on the board of Chevron; Don Evans, commerce secretary, has been CEO and chairman of an oil company), we would be foolish to suppose that a reinvigoration of these plans (oil pipelines) no longer figures in its strategic thinking.[74]

Taliban will 'Pay the Price'

After the 11 September attacks, the United States quickly began military strikes on Afghanistan. No trial, no evidence, that I have seen, to draw military force. Yet America has again stuck and killed more innocent Afghan civilians that the American civilians lost on 11 September.

And this is justice?

Eye for an eye makes the world blind, or that is what I have been told.

11 September, 2001 claimed the lives of 2,998 civilians (including the World Trade Center, Washington, D.C. and Flight 93).

A study by Professor Marc Herold of the University of New Hampshire concluded that between 7 October and 7 December, 2001, at LEAST 3,800 Afghanistan civilians (men, women, and children with NO connection whatsoever to 11 September) died from American and British attacks.[75] And that was more than one year ago.

If 11 September was the, "worst terrorist acts in history," what does that make the attacks on civilians in Afghanistan? Not to mention what will happen to innocent civilians in Iraq when Baby Boy Bush attack!

President Bush described the attacks as, "a new front," in the operation to combat terrorism.

The strike began with loud explosions and anti-aircraft fire in the Afghan capital Kabul, and later in the cities of Kandahar and Jalalabad. It still rages on, claiming to look for Osama bin Laden. If he was really so important to find, he would have been found already. But yet the U.S. Government has to keep a card up its sleeve to promote more massive innocent killing. More and more sacrifices to America's God: The Dollar.

Explosions and fires were also reported throughout Afghanistan. Videotapes and now audio tapes are presented almost weekly to show that bin Laden is still out there... somewhere....

Dodging the, "Greatest Military on Earth."

In addresses to the US nation, Baby Boy Bush said strikes by U.S. and British forces were taking place against training camps and military installations of the Al-Qaeda network in Afghanistan, and that they had been carefully targeted. Baby Bush also stated that the Taliban would, "pay the price," for sheltering terrorists. So when will America pay the price for sheltering terrorists? When will Great Britain, Germany, hell, the whole world?

Bush stated, "In this conflict there is no neutral ground, there can be no peace in a world of terror. We did not ask for this mission but we will fulfil it."[76] So, Mr. President, what are you doing the world wide to fulfil your mission? So far I have only seen you take on countries that have something you want… revenue from crude oil.

Baby Boy Bush added that operations were accompanied by deliveries of food, medicine and other supplies to the people of Afghanistan.[77]

So let me get this straight. The people who have just lost their cities, homes, loved ones, and more, are repaid with food, medicine and other supplies. I wonder if other supplies included staples for, "assuring America's victory," over Afghanistan. Like poison, small explosives, maybe even biological weapons, I wouldn't put it past them. Would you?

The U.S. administration has repeatedly rejected Taliban offers to bargain over the fate of its guest, Saudi-born militant Osama Bin Laden.[78]

I wonder why that could be? Perhaps they really don't want bin Laden, but a democratic form of government to proceed with the building of the pipeline, which by the way is back into production as this book is being written.

The Afghan war, it has been discovered, has an economic side to it.

Some writers, indeed, have gone further, suggesting that economic considerations provide the main, or at the very least a major, motivation for US and western involvement in Afghanistan.

If one discounts the more extreme and emotional versions of this theory, the argument boils down to this: Afghanistan has been proposed by more than one western oil company (the

US-based Unocal is often mentioned, but it is not the only one) as the best route by which to export the Central Asian republics' important output of oil and gas.

Given the increasing importance of finding and exploiting new sources of fossil fuel, governments like those of the US and the UK are enormously keen to gain influence in the Central Asian region in order to secure those supplies for the West.

In order to achieve that, and get those energy supplies moving out of Central Asia, they need to set up a pro-western government in Afghanistan.[79]

There is no doubt that Bush's decision to invade and bomb innocent civilians in Afghanistan have been influenced by oil money. This is the ultimate reason why 19 hijackers were able to board four commercial aircraft, and successfully hijack them, fly them into targets to bring an unstoppable revenge cry against its motivator. While all along that motivation was within the greed of the highest positions in the American and British Governments.

There is strong evidence of "surprisingly" close ties between Bush (Senior and Baby) and bid oil companies.

A majority of President Bush's new cabinet are millionaires and several are multimillionaires.

According to information from financial disclosure reports, released by the Office of Government Ethics, most cabinet appointees have amassed their fortunes in stock options.

Now a Washington-based think tank is questioning whether some of the cabinet members could face a possible conflict of interest.

It is not unusual for American politicians to be rich. For the last two decades more than half of all cabinet members have been millionaires.

Strong ties

But the number of millionaires in this new cabinet highlights the influence of money in American politics.

"You don't come to Washington and give up your life and business unless you have a lot of money," said Charles Lewis, executive director of the Center for Public Integrity.

What makes the new Bush administration different from previous wealthy cabinets is that so many of the officials have links to the same industry - oil.

112

The president, vice-president, commerce secretary and national security adviser all have strong ties to the oil industry.

Vice-President Dick Cheney amassed some £50m-$60m while he was chief executive of Haliburton oil company.

Commerce Secretary Donald Evans held stock valued between $5m and $25m in Tom Brown Inc, the oil and gas exploration company he headed.

Opening exploration

National Security Adviser Condoleeza Rice was a director of Chevron.

The concentration of energy connections is so pronounced that some critics are calling the Bush government the "oil and gas administration."

There are also questions about how energy policy decisions may be affected by the private financial interests of so many senior cabinet members.

The Bush administration has already made it clear that it would be interested in opening up oil exploration in Alaska.

It is a move opposed by environmental groups but favoured by energy companies. With oil prices rising in recent months this issue has taken on new urgency.

Political apathy

And this is not just the era of wealthy cabinet members.

One third of this senate are millionaires and 10 of the major presidential candidates also had financial fortunes in the millions.

If wealth is a prerequisite of political office, it appears that poverty is often a hallmark of political apathy.

Charles Lewis of the Center for Public Integrity said: "There is a perception of wealthy folks running the government and those who are not wealthy not participating in government."

Of the 100 million Americans who do not vote, the overwhelming majority are lower middle class or poor.

"During the 2000 elections, oil, gas and other energy interests donated more than $40 million to Republicans, including the Bush presidential campaign."

Bush in shares embarrassment

Mr. Bush sold shares in Harken Energy Corporation

113

The White House has acknowledged that US President George W Bush failed to follow the law and disclose details of shares he sold when he was a company director.

A spokesman blamed the omission on a clerical mistake by company lawyers.

The president's business dealings have sparked renewed interest since the accounting irregularities at WorldCom were revealed last week.

After those problems were announced, Mr. Bush said he was angry with company directors who abused their position.

Now his own actions have been called into question.

'A technicality'

In 1990, when he was a Texas businessman, Mr. Bush sold a large number of shares in the Harken Energy Corporation, just before the company announced news that made the share price fall.

Mr. Bush was on the auditing committee of the company at the time.

Previously the president has said that he had filed all the necessary forms regarding the sale on time with the accounting authorities.

But in a White House briefing on Wednesday, the president's spokesman acknowledged that one of the forms had, in fact, been filed late because of a clerical error.

The White House dismissed this as a technicality.

But it is enormously embarrassing in the current climate, where the spotlight has turned on good corporate governance, for the president to have failed to follow the law.[80]

I would like to offer everyone reading this book the opportunity to call for Baby Bush to make a public statement confirming that the oil pipeline issue did not influence his decision. But of course this public statement, no matter how many cry for it, will be ever made.

As such, the Bush administration's war on terrorism is, in fact, a war for resources, and the most precious resources are oil and gas.

Are you ready to try more pieces?

SOURCES

(1) http://www.rememberjohn.com/dawn.html
(2) http://www.gvnews.net/demo/html/Opinion/opin048.html
(3) http://www.satp.org/satporgtp/countries/pakistan/terroristoutfits/TNSM.htm
(4) http://www.unocal.com/uclnews/96htm/081396.htm
(5) http://www.hrw.org/backgrounder/asia/afghan-bck1023.htm
(6) http://irs.org.pk/IRSWEBSITE/spotlightEditions/sept2002.pdf
(7) http://www1.cnn.com/WORLD/9609/27/afghan.rebels/
(8) http://www.amnesty.org/ailib/aireport/ar97/ASA11.htm
(9) http://www1.cnn.com/WORLD/9609/27/afghan.rebels
(10) Ibid
(11) http://www.rawa.org/afg-info.htm
(12) http://www.shef.ac.uk/britfanfic/xICON.htm
(13) http://www.warresisters.org/talking_points.htm
(14) http://hotwired.lycos.com/netizen/netizenquote/96/40/index0a.html
(15) http://www.azadi.subnet.dk/President%20Najib.htm
(16) http://www1.cnn.com/WORLD/9609/27/afghan.rebels/
(17) Ibid
(18) Daily Press Briefing #156, U.S. Department of State, Sept. 27, 1996.
 http://www.hri.org/docs/statedep/96-09-27.std.html
(19) http://www.democraticunderground.com/forum_archive_html/DC
 ForumID45/1362.html
(20) http://www.globalresearch.ca/articles/PIL111B.html
(21) http://www.wsws.org/articles/2001/oct2001/tal2-o25.shtml
(22) http://www.globalresearch.ca/articles/AHM202Ap.html
(23) http://www.muslimedia.com/archives/special98/taliban.htm
(24) http://www.balochvoice.com/USA_The_pipeline_of_greed.html
(25) http://www.gvnews.net/demo/html/Opinion/opin048.html
(26) http://ist-socrates.berkeley.edu/~pdscott/q7.html
(27) http://www.rememberjohn.com/dawn.html
(28) http://www.greenleft.org.au/back/1996/254/254p23.htm
(29) http://www.chicagotribune.com/news/nationworld/chi-011021007
 1oct21.story
(30) http://www.ncf.ca/coat/our_magazine/links/issue46/articles/real_
 reasons_oil_us_taliban_relations.htm
(31) http://www.worldpress.org/specials/pp/pipeline_timeline.htm
(32) http://www.hartford-hwp.com/archives/51/119.html
(33) http://www.newsfrombabylon.com/article.php?sid=1483
(34) http://www.eariana.com/ariana/eariana.nsf/allArticles/A191070236E
 B441787256CDA00709DA8?OpenDocument
(35) http://www.scoop.co.nz/stories/HL0202/S00084.htm
(36) http://archive.tol.cz/transitions/oct98/pipeline.html
(37) http://www.thirdworldtraveler.com/Oil_watch/Oil_Empire_LGM.html
(38) http://www.unocal.com/uclnews/98news/082198.htm
(39) http://www.democraticunderground.com/forum_archive_html/DC

ForumID45/1362.html
(40) http://www.hartford-hwp.com/archives/51/119.html
(41) http://www.friendspartners.ru/friends/news/omri/1997/08/970801l.
html(opt,mozilla,unix,english,,new)
(42) http://www.worldpress.org/specials/pp/pipeline_timeline.htm
(43) Ibid
(44) Ibid
(45) Ibid
(46) http://www.tehelka.com/channels/currentaffairs/2001/oct/3/ca100301
us1.htm
(47) http://www.ncf.ca/coat/our_magazine/links/issue46/articles/real_
reasons_oil_us_taliban_relations.htm
(48) http://mail.sarai.net/pipermail/reader-list/2001-November/000760.html
(49) http://www.worldpress.org/specials/pp/pipeline_timeline.htm
http://www.tehelka.com/channels/currentaffairs/2001/oct/3/ca
100301us1.htm
(50) http://www.vcsun.org/~battias/911/20011006/20011003.ustaliban.txt
(51) http://www.ncf.ca/coat/our_magazine/links/issue46/articles/real_reasons
_oil_us_taliban_relations.htm
(52) This timeline has been based on Ahmed Rashid's excellent study,
Taliban: Militant Islam, Oil, and Fundamentalism in Central Asia (Yale
UP, 2000),Pratt's Oil Digest, Oil and Gas Magazine, Pravda, Moscow's
Interfax News Agency, the ITAR-TASS news agency, and the U.S.
Department of Energy)
(53) http://www.globalresearch.ca/articles/AHM202Ap.html
(54) Ibid
(55) Ibid
(56) Ibid
(57) BBC News Thursday, December 4, 1997
http://news.bbc.co.uk/hi/english/world/west_asia/newsid_37000/
37021.stm
(58) http://www.thirdworldtraveler.com/Central_Asia_watch/Don't%20Mess
_Unocal.html
(59) http://www.pbs.org/wgbh/pages/frontline/shows/binladen/bombings/
(60) http://www.tehelka.com/channels/currentaffairs/2001/oct/3/ca100301
us1.htm
(61) http://www.reliefweb.int/w/rwb.nsf/6686f45896f15dbc852567ae0053
0132/41bb9fd6cc6bae50c1256a50002f3ed7?OpenDocument
(62) http://www.unocal.com/uclnews/2001news/091401.htm
(63) http://www.globalresearch.ca/articles/AHM202A.html
(64) http://www.now.org/nnt/fall-98/global.html
http://www.preda.org/archives/2003/r03020401.html
http://www.counterpunch.org/tomenron.html
(65) http://www.worldpress.org/specials/pp/pipeline_timeline.htm
(66) http://www.balochvoice.com/USA_The_pipeline_of_greed.html
(67) http://www.angelfire.com/home/pearly/htmls1/osama-bio.html
(68) http://news.bbc.co.uk/hi/english/world/south_asia/newsid_1336000/
1336958.stm

The Taliban

(69) Ibid

(70) Ibid

(71) Source - U.S. Donates Wheat for Afghan Refugees, .c
The Associated Press

(72) the Washington Post, Monday, November 5, 2001 Page A01

(73) http://www.hinduonnet.com/thehindu/2001/10/13/stories/05132524.htm

(74) http://www.rememberjohn.com/dawn.html

(75) http://news.bbc.co.uk/hi/english/world/south_asia/newsid_1740000/
1740538.stm

(76) http://www.usnews.com/usnews/opinion/baroneweb/mb_011010.htm

(77) http://news.bbc.co.uk/hi/english/world/south_asia/newsid_1556000/
1556588.stm

(78) http://news.bbc.co.uk/onthisday/hi/dates/stories/october/7/newsid_
2519000/2519353.stm

(79) http://news.bbc.co.uk/1/hi/world/south_asia/1626889.stm

(80) http://news.bbc.co.uk/1/hi/business/2091642.stm121

Chapter 8
The Caspian Sea – Persian Gulf Pipeline
- It's *Not* About Oil

Just look at the irony of the situation: The tale of duplicity.

For years, the US Oil Company UNOCAL, with its Saudi partner Delta, competed with the Argentinean oil rival, Birdas, to build a gas pipeline from Turkmenistan to Pakistan through Afghanistan. And for that, it collaborated with the Taliban authorities in Afghanistan.

As for the US government, it wanted UNOCAL to build the oil and gas pipelines from Central Asian states to Pakistan through Afghanistan so that the vast untapped oil and gas reserves in the Central Asian and Caspian region could be transported to its markets in South Asia, South-East Asia, the Far East, and the Pacific.[1]

Consequently, the Clinton administration ignored the rise of the Taliban from October 1994 onwards, with the active backing of its allies Pakistan and Saudi Arabia. Especially after the fall of Kabul in September 1996.[2]

The United States was led to believe by Saudi Arabia and Pakistan that a Taliban regime would be able to herald an era of stable peace in Afghanistan, which did not occur as the Northern Alliance never allowed the Taliban to rule the country without any military challenge.

Washington also misjudged the Taliban resolve on the human rights front, hoping that they might soften their stand on women rights in the wake of the progress in the UNOCAL deal, and the millions of dollars and other financial benefits it entailed for them.

So did UNOCAL, which had donated $900,000 to the Center of Afghanistan Studies at the University of Omaha, Nebraska. The said Center set up a training and humanitarian aid program for the Afghans, opening a school in Kandahar, which began to train some 400 Afghan teachers, electricians, carpenters and pipe-fitters to help UNOCAL to lay out the pipeline. This was in addition to the millions of dollars of US official assistance to Taliban authorities as humanitarian assistance.[3]

The 2001 Bush administration contributed significantly to the humanitarian relief effort in Afghanistan in helping the Internally Displaced Persons (IDPs) prior to the September 11 tragedy.

As recently as July 2001, Christina Rocca, the U.S. Assistant Secretary of State for South Asia, met the Taliban officials in Islamabad and announced $43 million in food and shelter aid, brining the aid to $124 million that the U.S. contribution to Afghanistan's IDPs in 2001 alone. Since the humanitarian assistance was spent by the Taliban, without any accountability, the renewed US contacts with the Taliban, including a visit by seven U.S. officials to Kabul in late April 2001 preceded by another visit by three U.S. officials earlier in that month, before the terror-struck America on September 11 led to media speculations about a shift in the U.S. policy away from a single-focus on the Osama issue towards an approach based on a cautious engagement with Taliban even as they were under stringent sanctions by Washington and the U.N. Security Council.[4]

State Department spokesman Glyn Davies, said the U.S. found, "nothing objectionable," in the steps taken by the Taliban to impose Islamic law.

Senator Hank Brown, a supporter of the UNOCAL project, said, "The good part of what has happened is that one of the factions at least seems capable of developing a government in Kabul." UNOCAL's Vice President Miller called the Taliban's success a, "positive development."[6]

After capturing Kabul, as the Taliban started their northward military push, top U.S. officials continued to pay regular visits to Kabul. They included former US Assistant Secretary of State for South Asia Robin Raphel, her successor Karl Inderfurth, Deputy Secretary for Political Affairs Thomas Pickering, and the U.S. ambassador to the U.N. Bill Richardson. The U.S. policy towards Afghanistan, between the fall of Kabul until the November 1997 visit to Pakistan by Secretary of State Madeleine Albright, seemed to be primarily motivated by commercial concerns involving the realization of the UNOCAL pipeline project.

Tightening the noose around Iran, could be a political goal, but it was also appeared to be motivated by the economic factor, as Tehran had also concluded a couple of gas supply deals with the Turkmen government involving European oil companies. Albright was the first U.S. diplomat who came out categorically against the "despicable" attitude of Taliban on women rights; otherwise, all top U.S. leaders visiting the region, particularly Kabul, since it came under Taliban's occupation, had spoken altogether different words about Taliban.[7]

"We have an American company which is interested in building a pipeline from Turkmenistan through to Pakistan. This pipeline project will be very good for Pakistan and Afghanistan as it will not only offer job opportunities but also energy in Afghanistan," said Robin Raphel in Islamabad on 21 April, 1996 soon after visiting Kabul.[8] Later in October of that year, she was in Kabul once again for a week, and after returning from there, she told press-persons in Islamabad that the international community should, "engage the Taliban," instead of, "isolating them."[9]

Inderfurth, who succeeded Raphel in July 1997, was quoted by the Washington Post on 12 January 1998, even after Madeline Albright's remarks about Taliban, as saying, "We do believe they (Taliban) can modify their behavior and take into account certain international standards with respect to women's rights to education and employment."[10]

Bill Richardson was the highest-ranking U.S. diplomat to visit Afghanistan since Henry Kissinger. During his visit in April 1998, six months before the US embassies were attacked and two months after Al-Qaeda issued a declaration of jihad to, "kill the Americans and their allies: civilian and military," the U.S. ambassador to the U.N. was reported to have offered US recognition of the Taliban regime in Afghanistan in exchange for the handing over of Osama to the United States.[11]

Since then, even after the US embassies bombing in August 1998, the Taliban maintained their official contacts with the State Department through their representatives based in Washington, D.C., urging the U.S. administration that it should recognize their government since they were now in control of more than 90 percent of Afghanistan, meaning they were in a position to provide and safe and secure environment to the American oil concerns. It was only after the passing of the stringent U.N. Security Council resolutions in December of 1998 that they were asked to leave the United States, as the sanctions imposed a ban on international travel of Taliban officials.

U.S. gives silent backing the Taliban rises to power

Is it not ironic that Washington was courting the very force it is up against today for years in a bid to advance the commercial interests of

US oil barons?

I know what you are thinking, this is simply coincidence. Perhaps you can refer the friendship of the Americans with Iraq to fight Iran in the 1980's. But what if it isn't. What if the attack upon the United States on 11 September, 2001 was an event simply to oust the Taliban government?

Consider the following information brought before the House of Representatives, 12 February, 1998. Because of the length of this transcript, I will highlight the important statements with a **bold type**.

And because I do not want these statements to be taken out of contexts, the complete hearing is reprinted below:

U.S. INTERESTS IN THE CENTRAL ASIAN REPUBLICS HEARING BEFORE THE SUBCOMMITTEE ON ASIA AND THE PACIFIC OF THE COMMITTEE ON INTERNATIONAL RELATIONS HOUSE OF REPRESENTATIVES

ONE HUNDRED FIFTH CONGRESS SECOND SESSION

FEBRUARY 12, 1998

Next we would like to hear from Mr. John J. Maresca, vice president of international relations, Unocal Corporation. You may proceed as you wish.

STATEMENT OF JOHN J. MARESCA, VICE

PRESIDENT OF INTERNATIONAL RELATIONS, UNOCAL CORPORATION

Thank you, Mr. Chairman. It's nice to see you again. I am John Maresca, vice president for international relations of the Unocal Corporation. **Unocal, as you know, is one of the world's leading energy resource and project development companies.** I appreciate your invitation to speak here today. I believe these hearings are important and timely. **I congratulate you for focusing on Central Asia oil and gas reserves and the role they play in shaping U.S. policy.**

I would like to focus today on three issues.

First, the need for multiple pipeline routes for Central Asian oil and gas resources. Second, the need for U.S. support for international and regional efforts to achieve balanced and lasting political settlements to the conflicts in the region, including Afghanistan. Third, the need for structured assistance to encourage economic reforms and the development of appropriate investment climates in the

121

region. In this regard, we specifically support repeal or removal of section 907 of the Freedom Support Act.

Mr. Chairman, **the Caspian region contains tremendous untapped hydrocarbon reserves. Just to give an idea of the scale, proven natural gas reserves equal more than 236 trillion cubic feet. The region's total oil reserves may well reach more than 60 billion barrels of oil. Some estimates are as high as 200 billion barrels. In 1995, the region was producing only 870,000 barrels per day. By 2010, western companies could increase production to about 4.5 million barrels a day, an increase of more than 500 percent in only 15 years. If this occurs, the region would represent about 5 percent of the world's total oil production.**

One major problem has yet to be resolved: how to get the region's vast energy resources to the markets where they are needed. Central Asia is isolated. Their natural resources are land locked, both geographically and politically. Each of the countries in the Caucasus and Central Asia faces difficult political challenges. Some have unsettled wars or latent conflicts. Others have evolving systems where the laws and even the courts are dynamic and changing. In addition, a chief technical obstacle, which we in the industry face in transporting oil, is the region's existing pipeline infrastructure.

Because the region's pipelines were constructed during the Moscow centered Soviet period, they tend to head north and west toward Russia. There are no connections to the south and east. **But Russia is currently unlikely to absorb large new quantities of foreign oil.** It's unlikely to be a significant market for new energy in the next decade. It lacks the capacity to deliver it to other markets.

Two major infrastructure projects are seeking to meet the need for additional export capacity. One, under the aegis of the Caspian Pipeline Consortium, plans to build a pipeline west from the northern Caspian to the Russian Black Sea port of Novorossiysk. Oil would then go by tanker through the Bosporus to the Mediterranean and world markets.

The other project is sponsored by the Azerbaijan International Operating Company, a consortium of 11 foreign oil companies, including four American companies, Unocal, Amoco, Exxon and Pennzoil. This consortium conceives of two possible routes, one line would angle north and cross the north Caucasus to Novorossiysk.

The other route would cross Georgia to a shipping terminal on the Black Sea. This second route could be extended west and south across Turkey to the Mediterranean port of Ceyhan. But even if both pipelines were built, they would not have enough total capacity to transport all the oil expected to flow from the region in the future. Nor would they have the capability to move it to the right markets. Other export pipelines must be built.

At Unocal, we believe that the central factor in planning these pipelines should be the location of the future energy markets that are most likely to need these new supplies. Western Europe, Central and Eastern Europe, and the Newly Independent States of the former Soviet Union are all slow growth markets where demand will grow at only a half a percent to perhaps 1.2 percent per year during the period 1995 to 2010.

Asia is a different story all together. It will have a rapidly increasing energy consumption need. Prior to the recent turbulence in the Asian Pacific economies, we at Unocal anticipated that this region's demand for oil would almost double by 2010. Although the short-term increase in demand will probably not meet these expectations, we stand behind our long-term estimates.

I should note that it is in everyone's interest that there be adequate supplies for Asia's increasing energy requirements. If Asia's energy needs are not satisfied, they will simply put pressure on all world markets, driving prices upwards everywhere.

The key question then is how the energy resources of Central Asia can be made available to nearby Asian markets. There are two possible solutions, with several variations. One option is to go east across China, but this would mean constructing a pipeline of more than 3,000 kilometers just to reach Central China. In addition, there would have to be a 2,000-kilometer connection to reach the main population centers along the coast. The question then is what will be the cost of transporting oil through this pipeline, and what would be the netback, which the producers would receive.

For those who are not familiar with the terminology, the netback is the price, which the producer receives for his oil or gas at the

123

well head after all the transportation costs have been deducted. So it's the price he receives for the oil he produces at the well head.

The second option is to build a pipeline south from Central Asia to the Indian Ocean. One obvious route south would cross Iran, but this is foreclosed for American companies because of U.S. sanctions legislation. The only other possible route is across Afghanistan, which has of course its own unique challenges. The country has been involved in bitter warfare for almost two decades, and is still divided by civil war. From the outset, we have made it clear that construction of the pipeline we have proposed across Afghanistan could not begin until a recognized government is in place that has the confidence of governments, lenders, and our company.

Mr. Chairman, as you know, we have worked very closely with the University of Nebraska at Omaha in developing a training program for Afghanistan which will be open to both men and women, and which will operate in both parts of the country, the north and south.

Unocal foresees a pipeline, which would become part of a regional system that will gather oil from existing pipeline infrastructure in Turkmenistan, Uzbekistan, Kazakhstan and Russia. **The 1,040-mile long oil pipeline would extend south through Afghanistan to an export terminal that would be constructed on the Pakistan coast. This 42-inch diameter pipeline will have a shipping capacity of one million barrels of oil per day. The estimated cost of the project, which is similar in scope to the Trans-Alaska pipeline, is about $2.5 billion.**

Given the plentiful natural gas supplies of Central Asia, our aim is to link gas resources with the nearest viable markets. This is basic for the commercial viability of any gas project. But these projects also face geopolitical challenges. Unocal and the Turkish company Koc Holding are interested in bringing competitive gas supplies to Turkey.

The proposed Eurasia natural gas pipeline would transport gas from Turkmenistan directly across the Caspian Sea through Azerbaijan and Georgia to Turkey. Of course the demarcation of the Caspian remains an issue.

Last October, the Central Asia Gas Pipeline Consortium, called

124

CentGas, in which Unocal holds an interest, was formed to develop a gas pipeline, which will link Turkmenistan's vast Dauletabad gas field with markets in Pakistan and possibly India. The proposed 790-mile pipeline will open up new markets for this gas, traveling from Turkmenistan through Afghanistan to Multan in Pakistan. The proposed extension would move gas on to New Delhi, where it would connect with an existing pipeline. As with the proposed Central Asia oil pipeline, CentGas cannot begin construction until an internationally recognized Afghanistan Government is in place.

The Central Asia and Caspian region is blessed with abundant oil and gas that can enhance the lives of the region's residents, and provide energy for growth in both Europe and Asia. The impact of these resources on U.S. commercial interests and U.S. foreign policy is also significant. Without peaceful settlement of the conflicts in the region, cross-border oil and gas pipelines are not likely to be built. We urge the Administration and the Congress to give strong support to the U.N.-led peace process in Afghanistan. The U.S. Government should use its influence to help find solutions to all of the region's conflicts.

U.S. assistance in developing these new economies will be crucial to business success. We thus also encourage strong technical assistance programs throughout the region. Specifically, we urge repeal or removal of section 907 of the Freedom Support Act. This section unfairly restricts U.S. Government assistance to the government of Azerbaijan and limits U.S. influence in the region.

Developing cost-effective export routes for Central Asian resources is a formidable task, but not an impossible one. Unocal and other American companies like it are fully prepared to undertake the job and to make Central Asia once again into the crossroads it has been in the past. Thank you, Mr. Chairman. [12]

So let's take a look at the proposal before congress

(Please excuse the *slight* sarcasm.)

Unocal, as you know, is one of the world's leading energy resource and project development companies. And therefore one of the greediest.

I congratulate you for focusing on Central Asia oil and gas reserves and the role they play in shaping U.S. policy. And I'm sure you will also congratulate yourselves for assisting with our project with the over generous campaign contributions we are almost more than certain to repay you with. I would like to focus today on three issues. First, the need for multiple pipeline routes for Central Asian oil and gas resources. Second, the need for U.S. support for international and regional efforts to achieve balanced and lasting political settlements to the conflicts in the region, including Afghanistan.

I wonder if the conflict in the region is the Taliban, which you helped to create, sir. Or maybe, just maybe it's something else. Just maybe.

Third, the need for structured assistance to encourage economic reforms and the development of appropriate investment climates in the region.

Structured assistance to encourage economic reforms, or food, or supplies.

The Caspian region contains tremendous untapped hydrocarbon reserves. Just to give an idea of the scale, proven natural gas reserves equal more than 236 trillion cubic feet. The region's total oil reserves may well reach more than 60 billion barrels of oil. Some estimates are as high as 200 billion barrels. In 1995, the region was producing only 870,000 barrels per day. By 2010, western companies could increase production to about 4.5 million barrels a day, an increase of more than 500 percent in only 15 years. If this occurs, the region would represent about 5 percent of the world's total oil production.

200 billion barrels x \$30 per barrel = \$6,000,000,000.

I will bring this number up again later, but the price to rebuild the World Trade Center is... Come on, think about it.

Central Asia is isolated. Their natural resources are land locked, both geographically and politically. Each of the countries in the Caucasus and Central Asia faces difficult political challenges. Some have unsettled wars or latent conflicts.

Not to mention some conflicts we helped to establish.

Russia is currently unlikely to absorb large new quantities of foreign oil.

126

And why wouldn't this poor country want to become like the United States. It is claimed that Russia does not have enough technology or marketing skills to sell this oil. Come on, you don't think they will invest a few million rubbles for new products to sell nine trillion dollars worth of petroleum?

> The second option is to build a pipeline south from Central Asia to the Indian Ocean. One obvious route south would cross Iran, but this is foreclosed for American companies because of U.S. sanctions legislation.

Obviously.

> The only other possible route is across Afghanistan, which has of course its own unique challenges. The country has been involved in bitter warfare for almost two decades, and is still divided by civil war.

Thanks to our establishing the Taliban there.

> From the outset, we have made it clear that construction of the pipeline we have proposed across Afghanistan could not begin until a recognized government is in place that has the confidence of governments, lenders, and our company.

Unlike our competition, Birdas, who want OUR money and will build no matter what the state of the country is in.

> The 1,040-mile long oil pipeline would extend south through Afghanistan to an export terminal that would be constructed on the Pakistan coast. This 42-inch diameter pipeline will have a shipping capacity of one million barrels of oil per day. The estimated cost of the project, which is similar in scope to the Trans-Alaska pipeline, is about $2.5 billion.

One million barrels of oil per day x $30 per barrel = $30 million a day.

$2.5 billion divided by $30 million a day = 84 days to turn a profit.

After three months, $30 million a day. WOW!

> The Central Asia and Caspian region is blessed with abundant oil and gas that can enhance the lives of the region's residents, and provide energy for growth in both Europe and Asia. The impact of these resources on U.S. commercial interests and U.S. foreign policy is also significant. Without peaceful settlement of the conflicts in the region, cross-border oil and

127

gas pipelines are not likely to be built. We urge the Administration and the Congress to give strong support to the U.N.-led peace process in Afghanistan. The U.S. Government should use its influence to help find solutions to all of the region's conflicts.

Like, perhaps declaring war. Just, perhaps. Thank you Mr. Chairman.

The pipe dream becomes reality

The Afghanistan oil pipeline project was finally able to proceed in May 2002. This could not have happened unless America had not taken military action to replace the government in Afghanistan.

Afghan pipeline given go-ahead

The leaders of Afghanistan, Pakistan and Turkmenistan have agreed to construct a $2bn pipeline to bring gas from Central Asia to the subcontinent.

The project was abandoned in 1998 when a consortium led by US energy company Unocal withdrew from the project over fears of being seen to support Afghanistan's then Taliban government.

The President of Turkmenistan, Saparmurat Nayazov, the chairman of Afghanistan's interim administration Hamid Karzai and Pakistan's President General Pervez Musharraf signed a memorandum of understanding in Islamabad on Thursday.

President Musharraf said the 1,500km pipeline would run from Turkmenistan's Daulatabad gas fields to the Pakistani port city of Gwadar.

The Pakistani leader said once the project is completed, Central Asia's hydrocarbon resources would be available to the international market, including East Asian and other far eastern countries.

Pakistan has plans to build a liquid-gas plant at the Gwadar port for export purposes.

Call for interest

The three countries have agreed to invite international tenders and guarantee funding before launching the project.

Unocal has repeatedly denied it is interested in returning to Afghanistan despite having conducted the original feasibility study to build the pipeline.

There is also a question mark over stability in Afghanistan, but interim Afghan leader Hamid Karzai said peace was prevailing all over the country.

Afghan officials believe the pipeline could yield significant revenues for the impoverished country in the form of transit fees.

The pipeline could eventually supply gas to India.

President Musharraf also said he was committed to a proposed gas pipeline from Iran through Pakistan to India as it was in his country's economic interest.[13]

Is this a surprising coincidence, or a horrible and sickening CORRUPTION?

I don't know about you, but my puzzle pieces are beginning to create a whole different picture.

But, there are many more pieces to be examined and placed together.

SOURCES

(1) Covered in Chapter 7 of this book
(2) Ibid
(3) Ibid
(4) Ibid
(5) Ibid
(6) Ibid
(7) Ibid
(8) http://www.globalresearch.ca/articles/AHM202Ap.html
(9) http://www.users.dircon.co.uk/~nickhack/fpafghantime96.html
(10) http://www.khilafah.com/home/category.php?DocumentID=3640&TagID=1
(11) http://www.un.int/usa/98_96.htm
(12) http://www.worldpress.org/specials/pp/unocal.htm
(13) http://news.bbc.co.uk/1/hi/business/2017044.stm

Chapter 9
The Creation of Osama bin Laden
The Evil Osama Bin Laden

As the "terrorist" attacks were being broadcast live around the world, the media was already suggesting one person, and ONLY one, could have done this: Osama Bin Laden.

Then, when the President declared that Osama Bin Laden was in fact behind the "terrorist" attacks, the American people already had determined in their minds that he was guilty, and consequently must die.

The attack on Afghanistan then began. And may I kindly remind you, without the head of bin Laden. Imagine that.

But who was/is Osama bin Laden?

The creation of Osama bin Laden

According to a wonderful investigation by MSNBC, we can understand a little bit behind the smoke and mirrors who Osama Really is:

> NEW YORK, Aug. 24, 1998 — At the CIA, it happens often enough to have a code name: Blowback. Simply defined, this is the term that describes an agent, an operative or an operation that has turned on its creators. Osama bin Laden, our new public enemy Number 1, is the personification of blowback. And the fact that he is viewed as a hero by millions in the Islamic world proves again the old adage: Reap what you sow.

> Before you click on my face and call me naive, let me concede some points. Yes, the West needed Josef Stalin to defeat Hitler. Yes, there were times during the Cold War when supporting one villain (Cambodia's Lon Nol, for instance) would have been better than the alternative (Pol Pot). So yes, there are times when any nation must hold its nose and shake hands with the devil for the long-term good of the planet.

> But just as surely, there are times when the United States, faced with such moral dilemmas, should have resisted the temptation to act. Arming a multi-national coalition of Islamic extremists in Afghanistan during the 1980s - well after the destruction of the Marine barracks in Beirut or the hijacking of

TWA Flight 847 -was one of those times.

BIN LADEN'S BEGINNINGS

As anyone who has bothered to read this far certainly knows by now, bin Laden is the heir to Saudi construction fortune who, at least since the early 1990s, has used that money to finance countless attacks on U.S. interests and those of its Arab allies around the world.

As his unclassified CIA biography states, bin Laden left Saudi Arabia to fight the Soviet army in Afghanistan after Moscow's invasion in 1979. By 1984, he was running a front organization known as Maktab al-Khidamar - the MAK - which funneled money, arms and fighters from the outside world into the Afghan war.

What the CIA bio conveniently fails to specify (in its unclassified form, at least) is that the MAK was nurtured by Pakistan's state security services, the Inter-Services Intelligence agency, or ISI, the CIA's primary conduit for conducting the covert war against Moscow's occupation. By no means was Osama bin Laden the leader of Afghanistan's mujahedeen. His money gave him undue prominence in the Afghan struggle, but the vast majority of those who fought and died for Afghanistan's freedom - like the Taliban regime that now holds sway over most of that tortured nation - were Afghan nationals.

Yet the CIA, concerned about the factionalism of Afghanistan made famous by Rudyard Kipling, found that Arab zealots who flocked to aid the Afghans were easier to "read" than the rivalry ridden natives. While the Arab volunteers might well prove troublesome later, the agency reasoned, they at least were one dimensionally anti-Soviet for now. So bin Laden, along with a small group of Islamic militants from Egypt, Pakistan, Lebanon, Syria and Palestinian refugee camps all over the Middle East, became the "reliable" partners of the CIA in its war against Moscow.

WHAT'S 'INTELLIGENT' ABOUT THIS?

Though he has come to represent all that went wrong with the CIA's reckless strategy there, by the end of the Afghan war in 1989, bin Laden was still viewed by the agency as something of a dilettante - a rich Saudi boy gone to war and welcomed home by the Saudi monarchy he so hated as something of a hero.

In fact, while he returned to his family's construction business, bin Laden had split from the relatively conventional MAK in 1988 and established a new group, Al-Qaida, that included many of the more extreme MAK members he had met in Afghanistan.

Most of these Afghan vets, or Afghanis, as the Arabs who fought there became known, turned up later behind violent Islamic movements around the world. Among them: the GIA in Algeria, thought responsible for the massacres of tens of thousands of civilians; Egypt's Gamat Ismalia, which has massacred western tourists repeatedly in recent years; Saudi Arabia Shiite militants, responsible for the Khobar Towers and Riyadh bombings of 1996.

Indeed, to this day, those involved in the decision to give the Afghan rebels access to a fortune in covert funding and top-level combat weaponry continue to defend that move in the context of the Cold War. Sen. Orrin Hatch, a senior Republican on the Senate Intelligence Committee making those decisions, told my colleague Robert Windrem that he would make the same call again today even knowing what bin Laden would do subsequently. "It was worth it," he said.

"Those were very important, pivotal matters that played an important role in the downfall of the Soviet Union," he said.

HINDSIGHT OR TUNNEL VISION

It should be pointed out that the evidence of bin Laden's connection to these activities is mostly classified, though it's hard to imagine the CIA rushing to take credit for a Frankenstein's monster like this.

It is also worth acknowledging that it is easier now to oppose the CIA's Afghan adventures than it was when Hatch and company made them in the mid-1980s. After all, in 1998 we now know that far larger elements than Afghanistan were corroding the communist party's grip on power in Moscow.

Even Hatch can't be blamed completely. The CIA, ever mindful of the need to justify its "mission," had conclusive evidence by the mid-1980s of the deepening crisis of infrastructure within the Soviet Union. The CIA, as its deputy director Robert Gates acknowledged under congressional questioning in 1992, had decided to keep that evidence from President Reagan and his top advisors and instead continued to grossly exaggerate Soviet military and technological capabilities in its annual "Soviet Military Power" report right up to 1990.

132

Given that context, a decision was made to provide America's potential enemies with the arms, money - and most importantly - the knowledge of how to run a war of attrition violent and well-organized enough to humble a superpower.[1]

Osama Bin Laden and the CIA

Osama bin Laden, along with a small group of Islamic militants from Egypt, Pakistan, Lebanon, Syria, Palestine and other refugee camps all over the Middle East, were reliable partners and informants of the CIA:

Mon, 17 Oct 1994 02:04:32 -0400 (EDT)
The Independent December 6, 1993, Monday
HEADLINE: Anti-Soviet warrior puts his army on the road to peace

by ROBERT FISK

OSAMA Bin Laden sat in his gold- fringed robe, guarded by the Royal Arab mujahedin who fought alongside him in Afghanistan.

Bearded, taciturn figures - unarmed, but never more than a few yards from the man who recruited them, trained them and then dispatched them to destroy the Soviet army - they watched unsmiling as the Sudanese villagers of Almatig lined up to thank the Saudi businessman who is about to complete the highway linking their homes to Khartoum for the first time in history.

With his high cheekbones, narrow eyes and long brown robe, Mr. Bin Laden looks every inch the mountain warrior of mujahedin legend. Chadored children danced in front of him, preachers acknowledged his wisdom. "We have been waiting for this road through all the revolutions in Sudan," a sheikh said.

"We waited until we had given up on everybody - and then Osama Bin Laden came along."

Outside Sudan, Mr. Bin Laden is not regarded with quite such high esteem. The Egyptian press claims he brought hundreds of former Arab fighters back to Sudan from Afghanistan, while the Western embassy circuit in Khartoum has suggested that some of the "Afghans" whom this Saudi entrepreneur flew to Sudan are now busy training for further jihad wars in Algeria, Tunisia and Egypt. Mr. Bin Laden is well aware of this. "The rubbish of the media and the embassies," he calls it. "I am a construction engineer and an agriculturalist. If I had training camps here in Sudan, I couldn't possibly do this job."

And "this job" is certainly an ambitious one: a brand-new highway stretching all the way from Khartoum to Port Sudan, a distance of 1,200km (745 miles) on the old road, now shortened to 800km by the new Bin Laden route that will turn the coastal run from the capital into a mere day's journey. Into a country that is despised by Saudi Arabia for its support of Saddam Hussein in the Gulf war almost as much as it is condemned by the United States, Mr. Bin Laden has brought the very construction equipment that he used only five years ago to build the guerrilla trails of Afghanistan.

He is a shy man. Maintaining a home in Khartoum and only a small apartment in his home city of Jeddah, he is married - with four wives - but wary of the press. His interview with the Independent was the first he has ever given to a Western journalist, and he initially refused to talk about Afghanistan, sitting silently on a chair at the back of a makeshift tent, brushing his teeth in the Arab fashion with a stick of miswak wood. But talk he eventually did about a war which he helped to win for the Afghan mujahedin: "What I lived in two years there, I could not have lived in a hundred years elsewhere," he said.

When the history of the Afghan resistance movement is written, Mr. Bin Laden's own contribution to the mujahedin - and the indirect result of his training and assistance - may turn out to be a turning- point in the recent history of militant fundamentalism; even if, today, he tries to minimise his role. "When the invasion of Afghanistan started, I was enraged and went there at once - I arrived within days, before the end of 1979," he said. "Yes, I fought there, but my fellow Muslims did much more than I. Many of them died and I am still alive."

Within months, however, Mr. Bin Laden was sending Arab fighters - Egyptians, Algerians, Lebanese, Kuwaitis, Turks and Tunisians - into Afghanistan; "not hundreds but thousands," he said. He supported them with weapons and his own con- struction equipment. Along with his Iraqi engineer, Mohamed Saad - who is now building the Port Sudan road - Mr. Bin Laden blasted massive tunnels into the Zazi mountains of Bakhtiar province for guerrilla hospitals and arms dumps, then cut a mujahedin trail across the country to within 15 miles of Kabul.

"No, I was never afraid of death. As Muslims, we believe that when we die, we go to heaven. Before a battle, God sends us seqina, tranquillity.

"Once I was only 30 metres from the Russians and they were trying to capture me. I was under bombardment but I was so peaceful in my heart that I fell asleep. This experience has been written about in our earliest books. I saw a 120mm mortar shell land in front of me, but it did not blow up. Four more bombs were dropped from a Russian plane on our headquarters but they did not explode. We beat the Soviet Union. The Russians fled."

But what of the Arab mujahedin whom he took to Afghanistan - members of a guerrilla army who were also encouraged and armed by the United States - and who were forgotten when that war was over? "Personally neither I nor my brothers saw evidence of American help. When my mujahedin were victorious and the Russians were driven out, differences started between the guerrilla movements so I returned to road construction in Taif and Abha. I brought back the equipment I had used to build tunnels and roads for the mujahedin in Afghanistan. Yes, I helped some of my comrades to come here to Sudan after the war."

How many? Osama Bin Laden shakes his head. "I don't want to say. But they are here now with me, they are working right here, building this road to Port Sudan." I told him that Bosnian Muslim fighters in the Bosnian town of Travnik had mentioned his name to me. "I feel the same about Bosnia," he said. "But the situation there does not provide the same opportunities as Afghanistan. A small number of mujahedin have gone to fight in Bosnia-Herzegovina but the Croats won't allow the mujahedin in through Croatia as the Pakistanis did with Afghanistan."

Thus did Mr. Bin Laden reflect upon jihad while his former fellow combatants looked on. Was it not a little bit anti-climactic for them, I asked, to fight the Russians and end up road-building in Sudan? "They like this work and so do I. This is a great plan which we are achieving for the people here, it helps the Muslims and improves their lives."

His Bin Laden company - not to be confused with the larger construction business run by his cousins - is paid in Sudanese currency which is then used to purchase sesame and other products for export; profits are clearly not Mr. Bin Laden's top priority.

How did he feel about Algeria, I asked? But a man in a green suit calling himself Mohamed Moussa - he claimed to be Nigerian although he was a Sudanese security officer - tapped me on the arm. "You have asked more than enough questions," he said. At which Mr. Bin Laden went off to inspect his new road.[2]

Osama bin Laden was the creation of American and British intelligence. And wittingly or not, is doing their bidding.

In a November 1, 2001 Washington Times report by Elizabeth Bryant, it was reported alleged, ""that terrorist suspect Osama bin Laden met with a CIA officer in the United Arab Emirates in July."[3] The CIA dismissed this report as, "total absurdity."[4] Just like the President doesn't want anyone to listen to any outrageous conspiracy theories. Hmmm, I wonder why?

The news report continued stating this report by Radio France International, and a French Newspaper, Le Figaro alleging that, "A CIA agent met with bin Laden at a Dubai clinic, where the suspected terrorist was reportedly treated for kidney problems." The clinic, said to be the American Hospital in Dubai, also denied bin Laden had been a patient.[5]

Nonetheless, Radio France International, for one, said it stood by its report. This report continues:

> In a follow-up, the French radio station identified the alleged CIA agent as Larry Mitchell, "a connoisseur of the Arab world and specialist of the (Arab) peninsula."
>
> Mitchell's business card identified him as a "consular agent," the radio said. In fact, RFI alleged, he was a CIA agent and a prominent fixture in Dubai's expatriate community. According to both the radio and Le Figaro, Mitchell was recalled to the CIA's headquarters in McLean, Va., on July 15.
>
> The radio also gave the precise date of Mitchell's supposed encounter with bin Laden -- July 12, two days before the Saudi dissident reportedly checked out of the hospital.
>
> Neither the Figaro, nor Radio France offered independent confirmation of the report. The radio station also cited no source for its latest allegations. Earlier, the Figaro said its story was leaked by a partner of the hospital's management.[6]

The British newspaper, the Guardian also reported a similar story on November 1, 2001:

136

The CIA chief was seen in the lift, on his way to see Bin Laden, and later, it is alleged, boasted to friends about his contact. He was recalled to Washington soon afterwards.

Intelligence sources say that another CIA agent was also present; and that Bin Laden was also visited by Prince Turki al Faisal, then head of Saudi intelligence, who had long had links with the Taliban, and Bin Laden. Soon afterwards Turki resigned, and more recently he has publicly attacked him in an open letter:

"You are a rotten seed, like the son of Noah."

The American hospital in Dubai emphatically denied that Bin Laden was a patient there.

Washington last night also denied the story.

Private planes owned by rich princes in the Gulf fly frequently between Quetta and the Emirates, often on luxurious "hunting trips" in territories sympathetic to Bin Laden. Other sources confirm that these hunting trips have provided opportunities for Saudi contacts with the Taliban and terrorists, since they first began in 1994.

Bin Laden has often been reported to be in poor health. Some accounts claim that he is suffering from Hepatitis C, and can expect to live for only two more years.

According to Le Figaro, last year he ordered a mobile dialysis machine to be delivered to his base at Kandahar in Afghanistan.[7]

SOURCES

(1) http://msnbc.com/news/BODY
(2) http://inic.utexas.edu/menic/utaustin/course/oilcourse/mail/saudi/0007.html
(3) http://www.intellnet.org/news/2001/11/02/7975-1.htm
(4) http://www.pegmusic.com/news-binl-prcon.html
(5) http://mediastudy.com/articles/AVnov8-01.html
(6) Ibid
(7) http://www.unansweredquestions.org/background_44.shtml

Chapter 10
Osama and the Al-Qaeda

As I covered in Chapter 7, Al-Qaeda was created, armed, funded, and supported by the U.S. Government. Also covered in this chapter I pointed out how the U.S. Government trained, armed, funded and supported Osama bin Laden and his followers in Afghanistan after the Soviet invasion in 1979, and throughout the cold war.

Al-Qaeda emerged from an organization named Maktab al-Khidamar (MAK) in which bin Laden was running for the United States.[1]

With a huge investment of $3,000,000,000 (yes three billion) U.S. tax dollars, the CIA effectively created and nurtured bin Laden's Al-Qaeda terrorist network.[2] Using American tax-payers money! This money was funneled into Al-Qaeda hands by then CIA headman and soon be President of the U.S., dun dun dun.... Father George H. W. Bush.

Afghanistan is one of the world's poorest countries, where such an enormous sum of money would have had an extraordinary value. Hell it has an extraordinary value in a rich country.

> "In the 1980s, bin Laden left his comfortable Saudi home for Afghanistan to participate in the Afghan jihad, or holy war, against the invading forces of the Soviet Union - a cause that, ironically, the United States funded, pouring $3 billion into the Afghan resistance via the CIA."[3]

Between 1986 and 1987, the CIA Director William Casey (Iran-Contra) provided 900 Stinger missiles to Al-Qaeda.[4] And with this help from the CIA and the American tax dollars, the Soviets withdrew from Afghanistan. [5]. Then (also with help from the CIA and American tax dollars) the plantation and harvesting of opium began. This turned
Afghanistan into the largest producer of heroin on the planet.[6] And there is no doubt that many of that heroin turned up on the streets of America. All thanks to US tax dollars and the tax dollars which have funded CIA.

Osama bin Laden, labeled, "One of the most significant financial sponsors of Islamic extremist activities in the world,"[7] has been linked to terrorist actions and activity for years. And if you recall, bin Laden was even named a suspect for the Oklahoma City Bombing.[8]

Now the Bush administration is hunting him as the prime suspect in the 11 September terrorist attacks on the United States? Give me a break. But as I have exposed so many outrageous lies about 11 September, I will continue to expose this one too.

The Saudi exile is also suspected of playing large roles in the 1998 bombings of two U.S. Embassies in Africa and the attack on the USS Cole in the Yemeni port of Aden in October 2000.[9] But the nature of these attacks have no relativity against the mass destruction of the 11 September attacks.

Bin Laden has been a man on the run since a U.S.-led attack in late 2001 drove out Afghanistan's ruling Taliban party. May I remind you that the Taliban had offered to turn over bin Laden to U.S. custody with proof of his hands in the ordeal, but American demand him anyway, and as we all know . . . many thousands of innocent Afghanistan residents have been killed.

Bin Laden had been living in Afghanistan, and the United States asserts that he ran his terrorist operations out of that country. But there has been no confirmation of this, as he has been reported throughout many different regions including Kashmir, Pakistan, as well as Afghanistan.[10] And I believe I mentioned this before, but a man living and operating out of a cave who can plan, orchestrate and manipulate such a horrendous plan, is one brilliant mind!

As his whereabouts? One report claimed on September 10, 2001, that he had left Afghanistan for Kashmir.[11] And yet besides this information, the U.S. bombed the hell out of Afghanistan with no remorse what so ever for the men, women, and children who just months before were handed millions of dollars worth of food and aid from Secretary Collin Powell.[12] As I pointed out, Powell gave $43 million in aid to the Taliban regime, purportedly to assist hungry farmers who are starving since the destruction of their opium crop in January 2001 on orders of the Taliban regime.[13]

Bin Laden's al Qaeda organization is a loose umbrella association of radical groups and people believed to operate in dozens of countries around the world. So why did America attack Afghanistan. (Chapter 8! Chapter 8!!)

According to "official" stories, Al-Qaeda members were suspected of playing a role in several attacks against U.S. interests, including the 1993 World Trade Center bombing, failed plots to kill President Clinton and the pope, and even attacks on U.S. troops in Saudi Arabia and Somalia.[14] I have no doubt that any organization with $3,000,000,000 could do such things, but the question to really ask is, did they? Or were the Taliban and al-Qaeda just the scapegoats?

Bin Laden has also used his personal millions to bankroll terrorist training camps in Sudan, the Philippines and Afghanistan, sending holy warriors to foment revolution and fight with fundamentalist Muslim forces across North Africa, in Chechnya, Tajikistan and Bosnia.[15] You have all seen the Al-Qaeda training videos through main stream media I'm sure. And one thing I would like to know, is why are these tapes so important, when I can view a similar group of young men on a similar video tape provided to me by the local U.S. Armed Forces recruitment office? And the really funny thing about that is, that both tapes are produced with American Tax Dollars!

I always love how one country is always right and always the country without sin, i.e., America, and yet another country produces an army to protect itself, it is all the sudden branded a threat to the country with the largest arsenal on Earth. Wonderful country this United States of America! Bully to the world.

Born in 1957, bin Laden is the son of Saudi Arabia's wealthiest construction magnate.[16] Through the Carlyle Group of Father George Bush, the Bush family still have connections to the bin Laden Family.[17]

Saudi sources remember him as an ordinary young man whose intense religious nature began to emerge as he grew fascinated with the ancient, holy mosques of Mecca and Medina that his family's company was involved in rebuilding.

Bin Laden's family construction company is also connected to the excavation of the World Trade Center/Ground Zero.[18]

In the 1980s, bin Laden left his comfortable Saudi home for Afghanistan to participate in the Afghan jihad, 18 or holy war, against the invading forces of the Soviet Union. A cause that, ironically, the United States funded and pumped $3 billion into the Afghan resistance via the CIA.

Bin Laden quickly became the leader of the Arabs living in Afghanistan and a regional hero. Although a CIA informant, he was reportedly careful throughout to, "distance himself from U.S. influence."[19] The war radicalized bin Laden's politics, as does anyone who goes through the hell of war. [20]

140

Bin Laden then supposedly declared the Saudi ruling family, "insufficiently Islamic," and increasingly advocated the use of violence to force a movement toward extremism.[21] Sounds like any typical (fill in the blank here) extremist. So why do we have a problem with this Islamic one? Why not the extremist Christians who shout and yell that their way is the, "only way," and threaten your life with eternal damnation if you do not obey? And what about the Israeli extremist, who because of some crazy notion that they are God's chosen people, tear down the homes of Palestinians to build their own homes?

Saudi Arabia stripped bin Laden of his citizenship in 1994 for his alleged activities against the royal family, after he had left the country for Sudan.[22] Which I don't know what the difference between Afghanistan and Saudi Arabia is really. Simply one is on America's good side, and the other is on the bad side. The Islamic treatment of women is still the same in either country[23] yet Mrs. Bush and Mrs. Blair were against the Taliban's treatment of women.[24] Why not the Saudis?

Osama was later expelled from Sudan under U.S., Egyptian and Saudi pressure. Hell they probably just wanted their money back. In 1996, Osama took refuge in Afghanistan.[25]

A former mujahideen commanders close to the Taliban said that, in Afghanistan, bin Laden bankrolled the hard-line Islamic regime's capture of Kabul under the leadership of the reclusive Mullah Mohammed Omar. Bin Laden became one of Omar's most trusted advisers.[26] I smell a real hard core terrorist here.

Bin Laden is said to personally control about $300 million of his family's $5 billion fortune.[27] Not to mention what is left of the funds donated to Al-Qaeda from the cold war. His role as a financier of terrorism is pivotal, experts say, because he has revolutionized the financing of extremist movements by forming and funding his own private terror network. Sure, just like Baby Boy Bush, or any military leader can fund their own wars and terror networks.

Bin Laden has not only devoted his own fortune, but his business acumen to the cause, and through a nebulous network he calls the Foundation for Islamic Salvation, which sources say runs money through companies in the United States, Europe and the Middle East. The powerful recluse has funneled money into the promotion of terrorist causes around the world. Just like the promotion of a war against "terrorism" has funded an extremist movement also around the world.

141

Imagine that.

Bin Laden and the Smoking Gun Video

According to Osama bin Laden, as revealed in a November 9, 2001 "home video" released and officially translated by the U.S. Government (oh god here we go again) on December 13, 2001, only Osama bin Laden and a handful of others knew of the impending 11 September attacks.

But they knew only, "five days," before!!²⁸ Some mastermind. This would explain everything in the next chapter, you will see, surely. (You will see.)

> UBL: The brothers, who conducted the operation, all they knew was that they have a martyrdom operation and we asked each of them to go to America but they didn't know anything about the operation, not even one letter.
>
> But they were trained and we did not reveal the operation to them until they are there and just before they boarded the planes.²⁹

The video mentions also that most of the "hijackers" were unaware of their fate until the morning of their attacks. Had the "hijackers" not known their fate until that morning, why, as we saw in Chapter 4, did they go out of their way to be noticed and remembered?

That would explain the Quran in the strip bars... THEY WERE PLANNING ON COMING BACK TO GET THEM! Come on! Seriously! And what about the hand written letters found not only in Mohammed Atta's "checked luggage" but at the crash site of Flight 93?

We have seen how Atta was in a hurry to get to the Airport in Portland, so how could he write them all? Supposedly 19 letters if we believe the official story. And how did he deliver them to Washington in time to give to the "hijackers" that morning, then return to Portland, if they did not know anything until that morning?

Someone needs to consult a better script writer.

And the fact that Osama bin Laden knew of the timing on the previous Thursday, only five days prior to the attack? This confirms that Al-Qaeda cells are extremely isolated and information is very strictly withheld until the latest possible moment. Surely they, including Osama bin Laden, were not behind the attacks.

Also, the "hijackers" have been in Florida HOW LONG at the flight school to learn how to fly? SURELY they were learning for

MORE than five days. This video is surely a fraud!

After the release of the tape, many newspapers in the Arab world played down the significance of the video. Sure! I am doing that too!

Some Arabic news agencies questioned the authenticity of this video, which brought a strong response from U.S. President Bush who said;

> "This is bin Laden unedited. It's preposterous for anybody to think that this tape is doctored. That's just a feeble excuse to provide weak support for an incredibly evil man."[30]

OK Mr. President, lets look at what we know bin Laden looks like and compare that with the image seen on this video. (Please see Picture Section)

Clearly the person in the video is NOT the man the U.S. Government claims it is.

Look at bin Laden in this video compared to the last video filmed allegedly only one month before.

In the earlier video, bin Laden looks thinner, and healthy, but compared to the "Smoking Gun" video footage ALSO allegedly shot in December, shows Bin Laden A LOT fatter. Then a video released one month later shows bin Laden thinner and in not so good health. So why to sudden gain of weight to lose it so quickly? Must be the famous Hollywood 48-hour diet!

But we all know the intelligence level of President Baby Boy Bush anyway. And also as shown in previous chapters, Bush has more to do with the attacks than bin Laden.

Yet the "Smoking Gun" video represents, according to the mainstream media and U.S. Government, the "clearest evidence released" which "indicates that Osama bin Laden knew about the attacks."[31] But yet no where in the video does he claim responsibility for it. Only that he, if it *IS* bin Laden, only KNEW of the attacks. And yet thousands of innocent Afghanis were killed. Good move!

And here is another point that I would like to bring up. The main stream media constantly mentioned the "obvious glee and laughter" in the video bears witness to the "evil" that lurks within the men of Al-Qaeda. BULLSHIT. America and Britain are at war with Iraq. I don't know how many people I hear laughing and joking about the Iraqi soldiers that have been killed in this war. Please tell me what is the difference? People are dead! Period. It is always ok when

Americans laugh at others, but when someone laughs at them, god help us!

I'm no Rodney King, but, "Can't we all get along."

Shaykh: A plane crashing into a tall building was out of anyone's imagination. This was a great job. He was one of the pious men in the organization. He became a martyr. Allah bless his soul.

Shaykh (Referring to dreams and visions): The plane that he saw crashing into the building was seen before by more than one person. One of the good religious people has left everything and come here. He told me, "I saw a vision, I was in a huge plane, long and wide. I was carrying it on my shoulders and I walked from the road to the desert for half a kilometer. I was dragging the plane." I listened to him and I prayed to Allah to help him.

Another person told me that last year he saw, but I didn't understand and I told him I don't understand. He said, "I saw people who left for jihad...and they found themselves in New York...in Washington and New York." I said, "What is this?" He told me the plane hit the building. That was last year. We haven't thought much about it. But, when the incidents happened he came to me and said, "Did you see...this is strange." I have another man...my god...he said and swore by Allah that his wife had seen the incident a week earlier.[32]

This is absolutely great! America, the land of the godly Christian people, in many cases, are against psychics and fortune telling, yet they believe the "official" Government translation which talks about visions of the attack. One vision was even a year before. Come on, visions are justification for mass destruction? My god.

UBL: (...inaudible...) then he said: Those who were trained to fly didn't know the others. One group of people did not know the other group.[33]

Are we really to believe this video and the "official" story both?

As I mentioned earlier, Flight 93 supposedly had letters matching the handwriting of the letter found in Atta's "checked luggage" and yet Osama admits that they, "Didn't know the others. One group of people didn't know the other group." Come on!!! And this video is from the people controlling the life of millions in America and bombing millions as I write this! Wake up America! Wake up!!

> UBL: We were at a camp of one of the brother's guards in Qandahar. This brother belonged to the majority of the group. He came close and told me that he saw, in a dream, a tall building in America, and in the same dream he saw Mukhtar teaching them how to play karate. At that point, I was worried that maybe the secret would be revealed if everyone starts seeing it in their dream. So I closed the subject. I told him if he sees another dream, not to tell anybody, because people will be upset with him. (Another person's voice can be heard recounting his dream about two planes hitting a big building).

> UBL: They were overjoyed when the first plane hit the building, so I said to them: be patient.[34]

Here we have again more psychic predictions! Do I have to say anything again? Dear god.

The figure in this tape is shown writing with his right hand. According to the FBI MOST WANTED SITE, Osama bin Laden is LEFT HANDED and walks with a cane.[35]

> Editors note: To ensure the authenticity of the videotape, the U.S. utilized the latest voice and face identification techniques, and although the quality of the videotape is poor, teams of Arabic translators spent days listening to the tape to make sure the audible text of the conversations were accurately translated. [36]

Sure they did!

The translation is not only inaccurate, but also deliberately manipulative

Of course the U.S. mainstream media will not report this. By their own admission, they are censoring themselves at the request of the Bush White House (which explains why both Fox News and CNN were caught erasing stories about the Israeli spy scandal from their web sites).[37]

The following story broke all over Europe. Meanwhile the U.S. press has not picked up on this story at all, reporting instead that a new translation has revealed that Osama bin Laden even mentions the names of some of those involved. But the story was all over the German press.

From Germany's Channel One "Das Erste," the ones who broke this story which is equivalent to NBC or the BBC. Even "Der Spiegel" the equivalent of TIME or the Economist ran the same story:

Mistranslated OBL video - Germany's Channel One investigates

On 20 December 2001, German TV channel "Das Erste" broadcast its analysis of the White House's translation of the OBL video that George Bush has called a "confession of guilt."

On the show "Monitor," two independent translators and an expert on oriental studies found the White House's translation not only to be inaccurate, but "manipulative."

Arabist Dr. Abdel El M. Husseini, one of the translators, states, "I have carefully examined the Pentagon's translation. This translation is very problematic. At the most important places where it is held to prove the guilt of Bin Laden, it is not identical with the Arabic."

Whereas the White House would have us believe that OBL admits that "We calculated in advance the number of casualties from the enemy.", translator Dr. Murad Alami finds that: "'In advance' is not said. The translation is wrong. At least when we look at the original Arabic, and there are no misunderstandings to allow us to read it into the original."

At another point, the White House translation reads: "We had notification since the previous Thursday that the event would take place that day." Dr. Murad Alami: "'Previous' is never said. The subsequent statement that this event would take place on that day cannot be heard in the original Arabic version."

The White House's version also included the sentence "we asked each of them to go to America," but Alami says the original formulation is in the passive along the lines of "they were required to go." He also says that the sentence afterwards - "they didn't know anything about the operation" - cannot be understood.[38]

Prof. Gernot Rotter, professor of Islamic and Arabic Studies at the Asia-Africa Institute at the University of Hamburg sums it up:

"The American translators who listened to the tapes and transcribed them apparently wrote a lot of things in that they wanted to hear but that cannot be heard on the tape no matter how many times you listen to it."[39]

Instead, we read in the Washington Post of Friday, 21 December, 2001 (the day after the German TV show was broadcast) that a new translation done in the U.S. "Also indicates bin Laden had even more knowledge of the Sept. 11 attacks on the World Trade Center and the Pentagon than was apparent in the original Defense Department translation . . . Although the expanded version does not change the substance of what was released, it provides added details and color to what has been disclosed."[40]

I'll say. Aren't there any reporters in the U.S. who speak German (or Arabic, for that matter)? An article in USA Today of 20 December, 2001 sheds some light on why the original translation might not be accurate stating that, "The first translation was rushed in 12 hours, in a room in the Pentagon."[41] So why didn't the new U.S. translation find the same discrepancies as the German translators did? Read the article in USA Today against the grain:

> Michael, who is originally Lebanese, translated the tape with Kassem Wahba, an Egyptian. "Both men had difficulties with the Saudi dialect bin Laden and his guest use in the tape," Michael said.[42]

Why can't a Saudi translator not be found in a multi-cultural country like the U.S., especially with the close business relations between the U.S. and Saudi Arabia? Bush Sr. probably knows any number of them himself.

Of course, if we ever hear about the German analysis in the U.S. press, the reactions will be that some will never believe that bin Laden is behind the attacks no matter what you tell them. But actually, Americans are just as stubborn in refusing to face facts. One moderator on Fox News complained to his interviewee that the European media were focusing "too much" on civilian casualties in Afghanistan.[43] (I wondered which European languages this moderator could speak; a few weeks later, he happened to say on his show that he had had, "three years of German." This, he claimed, would allow him to "do the show in German.") His interviewee responded that, yes, the Taliban was very savvy manipulators of the media.[44] So there we have it: Europeans get their information straight from the Taliban Ministry of Propaganda.

No one knows you better than your Mother

> LONDON (Reuters) - Osama bin Laden's mother was quoted in a British newspaper on Sunday as saying she believes a videotape of her son, which the United States says proves he had prior knowledge of the September 11 attacks, was a fake.

"I believe the evidence against him is not solid. I think the video they produced is doctored," Alia Ghanem was quoted as saying by the Mail on Sunday tabloid in an interview conducted by a Saudi journalist.

"The voice is unclear and uneven. There are too many gaps and the statements are very unlike him," she said.

The Mail on Sunday said Ghanem was interviewed last week for the paper by Saudi journalist and bin Laden family friend Khalid Batarfi, the managing editor of Saudi newspaper Al Medina.

She was referring to a videotape released by the United States which officials say shows the Saudi-born militant celebrating the massive destruction and death caused when hijacked planes crashed into New York's World Trade Center.

Ghanem said she was convinced her son was not responsible for the attacks but feared he would be killed before his name was cleared.

"Osama is too good a Muslim and too good a person to say or do what the script of the video suggests he said and did," she said.

"But I don't agree with everything he says and he knows that. I pray to Allah that he will live until the truth is revealed."

The United States says the videotape was found in Afghanistan. It was shown around the world on December 13.

Bin Laden's current whereabouts is a mystery with no reported sightings of him for more than a week.

Pakistani President Pervez Musharraf said on Saturday there is a strong possibility that bin Laden was killed in the U.S. bombing of the Tora Bora mountains in eastern Afghanistan.

The United States has said it does not know his whereabouts but has vowed to pursue him until he is captured or killed. There is a $25 million bounty on his head.

Bin Laden is said to be 17th of 57 children born to his father, who was killed in an air crash when his son was a teenager.

His mother said in the newspaper interview he had not called her in six years, to prevent his location being traced through the telephone.

Saudi Arabia revoked bin Laden's citizenship in 1994 and his family has disowned him.[45]

Hatred for America

Somewhere in between the paychecks from America for $3 billion, and the 1991 Gulf War (Part I), Osama bin Laden, reportedly, developed a hatred for America. It is believed, that President Father George Bush, although a close friend and business partner with the bin Laden family,[46] starting the Gulf War was the event that turned Osama to the "dark side."

(Obi-wan never told you what happened to the your father.)

We also have the supposed hatred for America, as covered in the last chapter, because of American military presence in the Islamic "Holy Land" of Saudi Arabia, and also its support for Israel.

I don't agree with this "official story" of a mad man turning against his largest "employer" and being disinherited by his family. It just seams to me like another plot line in the B movie. Doesn't it?

He was and still is a valuable asset on the CIA payroll. I mean come on look at it. How many other helpless people and nations could American forces bomb the hell out of because the U.S. Government believes bin Laden is hiding out in their country?

This is why the best military on the planet couldn't find him when it invaded Afghanistan despite killing more than 5,000 innocent civilians while "searching" for him. This is why Clinton refused to put him on trial when "Slick Willie" had the chance and in turn went after Bill Gates. And this is precisely why Baby Boy Bush refused the offer of the Taliban to hand over bin Laden for evidence of his involvement,[47] when only days before Bush demanded the Taliban to hand him over.[48] What the #@$%! And why did the Baby Boy Bush Administration tell Congress to back off the investigations into the bin Ladens,[49] and also the 11 September attacks?[50]

Because Bush was involved! Plain and simple.

It is odd to mention that two years after people in Sudan reportedly offered bin Laden to President "Slick Willie" Clinton,[51] that he bombed a pharmaceutical plant in Sudan.[52] A simple, "Thanks, but no thanks," would have been acceptable. Clinton, almost sounding like Baby Boy Bush before the Gulf War (Part Due), claimed that the factory was producing chemical weapons and had ties to Osama. But it was later admitted as a mistake, and was not a factory for weapons of mass destruction, but simply an Aspirin factory.[53] Man do I have a headache.

Before the attacks, FBI's Deputy Director John O'Neill (and also head of anti-terrorism) resigned in July 2001 because of the USS Cole investigation being blocked.[54] This attack, "officially" was the "work" of Osama bin Laden.

Is it getting thick in here, or is it just me?

As I mentioned in the Taliban chapter, the Revolutionary Association of Women of Afghanistan, who challenged the regime's treatment of women, they released this statement three days after the "terrorist" attacks:

> The people of Afghanistan have nothing to do with Osama and his accomplices.
>
> But unfortunately we must say that it was the government of the United States who supported Pakistani dictator Gen. Zia-ul Haq in creating thousands of religious schools from which the germs of Taliban emerged. In the similar way, as is clear to all, Osama Bin Laden has been the blue-eyed boy of CIA. But what is more painful is that American politicians have not drawn a lesson from their pro-fundamentalist policies in our country and are still supporting this or that fundamentalist band or leader. In our opinion any kind of support to the fundamentalist Taliban and Jehadies is actually trampling democratic, women's rights and human rights values.
>
> Now that the Taliban and Osama are the prime suspects by the U.S. officials after the criminal attacks, will the U.S. subject Afghanistan to a military attack similar to the one in 1998 and kill thousands of innocent Afghans for the crimes committed by the Taliban and Osama? Does the US think that through such attacks, with thousands of deprived, poor and innocent people of Afghanistan as its victims, will be able to wipe out the root-cause of terrorism, or will it spread terrorism even to a larger scale?[55]

So who really is Osama bin Laden?

This puzzle piece is nothing what the "official story" would have us believe. One question I would like to know is: Is bin Laden really hiding out in a special room somewhere in Washington, D.C.?

I mean, I really wouldn't put it past this administration. Hell, Father and Baby Boy Bush probably have intimate dinners with him when they have the chance. What a wonderful paparazzi picture that would be!

SOURCES

(1) http://abcnews.go.com/sections/world/DailyNews/binladen_profile.html
(2) The Los Angeles Times, May 22, 2001.
(3) Ibid
(4) http://www.fas.org/irp/offdocs/walsh/chap_14.htm
(5) http://www.afsc.org/nomore/afghanistan.htm
(6) http://www.fao.org/giews/english/alertes/2001/SRAFG601.htm
(7) http://abcnews.go.com/sections/world/DailyNews/terror_binladin_
990110.html
(8) http://www.worldnetdaily.com/news/article.asp?ARTICLE_ID=22122
(9) http://www.pbs.org/newshour/bb/africa/july-dec98/bombings_9-30a.html
(10) http://www.ag.gov.au/www/attorneygeneralHome.nsf/Web+Pages/
F253EF5294C71004CA256C71001BDC30?OpenDocument
(11) http://www.metroactive.com/papers/metro/09.12.02/sept11a-0237.html
(12) http://www.cnn.com/2001/US/05/17/us.afghanistan.aid/
(13) http://www.aeronautics.ru/archive/linktrack/quaeda_attacks.htm
(14) http://abcnews.go.com/sections/world/DailyNews/binladen_profile.html
(15) http://www.howstuffworks.com/bin-laden.htm
(16) http://www.uni-muenster.de/PeaCon/global-texte/g-notes/BinLaden-
Carlyle.htm
(17) http://www.rense.com/general19/business.htm
(18) http://abcnews.go.com/sections/world/DailyNews/binladen_profile.html
(19) http://abcnews.go.com/sections/world/DailyNews/terror_binladin_
990110.html
(20) Ibid
(21) http://abcnews.go.com/sections/world/DailyNews/binladen_profile.html
(22) http://www.amnesty.ca/SaudiArabia/5.htm
(23) http://www.number-10.gov.uk/output/page2369.asp
(24) http://www.nsda.org/About/news/gumarabic.html
(25) http://www.satp.org/satporgtp/usa/Taliban.htm
(26) http://www.ict.org.il/articles/articledet.cfm?articleid=42
(27) http://www.cnn.com/2001/US/12/13/ret.bin.laden.quotes/
(28) http://www.usatoday.com/news/sept11/2001/12/14/tape-arabs.htm
(29) Ibid
(30) http://www.september11news.com/OsamaEvidence.htm
(31) http://abcnews.go.com/sections/world/DailyNews/OBL_transcript_
011213_3.html
(32) www.fbi.gov/mostwant/topten/fugitives/laden.htm
(33) Ibid
(34) Ibid
(35) http://www.whatreallyhappened.com/hatespeech.html
(36) Ibid
(37) http://dc.indymedia.org/front.php3?article_id=16389&group=webcast
(38) http://dc.indymedia.org/newswire/display/16801
(39) http://www.welfarestate.com/wtc/faketape/manipulative.txt
(40) Washington Post, Friday, 21 December, 2001

http://watch.windsofchange.net/2001_12.htm
(41) USA Today, 20 December, 2001
http://www.newworldpeace.com/coverup6a.html
(42) USA Today, 20 December, 2001
http://dc.indymedia.org/newswire/display/16801
(43) http://www.fair.org/activism/cnn-casualties.html
(44) http://www.abcnews.go.com/wire/US/reuters20011223_112.html
(45) http://www.americanfreepress.net/10_07_01/Bush___Bin_Laden_-
_George_W__B/bush___bin_laden_-_george_w__b.html
(46) http://www.guardian.co.uk/Print/0,3858,4277056,00.html
(47) http://www.rferl.org/nca/features/2001/09/19092001120229.asp
(48) http://www.russianatlanta.net/forums/topic.asp?TOPIC_ID=1904
(49) http://www.mikehersh.com/printer_65.shtml
(50) http://www.newsmax.com/showinside.shtml?a=2002/8/20/105933
(51) http://www.cin.org/archives/cinjust/199905/0025.html
(52) http://www.washingtondispatch.com/article_4686.shtml
(53) http://www.pbs.org/wgbh/pages/frontline/shows/knew/john/yemen.html
(54) http://www.rawa.org/ny-attack.htm
(55) http://www.satp.org/satporgtp/usa/Taliban.htm

Chapter 11
Prior Knowledge

With all the main stream media reports of prior knowledge, it is obvious that many people knew of the coming attacks. But just who knew, and when they knew, is what we must now discover.

One clue comes from the attack on the World Trade Center on February 26, 1993. The New York Times reported on the FBI recordings of Emad Ali Salem.[1]

Ali Salem was an FBI informer, who was also once an Egyptian Army officer, who informed the FBI about the coming first attack on the World Trade Center. According to this story, Salem informed them about the plot, and the FBI planned to somehow exchange the explosives in the truck bomb with a harmless powder. But according to Salem, an FBI officer named John Anticev stopped the plan cold in its feet. Salem then questioned why the attack was allowed to happen.

> Law-enforcement officials were told that terrorists were building a bomb that was eventually used to blow up the World Trade Center, and they planned to thwart the plotters by secretly substituting harmless powder for the explosives, an informer said after the blast.
>
> The informer was to have helped the plotters build the bomb and supply the fake powder, but the plan was called off by an F.B.I. supervisor who had other ideas about how the informer, Emad A. Salem, should be used, the informer said.
>
> The account, which is given in the transcript of hundreds of hours of tape recordings Mr. Salem secretly made of his talks with law enforcement agents, portrays the authorities as in a far better position than previously known to foil the Feb. 26 bombing of New York City's tallest towers. The explosion left six people dead more than 1000 injured and damages in excess of half a billion dollars. Four men are now on trial in Manhattan Federal Court in that attack.
>
> The transcript quotes Mr. Salem as saying that he wanted to complain to F.B.I. headquarters in Washington about the bureau's failure to stop the bombing, but was dissuaded by an agent he identified as John Anticev.
>
> "He said, I don't think the New York people would like the things

out of the New York office to go to Washington, D.C.," Mr. Salem said Mr. Anticev told him.

In another point in the transcripts, Mr. Salem recounts a conversation he said he had with Mr. Anticev, saying, "I said 'Guys, now you both saw this bomb went off and you both know that we could avoid that.'" At another point, Mr. Salem says, "You get paid, guys, to prevent problems like this from happening."[2]

The problem is that time and time again, secrets are leaked, and the exposure of such secrets are either stalled, or made to sound so ludicrous that the person revealing the information is made out to be an idiot. (Hence myself and my work in this book. What is the flavor of the pie that will hit me in the face this week?)

Time and time again, any "evidence" that the CIA or FBI acquires is later changed to support the prosecution of those who had nothing to do with what happened.

How many times do we see people released from prison many years later for crimes they did not commit? Or sadly how many die in prison and later evidence is released that that person was innocent?

Even in the events of 11 September, the FBI had an Algerian pilot Lotfi Raissi imprisoned for five months on the claims that he trained some of the "terrorists."[3] Evidence to support the FBI was never produced and he later was released. This again, my friends, is the same FBI telling the World what happened on 11 September, and why it happened, and who should be bombed and killed because of it. Absolutely brilliant.

On 14 August, 1995, FBI special agent Dr. Frederic Whitehurst testified in a trial to "support" the FBI's prosecution of the defendants for the 1993 WTC attacks.[4]

...The Justice Department is investigating complaints that workers in the bureau's crime laboratory have offered misleading or fabricated evidence in a number of major criminal cases.

The allegations were made by the supervisory special agent Frederic Whitehurst, who has complained to his FBI superiors that the lab work has been sloppy and that in some cases conclusions were altered to help the government's case. He aired some of his concerns publicly on Aug. 14 as a witness in a New York bombing conspiracy case.

The FBI yesterday said it was taking Whitehurst allegations seriously. But in a statement, the bureau said it has recently reviewed lab work in more than 250 cases and "to date the FBI has found no evidence of tampering, evidence fabrication, or failure to report exculpatory evidence... Any finding of such misconduct will result in tough and swift action by the FBI."[5]

Special agent Frederick Whitehurst is now a paint analyst after a demotion from the FBI.[6] Imagine that.

John Ashcroft stops flying on commercial airliners

On July 26, 2001, cbsnews.com reported that John Ashcroft had stopped flying on commercial airlines.

Ashcroft used to fly commercial, just as Janet Reno did. So why, two months before Sept. 11, did he start taking chartered government planes?

CBS News correspondent Jim Stewart asked the Justice Department.

Because of a "threat assessment" by the FBI, he was told. But "neither the FBI nor the Justice Department . . . would identify what the threat was, when it was detected or who made it," CBS News reported.

The FBI did advise Ashcroft to stay off commercial aircraft. The rest of us just had to take our chances.

The FBI obviously knew something was in the wind. Why else would it have Ashcroft use a $1,600-plus per hour G-3 Gulfstream when he could have flown commercially, as he always did before, for a fraction of the cost?

Ashcroft demonstrated an amazing lack of curiosity when asked if he knew anything about the threat.

"Frankly, I don't," he told reporters.

So our nation's chief law enforcement officer was told that flying commercially was hazardous to his health, and yet he appeared not to care what the threat was, who made it, how, or why?

Note that it was the FBI that warned Ashcroft before Sept. 11.

That's the same FBI now claiming it didn't "connect the dots" before Sept. 11.

Had we in the press been on our toes, we might have realized that if flying commercially posed a threat to John Ashcroft, it also posed a threat to the population at large.

But the CBSNews.com story was largely ignored. CBS ran it

155

once, briefly. A number of CBS affiliates repeated the story, even more briefly. That was it. As near as I can tell, no other major news outlet ran the story of danger to commercial air travel so severe that our attorney general was told to stay away from it.[7]

Echelon

Echelon is said to be a vast information collection system capable of monitoring all the electronic communications in the world. It is thought to be operated by the U.S., the U.K., Canada, Australia and New Zealand.

No government agency has ever confirmed or denied its existence. However, with the wake of the 11 September attacks has proved that this system does indeed exist.

So did Echelon cough up the nine or ten warnings?

The National Security Agency acknowledges that it had "intercepted" two messages (one said "tomorrow is zero hour") from "terrorists" indicating that the next day, 11 September, would be the date of a major attack.[8]

Unfortunately, and sadly appropriate, those messages weren't processed and evaluated until it was too late, on 12 September.

The NSA finally admitted that they maintain a sophisticated voice and keyword recognition computer system called Echelon.[9] A former NSA director told the French magazine *Le Nouvel Observateur* that Echelon uses automation to monitor every phone call, fax transmission, e-mail and wire transfer in the world.[10]

The acknowledgment of this is very frightening. And that is an understatement.

Is Echelon being used to monitor ordinary Americans? If the allegations that it is used to, "Monitor every phone call, fax transmission, e-mail and wire transfer in the world," are correct, the answer to that question is a sad and surprising, yes. So much for the Constitution.

As I raised the question in a previous chapter about where did the FBI get the cellular phone transcripts from the passengers on Flight 93, we now have a very possible answer.

Anyone who does not worry about the now admitted government spying ability to grow out of control and threaten freedom is a fool.

Is there even such a thing as freedom? I would like to know!

The Israeli Connection

It was reported that employees of Odigo, Inc., in Israel, one of the world's largest instant messaging companies, with offices in New York City, received threat warnings of an imminent attack on the WTC less than two hours before the first plane hit the World Trade Center.[11]

The Odigo Research and Development offices in Israel are located in the city of Herzliyya, a ritzy suburb of Tel Aviv which is the same location as the Institute for Counter Terrorism.[12]

Odigo says workers were warned of attack

Odigo, the instant messaging service, says that two of its workers received messages two hours before the Twin Towers attack on September 11 predicting the attack would happen, and the company has been cooperating with Israeli and American law enforcement, including the FBI, in trying to find the original sender of the message predicting the attack.

Micha Macover, CEO of the company, said the two workers received the messages and immediately after the terror attack informed the company's management, which immediately contacted the Israeli security services, which brought in the FBI.

"I have no idea why the message was sent to these two workers, who don't know the sender. It may just have been someone who was joking and turned out they accidentally got it right. And I don't know if our information was useful in any of the arrests the FBI has made," said Macover. Odigo is a U.S.-based company whose headquarters are in New York, with offices in Herzliya.

As an instant messaging service, Odigo users are not limited to sending messages only to people on their "buddy" list, as is the case with ICQ, the other well-known Israeli instant messaging application.

Odigo usually zealously protects the privacy of its registered users, said Macover, but in this case the company took the initiative to provide the law enforcement services with the originating Internet Presence address of the message, so the FBI could track down the Internet Service Provider, and the actual sender of the original messages.[13]

Massive spy ring linked to 11 September

Some people thought they had buried the story of Israeli foreknowledge of the impending 9-11 terrorist attacks, but now that story is taking on a new life of its own.

Exclusive To American Free Press
By Michael Collins Piper

There is strong evidence Israeli intelligence operatives engaged in clandestine dealings on American soil and almost certainly had advance knowledge of the impending terrorist attacks on Sept. 11.

Israel, however, did not report this information to the American authorities.

A sudden spate of news stories in the mainstream media over a three-day period cast new light on this story that first reached a national audience in the Dec. 17 issue of American Free Press which actually went to press on Dec. 7, 2001.

At that time, AFP noted that buried within a story in The Washington Post on Nov. 23 was the little-known fact that a number of Israeli nationals taken into custody by federal authorities after the Sept. 11 tragedy were suspected of having material knowledge relative to the terrorist attacks on New York and Washington.

Then, on Dec. 12, five days after the AFP story was published, Carl Cameron of Brit Hume's Special Report on Fox News, broke his report on a wide-ranging Israeli espionage ring uncovered on U.S. soil. Cameron reported that there was evidence that those Israeli agents were watching the 9-11 terrorists prior to the Sept. 11 tragedy. On Dec. 24, AFP summarized Cameron's report in which he stated in part: There is no indication the Israelis were involved in the Sept. 11 attacks, but investigators suspect that they may have gathered intelligence about the attacks in advance and not shared it. A highly placed investigator told Fox News there are "tie-ins," but when asked for details flatly refused to describe them. "Evidence linking these Israelis to 9-11 is classified. I cannot tell you about evidence that has been gathered. It is classified information."

During the segment, host Brit Hume asked Cameron: "What about this question of advanced knowledge of what was going to happen on 9-11? How clear are investigators that some Israeli agents may have known something?"

Cameron responded: "It's very explosive information, obviously, and there's a great deal of evidence that they say they have collected.

None of it necessarily conclusive. It's more when they put it all together. A bigger question, they say, is "How could they not have known?" [That is] almost a direct quote [from the investigators]."

The Fox report indicated that even prior to Sept. 11 as many as 140 other Israelis had been detained or arrested in what was described by reporter Cameron as "a secretive and sprawling investigation into suspected espionage by Israelis in the United States." According to Cameron: Investigators are focusing part of their efforts on Israelis who said they are art students from the University of Jerusalem or Bezalel Academy and repeatedly made contact with U.S. government personnel by saying they wanted to sell cheap art or handiwork.

Documents say they "targeted" and penetrated military bases, the Drug Enforcement Administration, the Federal Bureau of Investigation, dozens of government facilities and even secret offices and unlisted private homes of law enforcement and intelligence personnel.

After Fox made this amazing report, there was an angry response from the Israeli lobby in America. The Dec. 21 issue of the New Yorkbased Forward reported that Fox and Cameron were "under fire."

Whatever the case, Fox News pulled the transcriptions of Cameron's broadcast reports off its Internet web site, saying that "this story no longer exists," even though, at the time, Cameron had told Forward that he continued to stand behind his story. It appeared as though Cameron's story was destined for the Memory Hole, but for reports about it that had appeared in AFP and on the Internet.

However, on March 4, the story first pioneered by AFP and Fox News came back to life thanks to the famous French daily, Le Monde which hit the streets with a story charging that "a vast Israeli espionage network operating on American territory has been broken up," describing the network of "Israeli art students" that Fox had first reported.

Le Monde's story relied largely on reporting an independent investigation conducted by the Paris-based Intelligence Online (an Internet-based newsletter), which, in turn, had obviously been directed by the Fox report and the sources made available to Fox.

The story developed by Intelligence Online, according to Le

Monde, charged quite specifically that Israel had withheld information that it had developed, through its spying operations in the United States, about the impending Sept. 11 terrorist attacks.

LeMonde cited transcriptions of the previous work by Carl Cameron on Fox and pointed out how Fox itself refused to cooperate with Le Monde, saying that it was "a problem," but that Fox refused to be specific.

According to Intelligence Online, the suspects in the Israeli spying operation were all between 22 and 30 and had recently completed their Israeli military service. Six of the suspected spies had used portable telephones bought by a former Israeli vice consul in the United States. Many of the suspects were also linked to Israeli information technology companies.

Le Monde also noted that Intelligence Online had received a copy of a 61-page report prepared by an officer of the U.S. Drug Enforcement Administration and others from the Immigration and Naturalization Service. (A spokesman for the DEA, Will Glaspy, confirmed to Le Monde that the DEA "holds a copy" of that report.)

The report cited by Le Monde specifically pointed out that one-third of the suspected Israeli spies had been based in Florida, and at least five of them were on site in Hollywood, Fla., where accused Sept. 11 hijacker ringleader Muhammad Atta and four of his purported accomplices also lived.

The United States has deported 120 young Israelis posing as "art students" for visa violations. However, some officials do suspect them of spying.

On March 5, Reuters, the sometimes quite independent press service, carried a report describing Le Monde's article (even including the allegation of Israeli foreknowledge of the Sept. 11 terrorist attacks). Reuters, however, cited an un-named FBI spokesman who called it a "bogus story," saying—despite all the evidence to the contrary—that "there wasn't a spy ring."

On March 6, the Associated Press ran its own version (which appeared in some newspapers across the country) and reported that there had been allegations that so-called Israeli "art students" deported from the United States were "suspected" of spying.

AP's report, however, did not mention the implication that this spy ring had advance knowledge relating to the activities of the

160

9-11 terrorists.

On March 6 Washington Post staff writers John Mintz and Dan Eggen also wrote a story about the affair, but their version had a notably different spin.

The Post story was headlined "Reports of Israeli spy ring dismissed" and claimed that "a wide array of U.S. officials" had dismissed the reports that the U.S. government had broken up "an Israeli espionage ring that consisted of young Israelis attempting to penetrate U.S. agencies by selling artwork in federal buildings."

Mintz and Eggen reported that Attorney General Ashcroft's spokeswoman at the Justice Department, Susan Dryden, described the story as "an urban myth that has been circulating for months." She added: "The department has no information at this time to substantiate these widespread reports about Israeli art students involved in espionage."

The two Post writers suggest that the allegations appear to have been circulated in a memo written (and leaked) by a single "disgruntled" employee of the DEA who, Mintz and Eggen say, is "angry" that FBI and CIA sources have rejected what the Post duo dismissively calls his "theories."

The memo is presumably the same one that Intelligence Online used in as partial basis for its report.

So while the Post admits that the DEA memo does exist, the Post is trying to dismiss its reliability by charging that "a single employee" who is "disgruntled" and "angry" is its source.

However, even as it is trying to suggest that a DEA loner was behind the charges, the Post article does acknowledge in its closing paragraph: DEA spokesman Thomas Hinojosa said that multiple reports of suspicious activity on the part of young Israelis had come into the agency's Washington headquarters from agents in the fields. The reports were summarized in a draft memo last year, but Hinojosa said he did not have a copy and could not vouch for the accuracy of media reports describing its contents.

What is perhaps the most intriguing twist about the Post story is that co-author Mintz is the Post staffer who wrote in the Post on Nov. 23 that among a total of some 60 young Israeli Jews picked up by the FBI in the wake of the Sept. 11 terrorist attacks, there was at least a handful being held on suspicion of having material knowledge about the attacks themselves.

161

At that time Mintz pointed out that while most of the Israelis arrested and detained since Sept. 11 were held on immigration charges and not suspected of any involvement in terrorism, there were exceptions.

According to Mintz's previous Post article (published on Nov. 23) In several cases, such as those in Cleveland and St. Louis, INS officials testified in court hearings that they were "of special interest to the government," a term that federal agents have used in many of the hundreds of cases involving mostly Muslim Arab men who have been detained around the country since the terrorist attacks.

An INS official who requested anonymity said the agency will not comment on the Israelis. He said the use of the term "special interest" means the case in question is "related to the investigation of Sept. 11."

What Mintz did not say in his more recent Post article of March 6 was that some of these same Israelis that he was writing about on Nov. 23 have been implicated in the spy ring that his most recent article suggests is "an urban myth."

Now, Mintz's co-author, Dan Eggen, has revealed a new detail about yet another Israeli official to the events of 9-11. It turns out that another "former" Israeli operative was actually traveling on one of the ill-fated Sept. 11 flights alongside the Arab hijackers.

United Press International has yet to cover the developments in the Israeli spy ring story, which might be explained by the fact that its chief international correspondent, Eli Lake, is a devotee of Israel who previously worked for Forward, the Jewish community newspaper which bragged on Dec. 21 how the Fox story had been buried by other media. [14]

Fox News series on Israeli spying in the US

In mid December 2001, The Fox News Channel ran a blockbuster series on Israeli spying in the U.S. contending that Israeli intelligence had advanced information about the 11 September attacks before they occurred.

After significant pressure (from who?), Fox pulled the reports from their Website and went about deleting all references to the series of Fox's and other web sites. Fox has never given any explanation for this action. [15]

Fortunately, the original transcripts which appeared on Fox's

Website are reprinted in their entirety here:

The series was presented the investigative reporter Carl Cameron and presented on Special Report with Brit Hume.

Part 1: December 11, 2001

HUME: It has been more than 16 years since a civilian working for the Navy was charged with passing secrets to Israel.

Jonathan Pollard pled guilty to conspiracy to commit espionage and is serving a life sentence.

At first, Israeli leaders claimed Pollard was part of a rogue operation, but later took responsibility for his work.

Now Fox News has learned some U.S. investigators believe that there are Israelis again very much engaged in spying in and on the U.S.,who may have known things they didn't tell us before September 11. Fox News correspondent Carl Cameron has details in the first of a four-part series. (BEGIN VIDEOTAPE)

CARL CAMERON, FOX NEWS CORRESPONDENT (voice-over): Since September 11,more than 60 Israelis have been arrested or detained, either under the new patriot anti-terrorism law, or for immigration violations.

A handful of active Israeli military were among those detained, according to investigators, who say some of the detainees also failed polygraph questions when asked about alleged surveillance activities against and in the United States.

There is no indication that the Israelis were involved in the 9-11 attacks, but investigators suspect that they Israelis may have gathered intelligence about the attacks in advance, and not shared it.

A highly placed investigator said there are -quote – "tie-ins." But when asked for details, he flatly refused to describe them, saying, quote "evidence linking these Israelis to 9-11 is classified. I cannot tell you about evidence that has been gathered. It's classified information." Fox News has learned that one group of Israelis, spotted in North Carolina recently, is suspected of keeping an apartment in California to spy on a group of Arabs who the United States is also investigating for links to terrorism.

Numerous classified documents obtained by Fox News indicate that even prior to September 11,as many as 140 other Israelis had been detained or arrested in a secretive and sprawling investigation into suspected espionage by Israelis in the United

163

States.

Investigators from numerous government agencies are part of a working group that's been compiling evidence since the mid '90s.

These documents detail hundreds of incidents in cities and towns across the country that investigators say – quote – "may well be an organized intelligence gathering activity."

The first part of the investigation focuses on Israelis who say they are art students from the University of Jerusalem and Bazala (ph) Academy.

They repeatedly made contact with U.S. government personnel, the report says, by saying they wanted to sell cheap art or handiwork. Documents say they quote "targeted and penetrated military bases." The DEA, FBI and dozens of government facilities, and even secret offices and unlisted private homes of law enforcement and intelligence personnel. The majority of those questioned – quote - "stated they served in military intelligence, electronic surveillance intercept and or explosive ordinance units."

Another part of the investigation has resulted in the detention and arrests of dozens of Israelis at American mall kiosks, where they've been selling toys called Puzzle Car and Zoom Copter. Investigators suspect a front.

Shortly after "The New York Times" and "Washington Post" reported the Israeli detentions last months, the carts began vanishing. Zoom Copter's Web page says,"We are aware of the situation caused by thousands of mall carts being closed at the last minute. This in no way reflects the quality of the toy or its sale-ability.

The problem lies in the operators' business policies." Why would Israelis spy in and on the U.S.?

A general accounting office investigation referred to Israel as country A and said – quote -"According to a U.S. intelligence agency, the government of country A conducts the most aggressive espionage operations against the U.S. of any U.S. ally."

A defense intelligence report said Israel has a voracious appetite for information and said – quote -"the Israelis are motivated by strong survival instincts which dictate every possible facet of their political and economical policies.

It aggressively collects military and industrial technology and the

164

U.S. is a high priority target." The document concludes – quote – "Israel possesses the resources and technical capability to achieve its collection objectives." (END VIDEO CLIP)

A spokesman for the U.S. – excuse me, the Israeli embassy here in Washington issued a denial saying that any suggestion that Israelis are spying in or on the U.S. is – quote – "simply not true." There are other things to consider. And in the days ahead, we'll take a look at the U.S. phone system and law enforcement's methods for wiretaps. And an investigation that both have been compromised by our friends overseas – Brit.

HUME: Carl, what about this question of advanced knowledge of what was going to happen on 9-11? How clear are investigators that some Israeli agents may have known something?

CAMERON: It's very explosive information, obviously, and there's a great deal of evidence that they say they have collected – none of it necessarily conclusive.

It's more when they put it all together. A bigger question, they say, is how could they not have know? Almost a direct quote – Brit.

HUME: Going into the fact that they were spying on some Arabs, right?

CAMERON: Correct.

HUME: All right, Carl, thanks very much. We have to take a quick bread here for other headlines.

Part 2: December 12, 2001

HUME: Last time we reported on the approximately 6- Israelis who had been detained in connection with the September 11th terrorism investigation.

Carl Cameron reported that U.S. investigators suspect that some of these Israelis were spying on Arabs in this country, and may have turned up information on the planned terrorist attacks back in September that was not passed on.

Tonight, in the second of four reports on spying by Israelis in the U.S., we learn about an Israeli-based private communications company, for whom a half-dozen of those 60 detained suspects worked. American investigators fear information generated by this firm may have fallen into the wrong hands and had the effect of impeded the September 11th terror inquiry.

165

Here's Carl Cameron's second report. (BEGIN VIDEOTAPE)

CARL CAMERON, FOX NEWS CORRESPONDENT (voice-over): Fox News has learned that some American terrorist investigators fear certain suspects in the September 11th attacks may have managed to stay ahead of them, by knowing who and when investigators are calling on the telephone. How?

By obtaining and analyzing data that's generated every time someone in the U.S. makes a call.

UNIDENTIFIED FEMALE: What city and state, please?

CAMERON: Here's how the system works. Most directory assistance calls, and virtually all call records and billing in the U.S. are done for the phone companies by Amdocs, Ltd, an Israeli-based private telecommunications company.

Amdocs has contracts with the 25 biggest phone companies in America, and more worldwide. The White House and other secure government phone lines are protected, but it is virtually impossible to make a call on normal phones without generating an Amdocs record of it.

In recent years, the FBI and other government agencies have investigated Amdocs more than once. The firm has repeatedly and adamantly denied any security breaches or wrongdoing. But sources tell Fox News that in 1999, the super secret national security agency, headquartered in northern Maryland, issued what's called a Top Secret sensitive compartmentalized information report, TS/SCI, warning that records of calls in the United States were getting into foreign hands – in Israel, in particular.

Investigators don't believe calls are being listened to, but the data about who is calling whom and when is plenty valuable in itself.

An internal Amdocs memo to senior company executives suggests just how Amdocs generated call records could be used. Quote – "widespread data mining techniques and algorithms.... combining both the properties of the customer (e.g., credit rating) and properties of the specific behavior..." Specific behavior, such as whom the customers are calling.

The Amdocs memo says the system should be used to prevent phone fraud. But U.S. counterintelligence analysts say it could also be used to spy through the phone system.

Fox News has learned that the N.S.A has held numerous classified conferences to warn the F.B.I. and C.I.A. how Amdocs

166

records could be used.

At one NSA briefing, a diagram by the Argon national lab was used to show that if the phone records are not secure, major security breaches are possible.

Another briefing document said – quote – "It has become increasingly apparent that systems and networks are vulnerable.

Such crimes always involve unauthorized persons, or persons who exceed their authorization... citing on exploitable vulnerabilities." Those vulnerabilities are growing, because according to another briefing, the U.S. relies too much on foreign companies like Amdocs for high tech equipment and software.

Quote – "Many factors have led to increased dependence on code developed overseas.... We buy rather than train or develop solutions."

U.S. intelligence does not believe the Israeli government is involved in a misuse of information, and Amdocs insists that its data is secure.

What U.S. government officials are worried about, however, is the possibility that Amdocs data could get into the wrong hands, particularly organized crime. And that would not be the first thing that such a thing has happened.

Fox News has documents of a 1997 drug trafficking case in Los Angeles, in which telephone information, the type that Amdocs collects, was used to – quote – "completely compromise the communications of the FBI, the Secret Service, the DEO and the LAPD."

We'll have that and a lot more in the days ahead – Brit.

HUME: Carl, I want to take you back to your report last night on those 60 Israelis who were detained in the anti-terror investigation, and the suspicion that some investigators have that they may have picked up information on the 9-11 attacks ahead of time and not passed it on.

There was a report, you'll recall, that the Mossad, the Israeli intelligence agency, did indeed send representatives to the U.S. to warn, just before 9-11, that a major terrorist attack was imminent. How does that leave room for the lack of a warning?

CAMERON: I remember the report, Brit. We did it first internationally right here on your show on the 14th.

What investigators are saying is that that warning from the Mossad was nonspecific and general, and they believe that it

167

may have had something to do with the desire to protect what are called sources and methods in the intelligence community.

The suspicion being, perhaps those sources and methods were taking place right here in the United States. The question came up in select intelligence committee on Capitol Hill today. They intend to look into what we reported last night, and specifically that possibility – Brit.

HUME: So in other words, the problem wasn't lack of a warning, the problem was lack of useful details?

CAMERON: Quantity of information.

HUME: All right, Carl, thank you very much. Coming up next, more perspective on that B-1 bomber crash and on the show-down in eastern Afghanistan.

Part 3: December 13, 2001

HUME: Last time we reported on an Israeli-based company called Amdocs that generates the computerized records and billing data for nearly every phone call made in America. As Carl Cameron reported, U.S. investigators digging into the 9-11 terrorist attacks fear that suspects may have been tipped off to what they were doing by information leaking out of Amdocs.

In tonight's report, we learn that the concern about phone security extends to another company, founded in Israel, that provides the technology that the U.S. government uses for electronic eavesdropping. Here is Carl Cameron's third report.

(BEGIN VIDEOTAPE) CARL CAMERON, FOX NEWS CORRESPONDENT (voice-over): The company is Comverse Infosys, a subsidiary of an Israeli-run private telecommunications firm, with offices throughout the U.S. It provides wiretapping equipment for law enforcement. Here's how wiretapping works in the U.S.

Every time you make a call, it passes through the nation's elaborate network of switchers and routers run by the phone companies.

Custom computers and software, made by companies like Comverse, are tied into that network to intercept, record and store the wiretapped calls, and at the same time transmit them to investigators.

The manufacturers have continuing access to the computers so they can service them and keep them free of glitches. This

168

process was authorized by the 1994 Communications Assistance for Law Enforcement Act, or CALEA.

Senior government officials have now told Fox News that while CALEA made wiretapping easier, it has led to a system that is seriously vulnerable to compromise, and may have undermined the whole wiretapping system. Indeed, Fox News has learned that Attorney General John Ashcroft and FBI Director Robert Mueller were both warned October 18th in a hand-delivered letter from 15 local, state and federal law enforcement officials, who complained that - quote – "law enforcement's current electronic surveillance capabilities are less effective today than they were at the time CALEA was enacted."

Congress insists the equipment it installs is secure. But the complaint about this system is that the wiretap computer programs made by Comverse have, in effect, a back door through which wiretaps themselves can be intercepted by unauthorized parties. Adding to the suspicions is the fact that in Israel, Comverse works closely with the Israeli government, and under special programs, gets reimbursed for up to 50 percent of its research and development costs by the Israeli Ministry of Industry and Trade.

But investigators within the DEA, INS and FBI have all told Fox News that to pursue or even suggest Israeli spying through Comverse is considered career suicide.

And sources say that while various F.B.I. inquiries into Comverse have been conducted over the years, they've been halted before the actual equipment has ever been thoroughly tested for leaks.

A 1999 F.C.C. document indicates several government agencies expressed deep concerns that too many unauthorized non-law enforcement personnel can access the wiretap system.

And the FBI's own nondescript office in Chantilly, Virginia that actually oversees the CALEA wiretapping program, is among the most agitated about the threat.

But there is a bitter turf war internally at F.B.I. It is the FBI's office in Quantico, Virginia, that has jurisdiction over awarding contracts and buying intercept equipment. And for years, they've thrown much of the business to Comverse.

A handful of former U.S. law enforcement officials involved in awarding Comverse government contracts over the years now work for the company.

Numerous sources say some of those individuals were asked to leave government service under what knowledgeable sources call "troublesome circumstances" that remain under administrative review within the Justice Department.

(END VIDEOTAPE)

And what troubles investigators most, particularly in New York, in the counter-terrorism investigation of the World Trade Center attack, is that on a number of cases, suspects that they had sought to wiretap and surveil immediately changed their telecommunications processes. They started acting much differently as soon as those supposedly secret wiretaps went into place – Brit.

HUME: Carl, is there any reason to suspect in this instance that the Israeli government is involved?

CAMERON: No, there's not.

But there are growing instincts in an awful lot of law enforcement officials in a variety of agencies who suspect that it had begun compiling evidence, and a highly classified investigation into that possibility – Brit.

HUME: All right, Carl. Thanks very much.

Part 4: December 14, 2001

TONY SNOW: This week, senior correspondent Carl Cameron has reported on a longstanding government espionage investigation.

Federal officials this year have arrested or detained nearly 200 Israeli citizens suspected of belonging to a – quote – "organized intelligence-gathering operation."

The Bush administration has deported most of those arrested after September 11th, although some are in custody under the new antiterrorism law.

Cameron also an investigation into the possibility that an Israeli firm generated billing data that could be used for intelligence purposes, and describes concerns that the federal government's own wiretapping system may be vulnerable. Tonight, in part four of the series, we'll learn about the improbably roots of the probe: a drug case that went bad four years ago in L.A.

(BEGIN VIDEOTAPE) CARL CAMERON, FOX NEWS CORRESPONDENT (voice-over): Los Angeles, 1997, a major local, state and federal drug investigating sours.

170

The suspects: Israeli organized crime with operations in New York, Miami, Las Vegas, Canada, Israel and Egypt.

The allegations: cocaine and ecstasy trafficking, and sophisticated white collar credit card and computer fraud.

The problem: according to classified law enforcement documents obtained by Fox News, the bad guys had the cops' beepers, cell phones, even home phones under surveillance. Some who did get caught admitted to having hundreds of numbers and using them to avoid arrest. Quote: "This compromised law enforcement communications between LAPD detectives and other assigned law enforcement officers working various aspects of the case.

The organization discovered communications between organized crime intelligence division detectives, the FBI and the Secret Service."

Shock spread from the DEA to the FBI in Washington, and then the CIA. An investigation of the problem, according to law enforcement documents, concluded – quote -"The organization has apparent extensive access to database systems to identify pertinent personal and biographical information."

When investigators tried to find out where the information might have come from, they looked at Amdocs, a publicly-traded firm based in Israel. Amdocs generates billing data for virtually every call in America, and they do credit checks. The company denies any leaks, but investigators still fear that the firm's data is getting into the wrong hands.

When investigators checked their own wiretapping system for leaks, they grew concerned about potential vulnerabilities in the computers that intercept, record and store the wiretapped calls. A main contractor is Comverse Infosys, which works closely with the Israeli government, and under a special grant program, is reimbursed for up to 50 percent of its research and development costs by Israel's Ministry of Industry and Trade.

Asked this week about another sprawling investigation and the detention of 60 Israeli since September 11, the Bush administration treated the questions like hot potatoes.

ARI FLEISCHER, WHITE HOUSE PRESS SECRETARY: I would just refer you to the Department of Justice with that. I'm not familiar with the report.

COLIN POWELL, SECRETARY OF STATE: I'm aware that some Israeli citizens have been detained. With respect to why they're being detained and the other aspects of your question – whether it's because they're in intelligence services, or what they were doing - I will defer to the Department of Justice and the FBI to answer that.

(END VIDEOTAPE)

CAMERON: Beyond the 60 apprehended or detained, and many deported since September 11,another group of 140 Israeli individuals have been arrested and detained in this year in what government documents describe as – quote -"an organized intelligence gathering operation," designed to – quote – "penetrate government facilities."

Most of those individuals said they had served in the Israeli military, which is compulsory there. But they also had, most of them, intelligence expertise, and either worked for Amdocs or other companies in Israel that specialize in wiretapping.

Earlier this week, the Israeli embassy in Washington denied any spying against or in the United States – Tony.

SNOW: Carl, we've heard the comments from Ari Fleischer and Colin Powell. What are officials saying behind the scenes?

CAMERON: Well, there's real pandemonium described at both the FBI, the DEA and the INS.

A lot of these problems have been well-known to some investigators, many of whom have contributed to the reporting on this story.

And what they say is happening is supervisors and management are now going back and collecting much of the information, because there's tremendous pressure from the top levels of all of those agencies to find out exactly what's going on.

At the DEA and the FBI already a variety of administration reviews are under way, in addition to the investigation of the phenomenon.

They want to find out how it is all this has come out, as well as be very careful because of the explosive nature and very political ramifications of the story itself – Tony.

SNOW: All right, Carl, thanks. The Hart Senate office building, which was contaminated by anthrax, is scheduled to undergo some cleaning after more traces were found there.[16]

Insider trading

Believe it or not, another few pieces of the puzzle are the mysterious, but

172

purely coincidental I'm sure, profits made from insider trading in the stock market.

An Executive Director at the CIA named A. "Buzz" Krongard formerly worked for Bankers Trust in the banks top "Private Client Services Group" catering to the richest of the rich. Deutsche Bank purchased Bankers Trust, and in 1999, Mr. Krongard left Deutsche Bank for his present high-level job in the CIA.[17]

In the days immediately BEFORE 11 September, a number of very unusual stock trades were made in the two airlines whose planes were used in the attacks: American and United Airlines.

Also trades were made in two Securities Firms who had major offices in the World Trade Center: Morgan Stanley Dean Witter and Merrill Lynch.

The trades involved the purchase of enormous quantities of "put" options, which allow the option buyer to earn profits in the event the value of a stock goes down. And obviously, had anyone known of the coming attacks, and which airlines would be used, surely those stocks would fall.

Many of these unusual trades were handled through (you guessed it) Deutsche Bank, the place where Buzzy Krongard worked prior to becoming Executive Director of CIA. Coincidence I'm sure.

In fact, the appearance of "advance knowledge" is so strong, that to date $2.5 million of the $20 million in profits earned on those unusual trades, remains unclaimed by anyone. Perhaps taking the profits now, when people are watching, isn't such a good idea. Too many questions would have to be answered. I know I have a few for them.

Here are the pieces:

• Between September 6-7, 2001 4,744 puts were purchased on United Air Lines stock as opposed to only 396 call options (speculation that the stock will go up). This is a dramatic and abnormal increase in sales of put options. Many of the UAL puts are purchased through Deutsche Bank/A.B. Brown.[18]

   • September 10, 2001 4,516 put options are purchased on American Airlines as compared to 748 call options.[19]

For the month of September, until the 11th, no other airline company show any similar trading patterns to those experienced by United and American. The put option purchases on both airlines were 600% above normal. This, at a time when Reuters (September 10) issued

173

a business report stating, "Airline stocks may be poised to take off."[20] (Sure poised to take off into the World Trade Center and Pentagon.)

Again between September 6-10, 2001 highly abnormal levels of put options are purchased in Merrill Lynch, Morgan Stanley, AXA Re (insurance) which owns 25% of American Airlines, and Munich Re. All of these companies were directly impacted by the September 11 attacks. In fact, both Merrill Lynch and Morgan Stanley occupied 22 floors of the World Trade Center.[21]

Who else would have "suffered" enormous claims as the result of an attack on the WTC?

If this is not enough to already surprise you, guess who appointed Buzzy Krongrad to Executive Director? None other than George W. Bush in March 2001.[22]

May I propose an important question? (Of course I may, this is my book.) Who is more likely to have benefitted from these attacks and also these unusual put options?

Person A) Osama bin Laden who lives and operates out of a cave, or Person B) George W. Bush and his henchmen, including the vast financial network connected with the CIA?

Bush and his henchmen have been proven in the pages of this book that they are hiding the truth about the events of 11 September.

CNN announced, when wind broke of these unusual insider trades, that the CIA would conduct an investigation. Could someone please tell me how this investigation is going, because I can't find anything further on CNN, their website, or any other news network! I could use some help for the next edition of this book.

Duma warned citizens to cash out Dollars

The hearings in the Duma, which have become a rubber stump for President Putin, have been inspired, without doubt, by the Kremlin, "taking the necessary healthy measures" in advance of a U.S. crash and world crisis.[23]

The Kremlin was clearly thinking how it should operate in the "new world" after the expected U.S. crash.

It is my belief that the Kremlin provided Dr. Koryagina with a very small part of its information on the forthcoming attack against the U.S. Another article on this same theme was published by Pravda on July 17, 2001.[24]

It was an interview with Chairman of the Duma Commission on

Economic Politics Dr. Sergei Glazyev, one of the most prominent Russian economists.

This article was entitled, "The Dollar and the U.S. Could Fall at Any Moment."

Dr. Glazyev, in his answers, did not mention the forces preparing an attack on the U.S. and its financial system. But he merely discussed the forms and scales of the forthcoming financial catastrophe in the U.S. and its consequences for Russia, mostly beneficial ones if the necessary measures are taken in advance.

In particular, like Dr. Koryagina, Dr. Glazyev advised the Russian public to change dollars for rubles and predicted that, "The ruble will become the reserve currency for Eurasia, particularly in trade with China and India."[25]

The Russian Newspaper, Pravda, published an article on this theme on 31 July -1 August 2001 edition. This article, called, "The Dollar and the U.S. Will Fall," was in the form of an interview with the Malaysian ambassador in Russia.

Other Moscow newspapers published articles of this kind also. As a result, New York's Russian-language TV channel in early August was forced to state that, "The Moscow rumors are ungrounded." Within a few days the public forgot all about this story.[26] But I didn't.

The tone of Moscow economists predicting the crash of the U.S. financial-economic system was confident and somewhat delightful: "Finally, it is going to happen!"

They are not only discussing the future, they are evidently trying to issue a self-fulfilling prophecy, transforming this future into the present.

This is because the prospects described in the above articles are extremely attractive for the Russian elite for the following reasons:

A) It will become possible to pay off Russia's huge foreign debts with devalued dollars; it would be really easy enough if oil prices jumped to $100 per barrel or more.

B) Russia would become more equal among a weakened G-8 group of nations.

C) Investment conditions in Russia would become handsomely attractive in comparison to the bleak global background. Russia could become the goal of huge foreign investment.

D) If the U.S. military might is undermined (and it might be, if

175

the financial system collapses), Russia will regain its control over the former Soviet republics, spreading it to the Balkans and reacquire its former super-empire status.

Such a prize, such a temptation for the criminal Russian "elite!"

One small push, and such a great bounty! While reading these articles, it is almost possible to visualize how they are licking their lips with excitement.

So, those in Moscow had very serious reasons not to share information with the U.S. about the coming attack on the latter, if they indeed had such information.

Very likely they did, and the maximum amount of information was concentrated in the Kremlin. According to numerous statements published by prominent U.S. economists after the tragedy, the time and places of the attacks were chosen, more precisely extremely well calculated, as if the "terrorists" or those backing them had tried to do their best to undermine the U.S. financial system and political system and to cause a financial economic crisis in the US.[27]

There is some evidence that suggests that another aircraft, a TWA plane at JFK Airport, had been targeted for hijacking.[28] It did not take off, and if this evidence is true, another crash was thwarted. Was it intended for the New York Stock Exchange?

"It wasn't a healthy economy to begin with, and this could be just enough to push us into a mild recession and render a blow to consumer confidence," one of these economists told the UPI.[29]

He continued, "There has been a complete disruption of passenger flights. Besides the airline industry, tourism, retail and the shipping sectors will feel the negative effects of Tuesday's attack. Tougher security measures now in place at the nation's airports will increase shipping and travel expenses that will be passed along to the consumer."[30]

And the consumer confidence index, already low, declined additionally after the attacks.

However, those in Moscow, were probably waiting for much greater effects.

Remarkably, immediately after the events in New York and Washington, at approximately 6:00 p.m. Moscow time, the dollar exchange rate in Moscow street exchanges fell from 29 rubles to 15-20 rubles, as if the Moscow financial experts had awaited the strikes or expected a greater panic and/or collapse.[31]

176

It is important to note that such a great fluctuation in the exchange rate happened in no other world capital. The next day, the dollar in Moscow gradually returned to its previous exchange rate.

Clearly, we are made to believe something that is clearly not true.

Smoke and mirrors, and debris from the downed Towers will not prevent this knowledge getting out. You, with this knowledge can make a difference! The truth is in your hands. Not on your television or in your newspaper.

But the puzzle is not yet complete…

SOURCES

(1) Ralph Blumenthal New York Times October, 28 1993
(2) Ibid
(3) http://www.thisisthenortheast.co.uk/the_north_east/features/
    HEARALLSIDES9.html
(4) http://www.politikforum.de/forum/archive/15/2002/03/3/15396
(5) The Washington Post A Thursday, September 14, 1995
(6) http://www.devvy.com/200302211827.html
(7) http://www.sfgate.com/cgi-bin/article.cgi?file=/gate/archive/2002/06/
    03/hsorensen.DTL
(8) http://www.alternet.org/story.html?StoryID=13864
(9) http://www.newsfrombabylon.com/article.php?sid=2030
(10) http://www.metroactive.com/papers/metro/09.12.02/sept11a-0237.html
(11) http://www.xanga.com/home.aspx?user=davidandrew
(12) Source: CNN's Daniel Sieberg, 9/28/01; Newsbytes, Brian McWilliams,
    9/27/01; Ha'aretz, 9/26/01.
(13) http://www.haaretzdaily.com/hasen/pages/ShArt.jhtml?itemNo=77744
(14) http://www.americanfreepress.net/03_10_02/Massive_Spy_Ring/
    massive_spy_ring.html
(15) http://www.rense.com/general18/spypull.htm
(16) http://www.firefox.1accesshost.com/cameron.html
(17) http://www.tamil.net/list/2001-10/msg00704.html
(18) The Herzliyya International Policy Institute for Counterterrorism,
    http://www.ict.org.il/,
    September 21, 2001; The New York Times; The Wall Street Journal
(19) Ibid
(20) http://www.globalresearch.ca/articles/RUP112A.html.
(21) http://www.fromthewilderness.com/free/ww3/oct152001.html
(22) http://www.ndtceda.com/archives/200111/0770.html.
(23) http://www.rense.com/general13/russia.htm
(24) http://www.eionews.addr.com/psyops/news/didrussiaknow.htm
(25) Ibid
(26) http://www.newsmax.com/archives/articles/2001/9/16/103951.shtml
(27) http://www.eionews.addr.com/psyops/news/didrussiaknow.htm
(28) http://www.metroactive.com/papers/metro/09.12.02/sept11a-0237.html
(29) http://www.newsmax.com/archives/articles/2001/9/16/103951.shtml
(30) Ibid
(31) Ibid

Chapter 12
A Few More Suspicious Pieces

Here I have complied a few last pieces of our puzzle that needs to be answered.

Cockpit doors

Why didn't federal law require reinforced locked cockpit doors?

This common sense proposal had been adopted by carriers in other countries many years earlier, but not in the United States. Did the airlines lobby against the move because of increased costs? If so, which airlines? And which federal officials and/or members of Congress are criminally responsible for jeopardizing the safety of the flying public for the sake of a few bucks?

I can't hear you: Who skimped on NYFD communications?

Scores of New York firefighters died in the stairwells of the World Trade Center after they'd been ordered to evacuate the buildings because they couldn't hear those orders on their antiquated radio system. The fire department had requested up to date equipment years earlier. So, which city officials refused to allocate the necessary funding, causing firefighters to die needlessly? And do the NYFD and other urban fire departments have better communications now?

Other knives and other airplanes

What about the other knives?

After planes in the sky of America were grounded, investigators found box cutters attached under seats on several Delta flights out of Boston's Logan airport and from Atlanta bound for Brussels.[1] Was anyone ever arrested in connection with the would-be hijackings of these other flights? What were the intended targets of those aborted hijackings? Were those box cutters, and those on the four hijacked flights, placed there by personnel who service aircraft? Or were they smuggled aboard through lacked security checkpoints by would-be hijackers?

"These look like an inside job," a U.S. official told Time magazine.[2]

179

Were there other plots? American officials have questioned thousands of individuals in connection with 9/11.[3] Have they uncovered other schemes intended for that day, or for a later day?

Osama on 11 September

Where was Osama bin Laden on 9-11?

Afghanis told reporters that bin Laden and his entourage fled Afghanistan for Kashmir on 10 September, yet military officials were saying that as late as January that the world's most wanted man was held up in the Tora Bora region.[4]

Did the U.S. really know where Osama was on 9-11? And if so, where was he? And why wasn't he then captured? (But I think we already know why he wasn't captured. We need a boogie-man.)

Why weren't American commandos inserted in Kashmir and not Afghanistan?

Did anyone take responsibility or make demands? It's difficult to imagine that the group that carried out an act as expensive and carefully planned as 9/11 chose not to claim credit for it.

Furthermore, terrorist organizations typically make demands and requests for changes in policy, say, or the release of political prisoners. What demands and request, if any, are the American officials aware of?

No window seats available

One day when I was watching video of the second jet (Flight 175) turn and smash into the second tower, I noticed that the airplane was missing something . . . WINDOWS. I have not heard anyone else mention this, but was not one of the flight attendants not reporting what she was seeing out side of the window?

Maybe I am just seeing things . . . but if anyone out there can confirm this please contact me.

The "bubble" on the underbelly of the jet

Almost as weird as that there might not be any windows in the aircraft, there is also something mysterious that is on the bottom of the second jet as it crashes into the WTC. Just grab your copy of the September 12, 2001 newspaper and I am sure this infamous picture is on it. Look at the "bubble" between the wings and the fuselage.

Again, please contact me with additional information.

The World Trade Center

When the World Trade Center was attacked, many, if not all in the main stream media reported that the impact knocked out many of the elevators because the fuel shot down the shafts exploding the shafts and leaving only the stairs as an escape path.

In fact, says Hassan Astaneh, the towers would very likely still be standing had the impact been the only damage. But when the planes penetrated the buildings, they injected tens of thousands of gallons of extremely flammable jet fuel into each tower. "You just brought in very carefully a large amount of fuel, completely," he says. "Then let's ignite it. In this case, there was no struggle, the building sat there innocently and the plane went in. It went in like a bullet going into flesh."

He also came across severely scorched members from 40 or so floors below the points of impact. He believes that the planes obliterated the elevator walls, allowing burning fuel to pour down into the building, igniting blazes hundreds of feet below the main fire. "When the plane hit," he says, "the walls around the elevator shaft were gone, just thrown away." These lower-floor fires may have contributed to the collapse, and certainly added to the death toll.[5]

Yet six months later, CBS news released a documentary film that used footage from inside the World Trade Center titled *9/11*.[6] In case you were one of the ten people who didn't see this documentary, because when I was in Poland for two months I saw it four times, it was a documentary featuring a young firefighter of the Engine 7, Ladder 1 of the New York Fire Department. This footage shot by French film makers and brothers found themselves smack dab in the middle of groundbreaking history. One brother actually captured the first strike on video. (This must have been the life feed to Florida for Baby George Bush to watch, I'm sure.) When you watch the one brother and the firefighters enter the lobby, it is riddled with debris and cracks can be seen, some 96 floors BELOW impact. DAMN!

But as you watch this video, where are the burnt pages of important documents that should have caught on fire from the fuel shoot down the elevator shafts? Where are the carbon scored elevator doors? Where is the smoke shooting from the elevator doors? There is no evidence of what is claimed to have happened with the elevator shafts.

And what caused all the marble to crack and come off the walls in the lobby some 90 floors BELOW the plane's impact?

So here is another puzzle piece that doesn't go anywhere. The World Trade Center was made of metal and concrete. Designed, engineered, and constructed to survive an impact with a 707 jetliner.[7] So when the towers did collapse, why was the rubble almost disintegrated, and did not create clumps or blocks of concrete that is so common in demolished buildings? It appears as when you watch the video replays to simply become dust. Any I'm sorry, but we are made to believe that the enormous temperatures caused by the jet fuel caused the concrete to disintegrate and turn to dust?

Even to this day the remains of at least 1721 people have yet to be found. Only 289 intact bodies were found, and remains of 1102 people have been identified. And some 19,550 parts have been recovered.[8]

So where are the rest of the bodies? They became dust with the buildings I would imagine.

"When the planes hit the upper stories of the towers, there were explosions and bodies were fragmented," says Ellen Borakove, at the office of the chief medical examiner.

"Some of the victims were vaporised or rendered into dust. But we will go on testing until they stop bringing in remains."[9]

But yet someone disagrees with this theory, and the following makes more sense.

Dr. Michael Baden, New York State's chief forensic pathologist and an expert in pathology, said in September, 2001 that most of the victims' bodies should be identifiable, because the fires had not reached the 3200/F for 30 minutes necessary to incinerate a body. At a November press conference, Dr. Charles Hirsch, the chief medical examiner, told grieving relatives that many bodies had been "vaporized."

Are we to believe that the people killed on 9/11 were "vaporized" at 1700/ F?[10]

So are we led to believe that the people killed on 9/11 were "vaporized" at 1700/ F? What happened up there that "vaporized" and turned not only 1721 people "into dust" but also the whole building?

A very detailed and brilliant article from rense.com may shed some light on this:

Despite reports from numerous eyewitnesses and experts, including news reporters on the scene, who heard or saw explosions immediately before the collapse of the World Trade Center, there has been virtual silence in the mainstream media.

Television viewers watching the horrific events of Sept. 11 saw evidence of explosions before the towers collapsed. Televised images show what appears to be a huge explosion occurring near ground level, in the vicinity of the 47-story Salomon Brothers Building, known as WTC 7, prior to the collapse of the first tower.

Van Romero, an explosives expert and former director of the Energetic Materials Research and Testing Center at New Mexico Tech, said on Sept. 11, "My opinion is, based on the videotapes, that after the airplanes hit the World Trade Center there were some explosive devices inside the buildings that caused the towers to collapse."

The collapse of the structures resembled the controlled implosions used to demolish old structures and was "too methodical to be a chance result of airplanes colliding with the structures," Romero told The Albuquerque Journal hours after the attack.

Implosions are violent collapses inwards, which are used to demolish buildings in areas of high density, to prevent damage to surrounding buildings. Precision-timed explosives are placed on strategic load-bearing columns and beams to cause the controlled collapse.

Demolition experts say that towers are the most difficult buildings to bring down in a controlled manner. A tower tends to fall like a tree, unless the direction of its fall is controlled by directional charges.

The WTC towers "smokestacked" neatly, falling within the boundaries of their foundations.

Skeptics say this could not have happened coincidentally and it must have been caused by strategically placed and precisely timed internal charges. Videotape images may reveal these internal charges precipitating the controlled demolition of the towers and WTC 7.

Romero is vice president of research at New Mexico Institute of Mining and Technology, which studies explosive materials and the effects of explosions on buildings, aircraft and other structures, and often assists in forensic investigations into terrorist attacks, often by setting off similar explosions and studying the effects.

183

After being hit by the aircraft, the twin towers appeared to be stable. Then without warning, at 9:58 a.m. the south tower imploded vertically downwards, 53 minutes after being hit. At 10:28, 88 minutes after being struck, the north tower collapsed.

"It would be difficult for something from the plane to trigger an event like that," Romero said. If explosions did cause the towers to collapse, "It could have been a relatively small amount of explosives placed in strategic points," he said.

"One of the things terrorist events are noted for is a diversionary attack and secondary device," Romero said. Attackers detonate an initial, diversionary explosion, in this case the collision of the planes into the towers, which brings emergency personnel to the scene, then detonate a second explosion.

Ten days after the attack, following criticism of his initial remarks, Romero did an about-face in his analysis of the collapse, "Certainly the fire is what caused the building to fail," he told the Journal on Sept. 21.

The twin towers were struck by Boeing 767's carrying approximately 23,000 gallons of fuel.

However, there is other information that lends credence to Romero's controversial scenario. One eyewitness whose office is near the World Trade Center told AFP that he was standing among a crowd of people on Church Street, about two-and-a-half blocks from the South tower, when he saw "a number of brief light sources being emitted from inside the building between floors 10 and 15."

He saw about six of these brief flashes, accompanied by "a crackling sound" before the tower collapsed. Each tower had six central support columns.

One of the first firefighters in the stricken second tower, Louie Cacchioli, 51, told People Weekly on Sept. 24: "I was taking firefighters up in the elevator to the 24th floor to get in position to evacuate workers. On the last trip up a bomb went off. We think there were bombs set in the building."

Kim White, 32, an employee on the 80th floor, also reported hearing an explosion. "All of a sudden the building shook, then it started to sway. We didn't know what was going on," she told People. "We got all our people on the floor into the stairwell . . . at that time we all thought it was a fire . . . We got down as far as the 74th floor . . . then there was another explosion."

The accepted theory is that as the fires raged in the towers, the steel cores in each building were heated to 2,000 degrees Fahrenheit, causing the support beams to buckle.

A lead engineer who designed the World Trade Center Towers expressed shock that the towers collapsed after being hit by passenger jets.

"I designed it for a 707 to hit it," Lee Robertson, the project's structural engineer said. The Boeing 707 has a fuel capacity of more than 23,000 gallons, comparable to the 767's 23,980-gallon fuel capacity.

Another architect of the WTC, Aaron Swirski, lives in Israel and spoke to Jerusalem Post Radio after the attack: "It was designed around that eventuality to survive this kind of attack," he said.

Hyman Brown, a University of Colorado civil engineering professor and the World Trade Center's construction manager, watched in confusion as the towers came down. "It was over-designed to withstand almost anything including hurricanes, high winds, bombings and an airplane hitting it," he said.

Brown told AFP that although the buildings were designed to withstand "a 150-year storm" and the im pact of a Boeing 707, he said the jet fuel burning at 2,000 degrees Fahrenheit weakened the steel. Brown ex plained that the south tower collapsed first as it was struck lower with more weight above the impact area.

Brown told AFP that he "did not buy" the theory that the implosion was caused by the fires sucking the air out of the lower floors, which has been speculated.

The contractor who is reported to have been the first on the WTC collapse scene to cart away the rubble that remains is a company that specializes in the scientific demolition of large buildings, Controlled Demolition, Inc. (CDI) of Baltimore, headed by Mark Loizeaux. CDI is the same contractor that demolished and hauled away the shell of the bombed Oklahoma City Murrah building, actions that prevented independent investigators from pursuing evidence on leads suggesting that there were bombs set off inside the building.

In February 2000, a federal grand jury indicted Mark Loizeaux, Douglas Loizeaux and Controlled Demolition, Inc. on charges of falsely reporting campaign contributions by asking family members and CDI employees to donate to the campaign of Rep. Elijah E. Cummings (D-Md.).

The Baltimore Sun reported that the illegal contributions allegedly occurred between 1996 and 1998. The Loizeaux brothers and CDI were acquitted in Sept ember 2000. Cleaning up the estimated 1.2 million tons of rubble will reportedly cost $7 billion and take up to a year.

Removing the debris has also been controversial. The police said that some scrap metal has been diverted to mob-controlled businesses rather than the dump where investigators are examining rubble for clues and human remains.

The second plane nearly missed the South Tower, cutting through a corner. Most of its fuel burned in an outside explosion. However, this building collapsed first, long before the North Tower, into which a similar plane entered completely. [11]

Again, with all the evidence I have presented to this point, is there really any doubt that the "terrorists " attacks were planned years in advance, and that necessary U.S. Government explosive charges were placed in the towers to help bring them down?

Many other authors have detailed the Oklahoma City bombing as not being the work of a fertilizer bomb, but that of precisely placed U.S. Government explosives. So could the same be true this time?

And what kind of weapon could bring down such great engineering and construction?

An article released by the American Free Press sheds some light on this theory. And believe me, some of this is a little hard for me to believe, but seeing how almost anything, and everything is possible, I will let you see where this piece fits into our puzzle.

Physicist Explores WTC Collapse Scenarios

By Christopher Bollyn

Was the collapse of the World Trade Center caused by a laser beam weapon? A physicist who worked on the original "deep infrared" beam weapon has reason to believe so.

Amazingly, more than five months after the greatest terror attack on America in history, the cause of the towers' structural failure has yet to be investigated and re mains unexplained, according to America's leading fire engineering experts.

As part of an on-going investigation, American Free Press has interviewed a German physicist who believes a laser beam weapon, employing infrared technology originally developed in

186

the Soviet Union, may have caused the towers' collapse.

People are still trying to understand exactly what caused the towers to completely crumble. However, it now appears likely that the federal government will not conduct an open and comprehensive inquiry and that the most important questions may remain unanswered.

BUSH WANTS INVESTIGATION LIMITED

Both President Bush and Vice President Dick Cheney personally intervened and asked Senate Majority Leader Tom Daschle (D-S.D.) to "limit the congressional investigation into the events of Sept. 11," according to CNN. Bush made the unusual request at a private meeting with congressional leaders on Jan. 29. He asked that the House and Senate intelligence committees look only into "the potential breakdowns among federal agencies that could have allowed the terrorist attacks to occur," rather than conduct a comprehensive inquiry.

Cheney made a similar appeal to Daschle on Jan. 25. "The vice president expressed the concern that a review of what happened on Sept. 11 would take resources and personnel away from the effort in the war on terrorism," Daschle said. "I acknowledged that concern, and it is for that reason that the Intelligence Committee is going to begin this effort, trying to limit the scope and the overall review of what happened."

Privately, Democrats questioned why the White House feared a broader investigation to determine possible culpability.

A forensic investigation into what actually caused the buildings to collapse has not been opened and probably never will because the crucial evidence, such as steel from the building, was quickly removed rather than taken to a metallurgical laboratory to be examined. Fire Engineering magazine, a 125-year old respected journal which publishes technical studies of major fires, recently criticized the investigation by the Federal Emergency Management Agency (FEMA) as "a half-baked farce."

The journal said it "has good reason to believe that the 'official investigation' blessed by FEMA and run by the American Society of Civil Engineers is a half-baked farce, commandeered by political forces whose primary interests . . . lie far afield of full disclosure."

There are numerous indicators that something other than fuel fires caused the towers to collapse, including: the immense

187

clouds of dust and apparent disintegration of some 425,000 cubic yards of concrete; the short duration and low temperature of the jet fuel fires; the fact that the rubble burned for more than three months despite being constantly sprayed with water; the report from the medical examiner that many of the dead had been "vaporized" and the absence of any flight data from the planes' "black boxes."

Michael Baden, M.D., New York state's chief forensic pathologist and a top expert in the field, said most bodies should be identifiable because the fires had not reached the 3,200 degree (F), 30-minute level necessary to incinerate a body. "Recovered tissues will likely be identified," Baden said, because "bodies are not cremated—or burnt beyond the ability to be identified—in the type of fire that occurred at the World Trade Center."

A former East German physicist who was involved in the development of a infrared beam weapon in the Soviet Union told AFP that there is evidence that a directed energy weapon using "deep infrared" radiation was used to bring down the WTC.

The East German physicist told AFP, "From my experience as a physicist and research scientist with the GRU [Russia's equivalent to the CIA] I have enough experience to judge that the WTC towers have been burning too quickly, too hot, and too completely to have been caused by the kerosene [jet fuel] fires that resulted from the crashes.

Furthermore, the demolished buildings nearby [the 47-story Salomon Bros. Building] are an indication that there was a plasmoid cloud involved, which probably affected the buildings nearby."

A plasmoid cloud is a heated and ionized gas that can be created and projected using far infrared thermal waves. Plasma occurs when a gas is heated so that some electrons have been separated from their atoms or molecules. Ball lightning is considered by experts to be a plasmoid phenomenon.

The physicist told AFP that he believes that a plasmoid may have been projected onto the towers before the planes struck. "The planes may have had plasmoid in front of them. Just two or three seconds before the planes hit the towers, the plasmoids on the towers would have caused the Faraday cabin effect, like a car being hit by lightning.

"The thermal infrared plasmoid would have raised the heat of the building. One should examine the videos in slow motion to see when the fires started. A plasmoid would have affected the computers in neighboring buildings, because the plasmoid affects computers and cannot be targeted precisely," the physicist said.

If that were the case, another plasma expert says, "it seems evident that if the object [the plane] is moving at high speed in the dense lower levels of the atmosphere, the sudden collapse of the force free field and plasmoid would result in its thermal disintegration in a matter of seconds." The absence of any data from the black boxes is a further indication of the use of a plasmoid weapon, according to the physicist.

In 1991, before the Soviet military withdrew from East Germany, the GRU demonstrated for the U.S. Air Force Electronic Security Command (AFESC) the capabilities of its infrared beam weapon by reducing a ceramic plate into dust from a distance of one mile. This display of Soviet weapon technology was meant to impress upon the U.S. Air Force "how a stealth bomber could be turned into dust in the same way," the physicist said.

The physicist placed a slightly warmed plate on the floor of a kitchen in an apartment on the fifth floor, just below the roof. GRU headquarters, where the infrared beam originated was less than one mile away on the other side of the valley and the second transmitter or reflector was 200 meters away, with no obstacles between. An infrared beam weapon requires two sources. The TV and the oven were turned on and the TV's remote control was put in the refrigerator. The physicist left the room and watched the TV screen, which went black for a few seconds.

The physicist left the apartment for a half hour to allow AFESC personnel to examine the results. The plate had been reduced to such tiny pieces that it was difficult to pick them up even with a vacuum cleaner, according to the physicist.

"The plate was not destroyed suddenly as if hit by a bullet, rather it disintegrated in a process taking about 15 minutes."

Although such technology is not widely discussed in the West, the Soviet infrared beam weapon is nothing new and was used during a Soviet dispute with China in 1968 to destroy "a wall" at the Ussuri River, which separates Manchuria from Russia's Far East, according to the physicist.

Infrared light is heat producing and invisible and is found between visible light and microwave on the electromagnetic spectrum. Near infrared is closest to visible light and far or deep infrared is close to microwave.

Far infrared waves are thermal and cause increased molecular vibrational activity. In other words, infrared radiation is heat.

LASER WEAPON

There are indications, according to the physicist, that such a weapon was used when the KAL plane was shot down over Kamchatka in Sept. 1983. Since the early '90s, this technology returned to scientific discussions in the West and the technology appears to have been transferred from the Soviet Union.

Since 1995, the United States and Israel have actively developed an advanced infrared beam weapon under a joint "anti-missile" program known as the Tactical High-Energy Laser (THEL). The THEL is a mobile, high-energy laser weapon.

Lasers are the leading edge of directed energy weapons. Laser weapons have been under active development for 20 years and easily constitute the most advanced of the directed-energy devices. In 1984, Jeff Hecht, author of Beam Weapons: The Next Arms Race, wrote, "The military 'destructor beam' definitely is in our future tactical arsenal."

The advanced technology and plasma physics involved in directed energy weapons give them unprecedented lethal power. Among their more important features are: the ability to fire energy "bullets" at or near the speed of light; to redirect their fire toward multiple targets rapidly; their long range; and their ability to transmit lethal doses of energy in a fraction of a second. No conventional ammunition is required—only fuel for the power generator is needed.

THEL is part of a joint program known as Nautilus, in which the U.S. Army and the Israeli Ministry of Defense (IMOD) have developed infrared laser weapon systems. The prime contractor, TRW Space and Electronics Group, has been involved in the development of high energy laser systems since the early 1970s. A host of Israeli engineers and companies are involved in the program including the aerospace companies Rafael, Israel Aircraft Industries, and Tadiran.

THEL is a mobile system ostensibly designed to destroy rockets, such as the Russian-made Katyusha. The THEL employs the Mid-Infrared Advanced Chemical Laser (MIRACL). The MIRACL is a megawatt class, deuterium-fluoride chemical laser. The weapon's systems can be transported in one or two shipping

190

containers.

The THEL successfully destroyed a short range rocket in flight on Feb. 9, 1996. As a result, the United States and Israel began joint development of a Tactical High Energy Laser/Rapid Acquisition Demonstrator (THEL/ RAD) system. In April 1996, President Bill Clinton and Secretary of Defense William Perry met Israeli Prime Minister Shimon Peres. The United States made a commitment to assist Israel in the development of a THEL Advanced Concept Technology Demonstrator (ACTD) laser by the end of 1998. Congress gave more than $55 million for THEL development in 1997.

Expense to the U.S. taxpayer and U.S. national security are apparently not considerations at the political level when sharing the results of U.S. weapons development programs with Israel. Nautilus was offered to Israel in the form of a multimillion-dollar "research grant."

The funding for Nautilus research was part of a $2 billion military grants package Clinton offered to Peres. Israel's access to real-time U.S. satellite imagery and at least $50 million for accelerated development of the "Nautilus" laser system were included in the Clinton package.

"Our commitment to Israel's security is unshakable and it will remain so because Israel must have the right to defend itself, by itself." Clinton said while giving Israel an additional $200 million in U.S. taxpayer money above and beyond the "official" $5.5 billion figure.

Described as the "the world's first high-energy laser weapon system," THEL Advanced Concept Technology Demonstrator (ACTD) reportedly shot down a rocket with a live warhead on June 6, 2000, at the Army's High Energy Laser Systems Test Facility (HELSTF), White Sands Missile Range, N. M. The THEL-ACTD is a highly mobile "stand-alone defensive weapon system" unlike the earlier version. "We've just turned science fiction into reality," said Lt. Gen. John Costello, commanding general, U.S. Army Space and Missile Defense Command.

"The THEL/ACTD shoot-down is a watershed event for a truly revolutionary weapon," said Tim Hannemann, executive vice president and general manager, TRW Space & Electronics Group.

During the test of THEL/ACTD, an armed Katyusha rocket was fired from a rocket launcher placed at a site in White Sands

Missile Range. Seconds later, the THEL/ ACTD, located several miles away, detected the launch with its fire control radar, tracked the streaking rocket with its high precision pointer tracker system, then engaged the rocket with its high-energy chemical laser. Within seconds, the 10-foot-long, five-inch-diameter rock exploded.

This weaponry, which is usually described as defensive in the context of anti-missile applications, can be mounted on an airplane, ship, land-based station, or satellite. It can bombard its target with either beams that willdestroy it outright, or by beams of lesser strength to disable the target's electronics and cause it to go out of control.

If the WTC had been struck by a similar weapon, than it is very likely, according to the East German physicist that one of the transmitters would have been placed in a high building nearby and the second one on a ship or across the East River. Some of the questions that should be asked would be: How long did the towers' emergency power supply continue to function and had the computers in the towers been disturbed? [12]

We have seen time and time again throughout the pages of this book that anything we are told is to be questioned, and what we are not being told makes more since, once we start to put on our thinking caps.

Where will it end? Where does it even begin?

I am not that skilled on other conspiracy theories/facts and I will leave that to them. But what we must really decide is where is it going and what can we do to prevent outrageous Government cover-ups from hiding the true facts that the people need to know.

There once was a time when the people were the important part of the running of the country. Now it appears that the people are doing one thing, and the country is doing a totally different thing. And nobody cares.

Americans are bred to be better than their neighbor, to make more money than them, to drive a better car than them, to have a prettier wife than them. Meanwhile in this fun house of mirrors, the government is taking away more and more from both the neighbor and you and disguising it with planned "terrorists" attacks, and then introducing pre-written legislation to follow through with what the country's people think they want.

192

Locked doors on top of the World Trade Center

Who locked the roof doors at the World Trade Center? It is a well known fact that during the 1993 World Trade Center bombing, hundreds of workers escaped smoke by going to the roofs.[13] But on 11 September hundreds died when they went up dozens of flights of stairs only to find those same roof doors locked. Why did city fire officials order those doors locked between 1993 and 2001, and more importantly, why didn't they post notices through the World Trade Center complex to advise that roof doors would no longer be unlocked? Prosecutions may be in order for criminal negligence.

The Anthrax letters

As I am writing this chapter, America and Britain are at war with Iraq. And the press is reporting more and more about the concerns of Anthrax. And I am reminded of the Anthrax letters delivered to only Democrats at Capitol Hill, and also the scare in the post office outside of San Francisco.[14]

I was living in Santa Rosa, California at this time, and remember the fear of everyone in the area. One person died, a photo editor at Boca Raton, Florida's *the Sun* newspaper, and two others tested positive because of this "attack."[15] Is there any doubt that Bush and his henchmen were also behind this scare tactic to influence more pre-written legislation?

President Baby Boy Bush warned about letters coming from unknown senders,[16] and low and behold, letters containing the anthrax spores were sent to, coincidence I'm sure, Senate Democratic Leader Tom Daschle. Some fifty people, mostly members of Daschle's staff office across the street from the Capitol building were treated following the exposure. And twenty-nine of his staff were tested positive for the virus.[17]

This is the same Tom Daschle mind you that was personally asked from President Baby Boy Blue Bush to limit the congressional investigation into the events of 11 September, congressional and White House.[18] Coincidence, I'm sure.

Another anthrax-laced letter was sent to Senator Patrick Leahy, a Democrat from Vermont. Another purely coincidental incident, I'm sure. And just so that Bush wasn't eyed for being behind these letter, and talk about hate mail, other letters were also sent to NBC News anchor

Tom Brokaw, and the Editor at the *New York Post*.[19]

Also ironic, and purely "coincidental," is that White House personnel were given Cipro, an antibiotic for anthrax, some six weeks before the letters were found.[20]

And get this! On the night of the 11 September attacks, the White House Medical Office dispensed Cipro to staff accompanying Vice President Dick Cheney as he was secretly escorted off to the safety of Camp David, and told them it was only, "a precaution."

Bush even went so far as to boldly claim "Let me put it this way," Bush said. "I'm confident that when I come to work tomorrow, I'll be safe."[21]

And are you ready for this? *Remember the photo editor at The Sun* in Boca Raton, Florida? Ironically a gentle man named Peter Kawaja admitted on a radio program that he was involved with Product Ingredient Technology in Boca Raton.

Here is a transcript from that program:

"I got involved with a project called "Product Ingredient Technology" in Boca Raton, Florida. I was also involved throughout the United States with IBI (Ishan Barbouti International), the builder of Pharma 150, the chemical and biological weapons complex in Rabta, Libya. From my investigation, I found a lot of things that were not legitimate, and I ran. I was green about a lot of these things upon going in. I went to the CIA and FBI, and operated for the U.S. government under a code name, because they said these people were international terrorists and that they were going to prosecute them. However, they did not count on me bugging telephone lines, buildings, and certain other locations throughout the United States. I intercepted the Commodity Credit Corporation, the Banca Nazionale del Lavorro (CCC-BNL), the letters of credit of the BNL, which came from Switzerland, as well as a lot of other communications regarding the Gulf War that was to come. I recorded calls going to and coming from Baghdad, to and from the United States and London, CIA, FBI, FBI counter-intelligence, U.S. Customs, certain politicians and numerous other individuals. This is my information. It is not second-hand.

"What I found at the PIT plant was very heinous. I found that a strain of hydrogen cyanide called Prussian Blue was being tested on gas mask filters more than 1 year prior to the Persian Gulf War. This information was known to the President of the

194

United States, George Bush. It was arranged through Trevor Armbrister, a CIA asset and a Senior Editor of Reader's Digest, to fly me to the steps of the White House. Time does not permit me to tell my story, but the information that I want to get out to the American people is that the Gulf War illnesses are actually communicable diseases. The microbes will live almost indefinitely, but for a minimum of seven years. It's on the gas masks, the clothing, the weapons -- any of the materials brought back from the Gulf War. I have reports from several different states where civilians that bought some of the clothing went home and wore them, and now the entire family is in wheel chairs; there have been some deaths as a result of this."[22]

Chemical and biological weapons? Boca Raton, Florida? Coincidence, it has to be.

It is alleged that Product Ingredient Technology (PIT) has links to former President Father George Bush.[23] It is believed that PIT manufactured chemical warfare agents for the first Iraqi conflict,[24] eh heh war, sorry. What a coincidence that the anthrax scare should start in Boca Raton. Revenge? Or simply staged terror? All roads lead to Rome right?

It is obvious that whoever sent the "highly potent" forms of anthrax knew what they were doing. It was revealed to be a strain of AMES anthrax and the U.S. Army laboratory was revealed to be the main source of this strain.[25]

The existence of the secret army program was first revealed by the *Baltimore Sun* in an article published 12 December, 2001.[26] Until then, U.S. officials, including those investigating the anthrax attacks, had maintained that the American military stopped producing germ warfare materials in the late 1960s, before the signing of an international treaty banning the development of such weapons. So remind me why American invaded Iraq?

Wasn't it for allegedly creating weapons of mass destruction? Nahhh it couldn't be that America is guilty of doing what it blamed Iraq of, could it?

Nahhh.

But.... A Pentagon spokesmen later claimed that the development of weapons-grade anthrax is legal because the production of small quantities is permitted for "peaceful and protective" purposes. And what on earth is a "peaceful and protective" purpose with a biological weapon?

The United States is the only country that is known to have produced weapons-grade anthrax in the past 25 years.[27]

In June 2002, Baby Boy Bush signed the "bio-terrorism" law, which now devotes $4.3 billion to the storage of vaccines, food inspections, and special security for water supplies. Would it be safe to assume that this does not cover every man, women and child in the United States of America?

No, I take that back, all roads lead to Washington D.C..

Our puzzle is almost complete. Now we will look again, and in detail at the "official" reason for the attacks. Direct from the source. Piece by piece.

SOURCES

(1) http://www.metroactive.com/papers/metro/09.12.02/sept11a-0237.html

(2) http://www.sfreporter.com/archive/09-11-02truth.html

(3) http://www.google.com/url?sa=U&start=1&q=http://azeri-american.by.
ru/truth.htm&e=42

(4) http://www.alternet.org/story.html?StoryID=13864

(5) http://www.cbsnews.com/stories/2002/03/07/attack/main503218.shtml

(6) http://www.cbcraleigh.com/capcom/news/2002/wraltv_02/9_11_
documentary/9_11_documentary.htm

(7) http://www.engr.psu.edu/ae/WTC/NYTimes91801.htm

(8) http://www.cnn.com/2002/US/06/15/deutsche.building/?related

(9) http://news.bbc.co.uk/1/hi/in_depth/americas/2001/nyc_out_of_the_ashes
/1702336.stm

(10) http://www.pbs.org/wgbh/nova/wtc/letters.html

(11) http://www.rense.com/general17/eyewitnessreportspersist.htm

(12) http://www.americanfreepress.net/Conspiracy/Physicist_Explores_WTC
_Collaps/physicist_explores_wtc_collaps.html

(13) http://www.cephasministry.com/terror_the_truth_about_sept_11.html

(14) http://www.cbsnews.com/stories/2001/10/16/archive/main314795.shtml

(15) http://www.guardian.co.uk/Society/disasterresponse/story/0,1321,
574320,00.html

(16) http://news.bbc.co.uk/hi/english/world/americas/newsid_1601000/
1601093.stm

(17) http://news.bbc.co.uk/1/hi/world/americas/1601093.stm

(18) http://www.cnn.com/2002/ALLPOLITICS/01/29/inv.terror.probe/

(19) http://www.govexec.com/dailyfed/1002/100402gsn1.htm

(20) http://www.infowars.com/saved%20pages/Prior_Knowledge/bush_
cipro.htm

(21) http://www.washingtonpost.com/wp-srv/aponline/20011023/aponline
201158_000.htm

(22) http://www.alienobserver.com/files/text/kawa2.html

(23) http://www.alienobserver.com/files/text/kawa2.html

(24) http://www.cassiopaea.org/cass/signs24.htm

(25) http://www.washingtonpost.com/ac2/wp-dyn/A36408-2001Nov29

(26) http://www.wsws.org/articles/2002/jan2002/corr-j21_prn.shtml

(27) http://www.wsws.org/articles/2001/dec2001/anth-d28.shtml

Chapter 13
Conclusion

Not one person knows all the answers. To anything, or any subject.

I am not a full time author. This is not my full time job. This is my first book published. I am not an expert on what happened that September day, but as you have read, I have some serious problems with the "official" story.

The purpose of this book is in no way to say, "I am right and I know it all." This is just not the case. I admit I do not know everything. And although this is the conclusion to this book, there are even more pieces to find.

That is the reason for this book. For you to see the alternative information before you and make up your own mind.

I am not your controller. I am not twisting your arm to believe everything that I do. That is not my goal. My goal is to question the "official" story.

No one can say precisely how the events of 11 September were pulled off, who were on the planes, were there hijackers at all on the planes, did official pilots fly the aircraft, or were the aircraft flown by remote control.

No one knows except those behind the events. And with that in mind, we may never know.

As this book has shown, there have been cover-ups, tampering with evidence, half-truths, and even outrageous lies. Not the behavior of honest elected officials who have nothing to hide, is it? It is the behavior of someone hiding something. The truth.

No public investigation

How many years will pass before the American people, will know exactly what happened? If we will EVER know. There are still no plans for public investigation of how almost than 3,000 people lost their lives, and what could have been done to prevent the attacks or reduce their impact.

A very disturbing report was published through the Reuters Newswire U.K. And I find it amazing and surprising that the important stories are "expired" and the boring ones stay posted for years, taking up web space on the server, or the reason they say they "expire" stories. Susan Cornwell reported on 26 May, 2002:

> WASHINGTON (Reuters) - Both President Bush and Vice President Dick Cheney urged Senate Majority Leader Tom Daschle four months ago not to push for an investigation into the events of Sept. 11, Daschle said on Sunday.
>
> Appearing on the NBC program "Meet the Press," Daschle flatly contradicted Cheney, who last week denied he had warned Daschle off an investigation.
>
> Daschle and other Democrats favor a special commission into the official handling of pre-Sept. 11 terror warnings. Both Cheney and Bush have in recent days argued publicly against a the idea, opting instead for an ongoing inquiry by the intelligence committees of Congress.
>
> Daschle, a South Dakota Democrat, said Cheney telephoned him on Jan. 24 to urge that no Sept. 11 inquiry be made, and that Bush had followed up on January 28 with a similar request during a breakfast meeting at the White House.
>
> "I can tell you on January 24th, first, and on January 28th second, and on other dates following, that request was made, Daschle said. "I don't recall the exact words. The motivation was that they didn't want to take people off the effort to try to win the war on terror. They were concerned about the diversion of resources, the diversion of manpower in particular, and that was the reason given me by both the president and the vice president," Daschle said.
>
> Last week on the same program, Cheney denied calling Daschle to argue against a Sept. 11 probe, saying, "Tom's wrong. He has, in this case, let's say a misinterpretation. What I did do was ... say, we prefer to work with the intelligence committees."

Secrecy has been the watchword of the obsessively inscrutable Bush administration. So preoccupied are they with keeping their business away from the people that, rather than spark a national discussion of what went wrong and what we could do better, these public servants, OUR public servants, are asking members of Congress to take lie-detector tests to find out who's been leaking plans to attack Iraq.

Without a doubt, military intelligence requires secrecy. But there is no conceivable national security interest in keeping Americans in the dark about 11 September, a horribly public mass murder that devastated our national sense of invulnerability. A crisis whose first few weeks were marked by patriotic unity rapidly devolved into a divisive, "war on terrorism" marked by opportunistic assaults on the Bill of Rights, old-fashioned oil wars and a cynical neo-McCarthyism whereby those who question Bush and the Republican Party are smeared as "anti-American."

"United We Stand" bumper stickers and the waving flags aside, the "terrorists" have skillfully turned everyone against each other: Citizen against immigrant, Republican against Democrat, Christian against Muslim. Secrecy only deepens those divisions.

In conclusion

Under the Constitution of The United States, "treason" is defined very specifically as, "an overt act of war against The United States, witnessed by two or more people." The attacks of 11 September were certainly witnessed by two or more people. We even have them on videotape. Millions watched the horrors of that day. And besides what we are told to believe, it appears that various officials of our own Government have committed Constitutionally defined Treason. On the basis of Mr. Kennedy's remarks alone, there is probable cause to have a vast number of Government Officials taken into custody, charged, tried and, if convicted, executed.

But this will never happen. Not in our lifetime. UNLESS WE WAKE UP. Knowledge is power!

You have the knowledge and power to change the world and make the real people responsible for the attacks to responsibility for their actions!

Our puzzle is far from complete. The picture you see before you is not what you were made to purchase for almost two years now, is it?

What are you going to do with your picture?

You can make a difference in the world you live in.

Share this new picture with your family, your friends, and your elected officials.

The real war on REAL terrorism was started on you.

Thank you,

Eric D. Williams

Picture Section

Picture Section

Puzzle One: Flight 11, we are told, was a 767. Yet this image taken of the 'jet' is much smaller that a 767. Even eye witness accounts claim it was a small commuter plane.

Puzzle Two:
When 'Flight 175' was seen smashing into the second tower, many eye witnesses claimed to have seen a "missile." Further inspection of photos taken 1/3rd of a second before impact do in fact show something entering the building before the nose of the jet pierces the building.

Puzzle Three:
When 'Flight 175'is enlarged, we can also see a 'bubble' underneath the body of the plane. What is this anomaly?
If a missile was seen leaving the plane, could this be a missile pod? And if indeed a missile was launched from the plane, was this really United Airlines Flight 175? If this is not Flight 175, then what happened to the real commercial airliner?

Puzzle Four:
We are told the towers collapsed because of immense heat caused by the jet fuel. Jet fuel burns at less than 1800 F. Steel melts at 2500 F.
1) The fires did not burn evenly throughout the building, nor did
they reach the need 2500 F to begin to melt.
2) Steel is designed to pull heat throughout the beam to cool itself naturally.
3) 'Flight 175' lost most of its fuel outside of the building.

Puzzle Five:
The fires were so hot, they melted the steel and brought down the towers. . . yet this person, although is desperately trying to get help, is not melting.

Puzzle Six:
Many people do not know this, but the WTC was the first steel building to be brought down by fire, ever! EVER!

This is a photo of the 38-story One Meridian Plaza building in Philadelphia, PA.

In February 1991, an 18-hour fire gutted eight floors. Guess what, the building still stands!

Why did the WTC buildings fall?

Puzzle Seven:
This is the Interstate Bank Building in Los Angeles, CA.
In May 1988, four floors were destroyed in this 62-story building.
It burned for at least nine hours, and if you notice the fire is underneath many stories of weight, and yet this building also did not collapse. We are told that the WTC collapsed because of the weight of the floors above. Why did this building not fall?

Puzzle Eight:
When the towers collapsed, why did all the concrete turn to dust? Even the concrete below the impacts was 'pulverized' into a powder. Is this normal?

Puzzle Nine:
Another photo clearly showing steel beams, but no concrete chunks!! And we are told jet fuel did this? What really happened on 11 September?

2, 2001, 17:37:23   #4 impact

Puzzle Ten:
At the Pentagon, the largest office building in the world, and the most 'secure' building in the United States, had only one security camera on that day?

Also, notice the time on the lower left. The date implies that this image was taken on September 12, 2001 and at 5:37pm!

Are we to believe that the most 'secure' office and military complex is the US does not keep its own security cameras synchronized?

Puzzle Eleven:
Did Flight 77 REALLY hit the Pentagon? Please look carefully at this photo. 1) There is no plane wreckage. 2) Look closely at the intact window just to the right of the impact hole. 3) Notice for a jet, the impact hole is very, very small.

Puzzle Twelve:
This is a picture of a FedEx 727 jet which crashed in the summer of 2002. Clearly, we can see the remnants of the jet.
So why do we not see similar wreckage at the pentagon?

Puzzle Thirteen:
We have been told that the towers collapsed because of the thousands of gallons of jet fuel. So why did the jet fuel not cause more damage at the Pentagon?
Other than melting and disintegrating the entire plane?

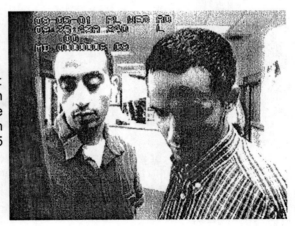

Puzzle Fourteen:
Dumb and Dumber: Majed Moqed with Hani Hanjour while using an ATM in Laurel, Maryland on 5 September.

Puzzle Fifteen: Who are these men boarding a plane in Portland, Maine? And why are there two times, 05:45:13 and 05:53:41, on the screen?

Puzzle Sixteen:
Is this really bin Laden or a Hollywood actor? The REAL Osama (pictured on both the left and right) has a much taller and narrower nose and lower and less full cheeks. A less rounded brow ridge, is less well nourished and his forehead slopes back more. Osama's face is also wider at the level of his eyes.

Comments on this book

"Dear Eric,

I have purchased 'The Puzzle of 9-11' and I think that it is a very important and fascinating book. I especially enjoyed how you melded a conversational style of writing with the facts, and your sources were a wonderland in themselves.

Whenever I read a book that I think should be read, I invariably purchase a second copy and insist (some would say foist upon) close friends read it. I have purchased a second copy of 'The Puzzle of 9-11,' a "lending" copy, if you will.

In closing, thank you for your efforts. I am sure that there are many other people who say to themselves when reading 'The Puzzle of 9-11'. . . "MY GOD, HE'S RIGHT."

Sincerely,
Kevin"

Summary of the 2nd Edition

What you have just read is the 2nd edition of my first book, *The Puzzle of 9-11*.

When I wrote this book, in the early months of 2003, I had no intention of ever really writing another book, so I tried to get it published for almost 18 months, until I gave up after rejection after rejection and self published it just to get my thoughts and question about 9/11 out in the public market.

Embarrassed now, I did not edit or even spell check the manuscript and published it anyway.

Four additional books later, thee dealing with 9/11, I was going to pull the book as I was quite embarrassed by it, but then I started to receive some emails about the book. The overall comments about the book were very positive, but the negative dealt with the spelling and grammatical errors. On 8 September, 2006, I heard Ralph Schoenman speak for two hours in NYC right before the 9/11 anniversary and many of the things he mentioned was in this book.

So, I thought differently about pulling this title, and wanted to revise it with new information, but then I thought I would just hire an editor and typesetting specialist and just correct the spelling and grammatical errors, and leave my original thoughts and commentary in tact.

Although some of my views on the information held within this book have changed, and after regaining faith in my first work, I decided to leave it the way I wrote it.

With that said, I hope you have enjoyed this edited and grammatically corrected edition.

Know the Truth, and may the Truth set us all FREE!

Eric D. Williams
September 2006

Contact the Author

You can contact the author by email at
williamsquire_ltd@yahoo.com

Please note, that in the event that this email address does not work,
please refer to the author's website

www.whatreallyisthematrix.com

or

www.geocities.com/williamsquire_ltd

for contact information.

Your comments and feedback are welcome.

Also available by Eric D. Williams

The Puzzle of the Matrix:
Intriguing explorations into the nature of reality
ISBN 1-419-60504-6

9/11 101:
101 key points that everyone should know and consider that prove
9/11 was an inside job
ISBN 1-419-62428-8

The Puzzle of Fascism:
Could fascism arise in America or could it already be a Fascist State?
ISBN 1-4196-3255-8

Tea with God:
A divinely inspired self-help book complete with workbook
ISBN 1-4196-0033-8

The Puzzle of 7/7:
An in-depth analysis of the London Bombings and Government
Sponsored Terrorism in the United Kingdom
ISBN 1-4196-4658-3

Available at:
www.whatreallyisthematrix.com
www.amazon.com
or bookstores everywhere.

388444

Made in the USA